DANIEL
BERRIGAN

To Alice —

In peace —

John Dear

D0062843

MODERN SPIRITUAL MASTERS
Robert Ellsberg, Series Editor

This series introduces the writing and vision of some of the great spiritual masters of the twentieth century. Along with selections from their writings, each volume includes a comprehensive introduction, presenting the author's life and writings in context and drawing attention to points of special relevance to contemporary spirituality.

Some of these authors found a wide audience in their lifetimes. In other cases recognition has come long after their deaths. Some are rooted in long-established traditions of spirituality. Others charted new, untested paths. In each case, however, the authors in this series have engaged in a spiritual journey shaped by the influences and concerns of our age. Such concerns include the challenges of modern science, religious pluralism, secularism, and the quest for social justice.

At the dawn of a new millennium this series commends these modern spiritual masters, along with the saints and witnesses of previous centuries, as guides and companions to a new generation of seekers.

MODERN SPIRITUAL MASTERS SERIES

DANIEL BERRIGAN

Essential Writings

Selected with an Introduction by

JOHN DEAR

ORBIS BOOKS

Maryknoll, New York 10545

Fifth Printing, May 2016

Founded in 1970, Orbis Books endeavors to publish works that enlighten the mind, nourish the spirit, and challenge the conscience. The publishing arm of the Maryknoll Fathers and Brothers, Orbis seeks to explore the global dimensions of the Christian faith and mission, to invite dialogue with diverse cultures and religious traditions, and to serve the cause of reconciliation and peace. The books published reflect the views of their authors and do not represent the official position of the Maryknoll Society. To learn more about Maryknoll and Orbis Books, please visit our website at www.maryknollsociety.org.

Library of Congress Cataloging-in-Publication Data

Berrigan, Daniel.
    [Selections. 2009]
    Essential writings / Daniel Berrigan ; selected with an introduction by
John Dear.
        p.   cm. – (Modern spiritual masters)
    Includes bibliographical references.
    ISBN 978-1-57075-837-9 (pbk.)
    1. Spirituality – Catholic Church. 2. Peace – Religious aspects – Christianity.
    I. Dear, John, 1959– II. Title.
    BX4705.B3845A25 2009
    261.8'73092 – dc22

                                                                    2009021053

For all those who create peace,
teach peace, work for peace, pray for peace,
walk for peace, speak for peace, vigil for peace,
act for peace, cross the line for peace,
get arrested for peace, go to prison for peace,
and give their lives for peace.

With gratitude and blessings of peace

Contents

Sources

AIHF   *America Is Hard to Find.* New York: Doubleday, 1972.

ARB   *And the Risen Bread: Selected Poems, 1957–1997,* edited by John Dear. New York: Fordham University Press, 1998.

BWB   "The Box within a Box: A Tale of Chastened Expectations," by Daniel Berrigan, in Dedria Bryfonski, ed., *Contemporary Authors: Autobiography Series,* vol. 1, Detroit: Gale Research Co., 1984.

CT   *Consequences: Truth and…* New York: Macmillan, 1967.

CW   *Cloud of Witnesses,* edited by Jim Wallis and Joyce Hollyday, see: "Daniel Berrigan: The Push of Conscience." Maryknoll, N.Y.: Orbis, 1991.

DNR   *The Dark Night of Resistance.* Eugene, Ore.: Wipf and Stock, 2007.

DUSG   *Daniel: Under the Siege of God.* Eugene, Ore.: Wipf and Stock, 2009.

EVID   *Ezekiel: Visions in the Dust.* Maryknoll, N.Y.: Orbis, 1997.

G   *Genesis: Fair Beginnings, Then Foul.* New York: Rowman and Littlefield, 2006.

JADND   *Job: And Death No Dominion.* Franklin, Wis.: Sheed and Ward, 2000.

JTWTWG   *Jeremiah: The World, the Wound of God.* Minneapolis: Fortress Press, 1999.

KTG   *The Kings and Their Gods.* Grand Rapids: Eerdmans, 2008.

LOIHD   *Lights On in the House of the Dead.* New York:
           Doubleday, 1974.

MPMT   *Minor Prophets, Major Themes.* Eugene, Ore.: Wipf
           and Stock, 2009.

NFH   *Night Flight to Hanoi.* New York: Macmillan, 1968.

NBM   *No Bars to Manhood.* Eugene, Ore.: Wipf and Stock,
           2007.

POTIL   *Portraits – Of Those I Love.* Eugene, Ore.: Wipf and
           Stock, 2007.

SS   *Steadfastness of the Saints.* Maryknoll, N.Y.: Orbis,
           1985.

ST   *Suspect Tenderness: The Ethics of the Berrigan
           Witness,* by William Stringfellow and Anthony
           Towne. Eugene, Ore.: Wipf and Stock, 2006.

TCN   *The Trial of the Catonsville Nine.* New York:
           Fordham University Press, 2004.

TDIP   *To Dwell in Peace.* Eugene, Ore.: Wipf and Stock,
           2007.

TMM   *Thomas Merton, Monk,* edited by Patrick Hart.
           Kalamazoo, Mich.: Cistercian Publications, 1983.

TWMF   *Testimony: The Word Made Fresh,* edited by John
           Dear. Maryknoll, N.Y.: Orbis, 2003.

WB   *Witness of the Berrigans,* edited by Stephen Halpert
           and Tom Murray. New York: Doubleday, 1972. "Ser-
           mon from the Underground," by Daniel Berrigan,
           140–43.

WS   *Whereon to Stand: The Acts of the Apostles and
           Ourselves.* Eugene, Ore.: Wipf and Stock, 2009.

WWA   *Where We Are: American Catholics in the 1980s,*
           edited by Michael Glazier. "Christian Peace-
           making in a Warmaking State," by Daniel Berrigan.
           Wilmington, Del.: Michael Glazier, 1985, 200–211.

Permissions

The publisher thanks Daniel Berrigan and acknowledges the following publishers for permission to reprint copyrighted material.

Augsburg Fortress Press for selections from *Jeremiah: The World, the Wound of God* by Daniel Berrigan, copyright © 1999 Fortress Press. Reproduced by special permission of Augsburg Fortress Press.

Wipf and Stock Publishers, for selections from *The Dark Night of Resistance*, Wipf and Stock edition © 2007; *Minor Prophets, Major Themes,* Wipf and Stock edition © 2009; *No Bars to Manhood,* Wipf and Stock edition © 2007; *To Dwell in Peace,* Wipf and Stock edition © 2007; *Portraits of Those I Love,* Wipf and Stock edition © 2007; *Whereon to Stand: The Acts of the Apostle and Ourselves,* Wipf and Stock edition © 2009.

Wm. B. Eerdmans Publishing Co. for selections from Daniel Berrigan, *The Kings and Their Gods* © 2008 by Wm. B. Eerdmans Publishing Company, Grand Rapids, Michigan. Reprinted by permission of the publisher. All rights reserved.

Michael Glazier for permission to reprint "Signs of Peace" by Daniel Berrigan from *Where We Are: American Catholics in the 1980s,* ed. Michael Glazier, Michael Glazier, Inc., 1985.

Sheed & Ward, an imprint of Rowman & Littlefield, for selections from *Genesis: Fair Beginnings, Then Foul,* © 2006; and *Job: And Death No Dominion,* © 2000.

Fordham University Press for selections from *And the Bread Is Risen: Selected Poems 1957-1997,* ed. John Dear © 1998.

Daniel Berrigan's Life and Work: A Brief Overview

1921   Born on May 9, in Virginia, Minnesota, the fifth of six sons of Frida Fromhart and Thomas Berrigan.

1926   Family moves to a farm near Syracuse, New York.

1926–39   Attends St. John the Baptist Academy, Syracuse, New York.

1939–43   Enters the Society of Jesus on August 14, 1939; St. Andrew-on-Hudson novitiate near Poughkeepsie, New York, until 1941; then classical studies until 1943.

1943–46   Jesuit studies at Woodstock College, near Baltimore, Maryland.

1946–49   Teaches at St. Peter's Prep, Jersey City, New Jersey.

1949–53   Jesuit theological studies, Weston, Massachusetts.

1952   June 19, ordained a priest.

1953–54   Jesuit studies and ministerial work in France.

1954–57   Teaches French and philosophy at Brooklyn Prep, Brooklyn, New York.

1957   First book published, *Time without Number*; wins the Lamont Poetry Award.

1957–62   Teaches New Testament at Le Moyne College, Syracuse, New York.

1959   *The Bride: Essays in the Church.*

1960   *Encounters* (poetry).

1961   *The Bow in the Clouds: Humanity's Covenant with God.*

1962   *The World for Wedding Ring* (poetry).

1963–64   Sabbatical year in France; travels to Czechoslovakia and South Africa; co-founds Catholic Peace Fellowship.

1965   Assistant editor, *Jesuit Missions;* co-founds Clergy and Laity Concerned about Vietnam; in November, exiled to Latin America following the death of Roger LaPorte.

1966   Returns to New York City. *No One Walks Waters* (poetry); *They Call Us Dead Men: Reflections on Life and Conscience.*

1967   Teaches in Colorado and California; September, joins Cornell United Religious Work at Cornell University, Ithaca, New York; October, arrested at the massive antiwar protest at the Pentagon, first priest in U.S. history to be arrested for a protest against war. *Consequences: Truth and...*

1968   February, to Vietnam with Howard Zinn; May 17, burns draft files with others, including his brother Philip, at Catonsville, Maryland; stands trial in October. *Night Flight to Hanoi; Love, Love at the End* (poetry).

1969   *No Bars to Manhood; False Gods, Real Men* (poetry).

1970   April, goes underground; August 11, arrested on Block Island, Rhode Island, sent to Danbury Federal Prison, Connecticut, as prisoner #23742–125. *The Trial of the Catonsville Nine* (Drama); *Trial Poems* (poetry); *The Holy Outlaw* (film).

1971   *The Geography of Faith: Conversations between Daniel Berrigan, when Underground, and Robert Coles; The Dark Night of Resistance.*

1972   February, released on parole from Danbury federal prison; Harrisburg trial of Philip and other defendants; teaches at Union Theological Seminary; *America Is Hard to Find* (letters, poems, essays); *Absurd Convictions, Modest Hopes: Conversations after Prison* (with Lee Lockwood); *Jesus Christ* (poetry).

1973   *Selected and New Poems; Prison Poems* (poetry); October, addressed Association of Arab University Graduates, Washington, D.C.; teaches at University of Manitoba; arrested at the White House.

1974   Lives with Thich Nhat Hanh in Paris; *Lights On in the House of the Dead: A Prison Diary.*

1975   *The Raft Is Not the Shore: Conversations towards a Buddhist/Christian Awareness* (with Thich Nhat Hanh); travels to Lebanon, Israel, Palestine, and Syria.

1976   Arrested at the Pentagon, the United Nations, and various arms manufacturers; teaches, lectures, and leads retreats at universities and churches around the United States, a pattern that will continue for the next thirty years. Joins the West Side Jesuit Community in Manhattan.

1977   *A Book of Parables.*

1978   *Uncommon Prayer: A Book of Psalms; Beside the Sea of Glass; The Words Our Savior Gave Us.*

1979   Begins working at St. Rose's Cancer Home, New York City; teaches at Yale University and College of New Rochelle. *The Discipline of the Mountain: Dante's Purgatorio in a Nuclear World.*

1980   September 9, arrested with the Plowshares Eight at GE missile plant, King of Prussia, Pennsylvania; teaches in Berkeley; visits Northern Ireland. *We Die before We Live: Talking with the Very Ill.*

1981   *Ten Commandments for the Long Haul.*

1982   Plowshares Eight trial; *Portraits – Of Those I Love; In the King of Prussia* (film, with Martin Sheen); lectures in Germany and Ireland.

1983   *The Nightmare of God.*

1984   June–July in El Salvador and Nicaragua; begins work at St. Vincent's hospital, New York, with people with AIDS.

1985   *Steadfastness of the Saints;* April–July, making a film, *The Mission,* in South America; in Australia. *Block Island* (poetry).

1986   *The Mission: A Film Journal.*

1987   Teaches at Berea College, Kentucky; *To Dwell in Peace: An Autobiography.*

1988   Teaches at Yale; *Stations.*

1989   Teaches at Loyola Univ., New Orleans; arrested November 17 after the deaths of six Jesuit priests in El Salvador.

1990   Sentenced to time served for the Plowshares Eight disarmament action, Philadelphia.

1991   *Whereon to Stand: The Acts of the Apostles and Ourselves; Jubilee* (poetry).

1992   *Tulips in the Prison Yard* (poetry).

1993   *Homage to Gerard Manley Hopkins* (poetry).

1995   *Minor Prophets, Major Themes.*

1996   *Isaiah: Spirit of Courage, Gift of Tears; Apostle of Peace: Essays in Honor of Daniel Berrigan* (edited by John Dear)

1997   *Ezekiel: Vision in the Dust;* nominated for the Nobel Peace Prize by Mairead Maguire, in Belfast, Northern Ireland.

1998   *And the Risen Bread: Collected Poems, 1957–1997* (edited by John Dear); *Daniel: Under the Siege of the Divine.*

1999   *Jeremiah: The World, the Wound of God.*

2000   *Job: And Death No Dominion; The Bride* (with icons by William Hart McNichols).

2001   *Wisdom: The Feminine Face of God; Investigation of a Flame* (film)

2002   Brother Philip dies, December 6; *Lamentations: From New York to Kabul and Beyond.*

2003   Teaches at Fordham University, New York.

2004   *Testimony: The Word Made Fresh* (edited by John Dear).

2006   *Genesis: Fair Beginnings, Then Foul; A Sunday in Hell.*

2007   *The Trouble with Our State* (CD); *Exodus: Let My People Go; Prayer for the Morning Headlines* (poetry).

2008   *The Kings and Their Gods: The Pathology of Power.*

2009   *No Gods But One.*

Daniel Berrigan — Poet, Prophet, and Peacemaker

"We have assumed the name of peacemakers," Daniel Berrigan famously wrote at the height of the Vietnam War in his classic work *No Bars to Manhood,* "but we have been, by and large, unwilling to pay any significant price. And because we want the peace with half a heart and half a life and will, the war, of course, continues, because the waging of war, by its nature, is total — but the waging of peace, by our own cowardice, is partial. So a whole will and a whole heart and a whole national life bent toward war prevail over the velleities of peace. There is no peace because there are no peacemakers. There are no makers of peace because the making of peace is at least as costly as the making of war, at least as exigent, at least as disruptive, at least as liable to bring disgrace and prison and death in its wake."[1]

With such pointed observations, my friend and Jesuit brother Daniel Berrigan staked out the cost of Gospel peacemaking and set a new course for the North American church, if the faithful would only join the campaign. With his brother Philip, Dan waged peace with his whole heart, will, and life, and paid the cost. Time and time again, he has been denounced and exiled, arrested and imprisoned, and yet he stands at the center of the culture of war with the good news of Christ the peacemaker, and in doing so, he makes peace possible at home and abroad. Through his poetry, journals, essays, and scripture studies — and a lifetime of committed action — he invites us all to abandon war for a new life of peace.

And so Daniel Berrigan remains one of this century's leading voices for peace and disarmament, in a rare pantheon with

Dorothy Day, Martin Luther King Jr., Thomas Merton, Mairead
Maguire, Cesar Chavez, Dom Helder Camara, Hildegard Goss
Mayr, Archbishop Desmond Tutu, Mohandas Gandhi, Bishop
Thomas Gumbleton, and Thich Nhat Hanh. He has come to
embody the Christian insistence on peace and disarmament in a
world of war, empire, and nuclear weapons.

Dan exemplifies a Christianity that works for peace, speaks
for peace, and welcomes Christ's resurrection gift of peace, first
of all to the poor and the enemy. Through word and deed, he
sheds new light on the Gospel of Jesus, pointing us toward a new
world of nonviolence, a new future of peace if we but welcome
the gift. His life work, he would say, is modest, but the cumula-
tive effect of his writings and actions, I suggest, show us what the
church might look like, what a Christian looks like in such times,
indeed, what a human response looks like in an inhuman world.
An amazing gift.

Dan knows by heart that God does not bless war, justify war,
or create war. He points to a nonviolent Jesus who blesses peacemakers, not warmakers; who calls us to love enemies, not kill
them; who commands us to take up the cross of nonviolent
resistance to empire — not put others on the cross.

From the days of the "war on communism" to the even darker
days of the "war on terror," from Nixon's doctrine of "Mutually
Assured Destruction" to Bush's "surge" in Iraq, Dan has kept
vigilant. Across these tortured decades, against the odds, Dan
has steadfastly said "No" to war, empire, and nuclear weapons.
Through his poetry, books, retreats, and talks, indeed, by his very
life, he has offered an affirming "Yes" to the God of life and
peace. Dan's genius is the combination of the two. You can't have
one without the other, as many attempt to do.

This collection includes selections from his poems, journals,
seminal essays on peacework and resistance, and groundbreaking scripture commentaries. I culled these essential writings from
his fifty books and countless articles and poems and from the
massive archives of letters and original manuscripts at Cornell University library. I placed these selections by and large in

chronological order, to show how his thought and spirit evolved as his peacemaking path unfolded.

To my mind, Dan's writings are best understood as the fruit of his nonviolent actions and resistance, and as such they stand within the tradition of resistance literature. But more, they join a legacy of spiritual writing that stretches from the Acts of the Apostles and the letters of St. Paul through the poetry of St. Francis to the sermons of Archbishop Romero and Dr. King. Dan's writings fit in both categories: as resistance literature and spiritual writing. For Daniel Berrigan, they are one and the same. All spiritual writing is political, for it resists the culture of war and injustice by its very nature. All political writing for peace and justice is therefore quintessentially spiritual, for it points us toward the reign of God. This, I suggest, is the mark of a true spiritual master.

In this introduction, I shall review the facts of Dan's life and then look at his message from three angles — as a poet of peace, a prophet of peace, and a peacemaker at work in the belly of the American empire. These remarks are offered as a way of preparing us to read Dan's words in a prayerful, reflective manner, so that we might understand his message, take it to heart, and deepen our own journey toward the God of peace and a new world of peace.

A Life of Peace in a World of War

As a member of the Society of Jesus, Dan lives the Jesuit mission to promote a universal faith that serves those in need, points others to the peacemaking Christ, and welcomes God's reign of peace on earth here and now with all its glorious social, economic, and political implications. He has tried many avenues to spread the Gospel of peace, from his poetry and books, to his retreats and lectures, to his civil disobedience and periodic imprisonments. A prize-winning poet, an acclaimed Broadway playwright, a best-selling memoirist, a theologian, a professor, an actor, a social critic, a radical resister, a fugitive, an ex-con, a Nobel Peace Prize nominee, and in the words of Amy Goodman of *Democracy Now,* "a national treasure," Dan remains a beacon of hope to peace-loving people everywhere.

By the late 1960s and 1970s, Dan's deeds were featured regularly on the front page of the *New York Times;* he even appeared on the cover of *Time* magazine. His actions were followed, monitored, and debated by people everywhere. But what the media and the masses missed was the spiritual commitment underlying his witness. It is that spiritual base, that openness to the God of peace, that makes all the difference in Dan's life and message.

Born on May 9, 1921, in Virginia, Minnesota, the fifth of six boys, to Frida and Thomas Berrigan, Dan grew up in Syracuse, New York. When his childhood friend Jack St. George announced he was going to enter the Society of Jesus in 1939, Dan followed him into the novitiate at St. Andrew's on the Hudson, next door to Franklin and Eleanor Roosevelt's mansion near Poughkeepsie, New York. Three weeks later, World War II began.

After philosophy studies in Woodstock, Maryland, teaching high school in Brooklyn, and theology studies at Weston in Massachusetts, Dan was ordained a priest on June 21, 1952. He was, by his own admission, quite "conventional," wearing the black Jesuit robes and beret. But his 1953 Jesuit sabbatical year, known as "tertianship," opened a new world for him. He studied in France, where he encountered the Worker Priest movement, a controversial experiment in which priests, who usually stood above the fray, entered factories and worked alongside low-skilled workers and, on their behalf, advocated for reasonable hours and decent pay. Years of high school teaching and then undergraduate teaching at Le Moyne College in Syracuse followed, where a spirit of new possibility was percolating within him.

Throughout those years, Dan wrote poetry, an interest fostered somewhat by his father's frustrated efforts to memorize and write poems. In the mid-1950s, Dan showed a collection of his poems to a publisher, who in turn passed them on to renowned poet Marianne Moore, who took to them instantly. His first book, *Time without Number,* published in 1957, won the prestigious Lamont Poetry Award. By the early 1960s, he was a widely read poet, much in demand speaker, and one of the nation's most prominent priests. He grew close to church activists and writers Dorothy Day, Thomas Merton, and William Stringfellow. After another sabbatical year in France and travels to South Africa, Czechoslovakia, and the Soviet Union, he marched in Selma with his brother Philip. He then turned his attention toward U.S. war-making and co-founded both the Catholic Peace Fellowship and Clergy and Laity Concerned about Vietnam.

As the United States escalated its horrific bombing campaigns over Vietnam, Dan started speaking publicly against the war, a first venture for a U.S. Catholic priest. After Roger LaPorte, a young Catholic Worker, burned himself to death in protest in front of the United Nations, Dan presided at a Mass for him and spoke of compassion and forgiveness. His Jesuit superiors immediately ordered him to leave the country — indefinitely. Off he went on a six-month tour of Latin America. Public outrage, including a full-page ad in the *New York Times,* forced his embarrassed Jesuit superiors to let him return. When he did, Dan took a new assignment as a teacher and chaplain at Cornell University in Ithaca, New York. The poverty he had witnessed throughout Latin America only fueled his passion for justice and peace.

In January 1968 Dan flew to Hanoi on a peace mission with historian Howard Zinn. There they endured in shelters a U.S. bombing raid and eventually brought back several U.S. prisoners of war. The shock of this experience, along with the April 4 assassination of Dr. King, led Dan to join his brother Phil and others members of the "Catonsville Nine" on May 19, 1968, to burn draft files with homemade napalm near Baltimore. Their action attracted enormous media coverage across the country and shocked the nation, inspiring millions to speak out and act against the U.S. war. It dramatically challenged pro-war Catholics and Christians with the antiwar Gospel message of universal, nonviolent love, and the image of rebellious priests disturbing the so-called peace of the status quo.

"Our apologies, good friends," Dan wrote in their statement, "for the fracture of good order, the burning of paper instead of children, the angering of the orderlies in the front parlor of the charnel house. We could not, so help us God, do otherwise."[2]

For their creative nonviolence, Dan was tried, convicted, and sentenced to several years in prison. While awaiting sentencing, Dan took the court transcripts of their trial and turned them into a play, *The Trial of the Catonsville Nine,* which was later performed on Broadway. Today it continues to be produced and to inspire audiences around the world. It led folksinger Dar Williams, for example, to write a moving tribute to Dan called, "I Had No Right."

Instead of turning himself in to the authorities, Dan went underground in April 1970 to carry on his public protest against the war. He eluded the FBI, traveled throughout the Northeast, and spoke out periodically in the media against the ever-escalating war. His action again drew national media interest to his antiwar message, as well as the wrath of President Nixon, J. Edgar Hoover, and the FBI. He was finally arrested on August 11, 1970, and imprisoned in Danbury, Connecticut, until February 1972. While in prison, he nearly died during a routine dental procedure, when Novocain was accidentally shot into a blood vessel.

Throughout the 1970s, Dan continued to write and speak out against war, with increasing focus on the global specter of nuclear weapons. On September 9, 1980, again with his brother Philip, he participated in the first "Plowshares" disarmament action, a protest at the General Electric Plant at King of Prussia, Pennsylvania, where they hammered on an unarmed nuclear warhead. As they told their judge, they were simply trying to fulfill Isaiah's prophecy to "beat swords into plowshares." He faced ten years in prison, but was eventually sentenced to time served.

Over the years, Dan has traversed the war zones of the world, been arrested in hundreds of acts of civil disobedience, and consistently held aloft the Gospel vision of peace with justice. Again and again he finds himself with friends before some judge or sitting on ice in some dismal holding cell, jailed because he dared question the nation's warmaking. I have joined him many times, in dozens of such protests — at New York City's Riverside Research Institute, Times Square's Armed Forces Recruiting Station, and the U.S.S. Intrepid War Museum, as well as at the Nevada Nuclear Weapons Test Site. In each instance, his good humor and gentle wit kept our spirits high, as we were led around in handcuffs, sometimes even in chains. Inevitably, he transformed each dreadful episode into a blessing of peace.

Along the way, Dan has worked in New York at St. Rose's Home for the dying and later on at St. Vincent's hospital serving people with AIDS. For decades, he could be found teaching for a semester or a summer session at campuses across the country, from Yale to U.C. Berkeley, from Loyola New Orleans to Fordham. He meets with a steady stream of daily visitors, including family and friends, students and young people, journalists and activists, Catholic Workers and celebrities. He works every day, writing in the morning, walking in the afternoons, and meeting people in the evenings — a peaceful contemplative in downtown New York City, keeping watch with one eye on the warring world, a second eye on friends and those in need, and a third eye on the spiritual realm of peace breaking through the darkness.

Since the early 1970s, Dan has lived in New York City with a group of twenty other Jesuits who teach and serve throughout the city. He attends regular meetings of his local peace group, *Kairos,* every other week, to pray over scripture, discuss some social issue, and plan some public action. He has given a thousand lectures, led hundreds of retreats, and been arrested every year for protests against war, injustice, and nuclear weapons. He has stood with those on death row, in soup kitchens, and homeless shelters, with the dying in Northern Ireland and El Salvador, Nicaragua, and South Africa. Throughout this past decade, he has been a fearless opponent of the U.S. wars in Iraq and Afghanistan.

Now at age eighty-eight, he remains faithful to his vocation and vision of peace, calling us to do the same — whether we're successful or not. The focus, he teaches, is on the God of peace, and so, Dan avers, "The outcome is in better hands than ours." With that, he insists, we can live in hope. And struggle on.

Keeper of the Word: A Poet Who Imagines Peace

Dan's first book of poetry, *Time without Number,* attracted enormous interest, especially from noteworthy poets. After that first book, Dan took up writing as a natural response to his love of the Word of God. He has published a book a year, including some eighteen books of poetry, winning a wide readership and respect. His journals, essays, plays, and scripture studies all bear the hallmark of a surpassing poetic mind, brimming with talent, creativity, lucidity, and possibility.

"Daniel Berrigan is evidently incapable of writing a prosaic sentence," biblical scholar Walter Brueggemann once observed. "He imitates his Creator with his generative word...that bewilders, dazzles, and summons the reader." "For me, Father Daniel Berrigan is Jesus as a poet," Kurt Vonnegut wrote.

Dan's poems are the fruit of his long pursuit of peace and justice, indeed of the God of peace and justice. Recently, he recorded a CD of his best poems, *The Trouble with Our State,* where he explains that they are mainly about war and the culture of perpetual war. As I wrote in the liner notes, I think they also concern peace, and the hope and life and vision of nonviolence.[3] Reading and hearing his poems confronts, inspires, uplifts, and heals. They offer hope to those struggling with cultural despair. That for me is the best clue to appreciating his poetry. Dan invites us to hope. He insists on hope. Despite all. And he can do this because he himself is essentially hopeful. He keeps a long haul view toward resurrection.

And thus we hear about the "the slight edge of life over death." We read about a "strictly illegal" way of seeing the world, about "not letting blood." We "learn to put on like glasses" Dan's "second sight" and "see washed ashore the last hour of the world, the murdered clock of Hiroshima." Here we reclaim our "natural powers" and join those who "deceive no one, curse no one, kill no one," "because the cause is the heart's beat and the children born and the risen bread." Dan's poems help us look anew at our broken world, to get beyond our anger and grief, and step into a new realm of nonviolence.

In this collection I have included some of Dan's greatest poems, such as "Peacemaking Is Hard," "Less Than," "The Trouble with Our State," "Prophecy," "Some," and "Zen Poem." When I edited a massive anthology of Dan's poems, *And the Risen Bread: Selected Poems, 1957–1997*, I studied all his poems, starting with the early poems that caught the attention of critics, such as "Credentials" and "Each Day Writes," through the mid-1960s collections, *Encounters, The World for Wedding Ring, No One Walks Waters,* and *Love, Love at the End,* with their biblical themes of creation, saints, and scripture.[4] With *False Gods, Real Men,* his poems, like his life, took a turn into full-blown nonviolent resistance to war. The poetry of *Night Flight to Hanoi, Trial Poems, The Dark Night of Resistance, America Is Hard to Find,* and *Prison Poems* emerged from his journeys to Vietnam, Catonsville, court, and prison.

In the 1970s and 1980s, his poetry integrated that earlier love of life with his public confrontation with death as he wrote about the psalms, Dante's *Purgatorio,* the filming of the movie *The Mission,* the poetry of Gerard Manley Hopkins, and the Plowshares movement. Much of his poetry over the last two decades involves his groundbreaking work with the Hebrew Bible.

Dan uses the language of poetry to help us break through the cultural mindset to reclaim our imaginations for peace. In this nuclear age, few can imagine a world without war or weapons — much less a nonviolent God — but Dan's gift of language helps us hear the good news in a new way. Like a Zen master, he offers koans of nonviolence that enlighten and open us to the gift of peace. It is this gift of unpacking the Word of God that led to his prophetic ministry: announcing God's word of peace to the culture of war.

Prophet of Peace to the World of War

Dan's astonishing gift of language combined with his keen critique of the culture of war make for a unique contribution to American history and Catholic spirituality. His vision of "the human," coupled with his public resistance toward inhumanity, has led many to call him a prophet.

Does it go too far in suggesting that Dan has earned his place among the venerable prophets? I think not. A prophet, says Dan, is nothing more than "a truth teller, who says it and pays up."[5] Under this definition, Dan surely qualifies. He has spent his life listening to the truth of God, sharing it widely — often with people inhospitably disposed — and paying a hefty price.

Dan's contemplative rhythm of first listening and then "going public" places him in the tradition of the towering prophets — Isaiah, Daniel, Jeremiah, and Ezekiel — each of whom, notwithstanding the vast distance in time, have become Dan's mentors and models. Like them, he denounces war, weapons, arms races, corrupt regimes, miscarriages of justice, assaults on human rights, as well as threats to widows, orphans, the unborn, and prisoners. What makes Dan's critique so unique, according to one of his biographers, Francine du Plessix Gray, is his "startling" use of language. Even his opponents sit up and take note.

For Dan, the spiritual life demands our encounter with the world and thus nonviolent resistance to its violence in the tradition of the peacemaking Jesus. His early poems were, in his words, "sacramental," but his later poems took on the world and its wars and suffering, he says, because he himself began to taste some of that suffering. And so, Dan teaches not a comfortable spirituality — with its private, one-to-one relationship with God — but an uncomfortable spirituality that finds God in the poor, in the marginalized, and in the enemy and evokes loving action on their behalf.

"Some people today argue that equanimity achieved through inner spiritual work is a necessary condition for sustaining one's ethical and political commitments," Dan writes. "But to the prophets of the Bible, this would have been an absolutely foreign language and a foreign view of the human. The notion that one has to achieve peace of mind before stretching out one's hand to one's neighbor is a distortion of our human experience, and ultimately a dodge of our responsibility. Life is a rollercoaster, and one had better buckle one's belt and take the trip. This focus on equanimity is actually a narrow-minded, selfish approach to reality dressed up within the language of spirituality."[6]

"I know that the prophetic vision is not popular today in some spiritual circles," he continues. "But our task is not to be popular or to be seen as having an impact, but to speak the deepest truths that we know. We need to live our lives in accord with the deepest truths we know, even if doing so does not produce immediate results in the world."[7]

Dan finds the wherewithal to set his face against the tide of war in large part because of his daily Bible study. Indeed, like his brother Philip, Dan is a rare biblical person, one who wrestles with the Word of God day and night and tries to live according to that troublesome, peacemaking Word. "Open up the book of Jeremiah and you do not find a person looking for inner peace," Dan notes. Jeremiah cries out against injustice and then rejoices in the fulfillment of God's justice, Dan observes. "Jeremiah goes through mountains and valleys. That kind of richness I find very appealing, whereas the kind of spirituality that looks for a flat emotional landscape brought on by the endless search for inner peace and equanimity I find disturbing, a quest that goes nowhere."[8]

"I draw from the prophets a very strong bias in favor of the victim and a very strong sense of judgment of evil structures and those who run them," Dan says. The prophets and Christ talk "about the God who stands at the bottom with the victims and with the 'widows and orphans' and witnesses with them in the world, from that terrifying vantage point which is like the bottom of the dry well that Jeremiah was thrown in. That vantage point defines the crime and sin; that point of view of the victim indicts the unjust, the oppressor, the killer, the warmaker. And the message is very clear. It's a very clear indictment of every superpower from Babylon to Washington."[9]

Dan reaches such unlikely conclusions because he is thoroughly immersed in the text and the praxis that the text demands. He dares think that God can be taken at God's Word, most notably, in the Gospel message of Jesus. "I've been maintaining a new discipline," he told me casually a few years ago, at the height of Bush's war on Iraq. "First, I get as little of the bad news as possible. I only look at the *New York Times* once a week, if that, and occasionally BBC TV.

Second, I spend more time than ever with the good news, reading and meditating on the Gospel every morning, to be with Jesus."

That, to my mind, is the job description of the modern-day biblical prophet — aware of the world, immersed in the Word of God, a kind of Barthian recipe for readying oneself to announce the Gospel in word and deed. Deed especially. It is Dan's nonviolent direct action that gives Dan's words such vigor and power. But it is his words that expose his deeds and vision and inspire so many others.

"The Word of God is spoken for the sake of today," Dan writes in a recent book, *The Kings and Their Gods*, "for ourselves. If not, it lies dead on the page. Lift the Word from the page, then — take it to heart. Make of it the very beat of the heart. Then the Word comes alive — it speaks to commonality and praxis. Do it — do the Word."[10] This is the advice of a postmodern spiritual master. And it rings true because its ancient wisdom was first tested by the early saints and martyrs.

His message has been a consistent Gospel word — "Do not kill. Do not support the culture of killing. Do all you can to stop the killing." He put it succinctly in an influential open letter to the Weathermen: "The death of a single human being is too heavy a price to pay for the vindication of any principle, however sacred."

Dan summed up his prophetic message of peace during his 1981 trial for his Plowshares action. These words, offered in the face of a ten-year prison sentence, challenge all of us to pursue God's reign of nonviolence as the main task of the spiritual life.

The only message I have to the world is: we are not allowed to kill innocent people. We are not allowed to be complicit in murder. We are not allowed to be silent while preparations for mass murder proceed in our name, with our money, secretly.... It's terrible for me to live in a time where I have nothing to say to human beings except, "Stop killing." There are other beautiful things that I would love to be saying to people. There are other projects I could be very helpful at. And I can't do them. I cannot. Because everything is endangered. Everything is up for grabs. Ours is a kind of primitive situation, even though we would call ourselves sophisticated. Our plight is very primitive from a Christian point of view. We are back where we started. Thou shalt not kill; we are not allowed to kill. Everything today comes down to that — everything.[11]

The Christian Peacemaker in a Warmaking Culture

In 1984, after I first met Daniel Berrigan, I asked him for a piece of advice. "Make your story fit into the story of Jesus," he told me. "Ask yourself: does your life make sense in light of the life of Jesus? All we have to do is close our eyes to the culture and open them to our friends. We have enough to go on. We can't afford the luxury of despair." His words were enormously helpful and encouraging to a young Jesuit and would-be peacemaker. Later, he put it another way for a group: "The best way to be hopeful is to do hopeful things."

Over the next twenty-five years, I watched Dan practice his own teaching. Because he took public risks to fit his life into the story of Jesus, he became the first priest to go to jail for opposing war, and one of the most consistent antiwar priests in church history. He broke new ground by his peacemaking activity in a world of total war. In the process, he showed us not just what every priest, minister, and bishop should say and do, but how all of us can follow Jesus in these difficult times. He encourages us to become mature Christians who do not run from the Gospel's risky, political message of justice for the poor and peace for all.

"As a priest who is attempting to be faithful to the Gospel," Dan told one interviewer, "I think that Christians, according to our testament, are not allowed to kill. It is boldly stated in the Sermon on the Mount and in the behavior of Jesus before his execution. I proceed on that assumption — 'Love your enemies and do good to those who do bad to you.' That's a political gift that the church can offer to an aggrieved and tormented public."[12]

"Dorothy Day taught me more than all the theologians," Dan continues. "She awakened me to connections I had not thought of or been instructed in — the equation of human misery and poverty with warmaking. She had a basic hope that God created the world with enough for everyone, but there was not enough for everyone *and* warmaking."[13]

Dan took up Dorothy's mantle and carried on her work for peace. From his journeys in the American South with the civil rights movement, to South Africa at the height of apartheid, to the Soviet Union and the Eastern Bloc at the height of the Cold War, to Vietnam, Palestine, and Central America — Dan tried to bring the Gospel to life. He attempted to love enemies, make peace, and seek God's reign of justice. But his bold witness at Catonsville, his trial, months underground, imprisonment, subsequent Plowshares actions, and repeated smaller civil disobedience actions took Dan deeper into the story of Jesus. It broke new ground by showing us that if we want to follow the peacemaking Jesus here in the U.S. empire, we have to take up the cross as active nonviolent resistance to imperial warfare and risk the consequences.

What's more, Dan has stayed faithful to that Gospel journey. He keeps on walking the road to peace, one mindful step at a time, whether others do or not. Whether the media is interested or not. Whether the church agrees or not. "We walk our hope and that's the only way of keeping it going," he says. "We've got faith, we've got one another, we've got religious discipline and we've got some access that goes beyond the official wall."[14] In that spirit, Dan keeps at it.

"Peacemaking is tough, unfinished, blood-ridden," he told one interviewer not long ago. "Everything is worse now than when I started, but I'm at peace. I don't have to prove my life. I just have to live."[15] In the end, the point for Dan is to be faithful to the God of peace and the Gospel of Jesus.

"Nobody can sustain him or herself in the struggle for a nonviolent world on the basis of the criterion of immediate success," Dan writes. "The Bible gives us a long view rather than the expectation of a quick fix. All of us are in grave danger of being infected by this American ethos that good work brings quick change, rather than the older spiritual notion that good work is its own justification and that the outcome is in other hands besides ours."[16]

Today, Dan continues to live in community, spend several hours a day studying the scriptures, meet with people and give lectures and retreats. He calls us to be human in inhuman times, to be peacemakers in a warmaking culture, and to resist death and the metaphors of death, as Jesus did, with our very lives.

"The good is to be done because it is good, not because it goes somewhere," he insists. "I believe if it is done in that spirit it will go somewhere, but I don't know where. I don't think the Bible grants us to know where it goes, in what direction. I have never been seriously interested in the outcome. I was interested in trying to do it humanly and carefully and nonviolently and let it go."[17]

Concluding Notes

This collection has taken many years of reading, research, and collating. For these essential writings, I gathered some of Daniel Berrigan's classic texts from bestsellers like *No Bars to Manhood* and *To Dwell In Peace,* as well as *The Trial of the Catonsville Nine* and *The Dark Night of Resistance,* sprinkled his poems throughout, and concluded with excerpts from his many recent scripture commentaries, the major work of his last twenty years. Several selections are published here for the first time, such as his homily at the memorial Mass for Roger LaPorte, remarks that led to his exile in Latin America.

I encourage readers to share these writings with friends, neighbors, activists, and other church workers, and to study other collections of Dan's writings that I have edited, including: *And the Risen Bread: The Selected Poems of Daniel Berrigan, 1957–1997* (Fordham University Press, 1998); *Testimony: The Word Made Fresh* (Orbis); and *Apostle of Peace: Essays in Honor of Daniel Berrigan* (Orbis, 1996). A great new CD, *The Trouble with Our State,* features Dan reading his best poetry and is available at *www.yellowbikepress.com.* Also, Wipf and Stock Publishers have just republished over a dozen of Dan's classic works, in a new series that I edited, available at: *www.wipfandstock.com.*

I would like to thank my friends who helped me with this project: Ellie Voutselas, who typed most of the manuscript; Ted Gordon, who helped with this introduction; Robert Ellsberg, who guided me through the process and helped with the manuscript; and the Jesuit Community at the University of Hawaii in Honolulu, where I sorted through and organized the massive amount of material for this book.

And I thank Father Daniel Berrigan, friend and brother, for holding aloft this Gospel vision of peace and disarmament, and showing us, through faith and courage, friendship and hope, word and deed, that on such a vision we can stake our lives.

May these essential writings of Daniel Berrigan help us all, like Dan, to follow the nonviolent Jesus on the road of peace in pursuit of a new world without war, poverty, or nuclear weapons, "because the cause is the heart's beat and the children born and the risen bread," that we might fulfill our vocations as sons and daughters of the God of peace and become Gospel peacemakers.

— John Dear, S.J.
Santa Fe, New Mexico
May 9, 2009

Notes

1. Daniel Berrigan, *No Bars to Manhood* (Eugene, Ore.: Wipf and Stock, 2007), 57–58.

2. Daniel Berrigan, *Night Flight to Hanoi* (New York: Macmillan, 1968), xvi.

3. Daniel Berrigan, *The Trouble with Our State*. CD available from *www.yellowbikepress.com*.

4. See *And the Risen Bread: Selected Poems of Daniel Berrigan, 1957–1997*, ed. John Dear (New York: Fordham University Press), 1998.

5. "Daniel of the Lion's Den," *The Rail*, Brooklyn, N.Y. (May–June 2001): 10.

6. "Daniel Berrigan on Contemporary Developments in American Spirituality," *Tikkun* 13, no. 5 (September–October 1998): 48.

7. Ibid.

8. Ibid.

9. "A Conversation between Daniel Berrigan and Alan Fox," *Rattle* Bombshelter Press, 5, no. 1 (Summer 1999): 152.

10. Daniel Berrigan, *The Kings and Their Gods* (Grand Rapids, Mich.: Eerdmans, 2008), 9.

11. "The Push of Conscience," in *Cloud of Witnesses*, ed. Jim Wallis and Joyce Hollyday (Maryknoll, N.Y.: Orbis, 1991), 230.

12. "Daniel Berrigan on Terrorism and Its Cause," *Block Island Times*, October 27, 2001, 18.

13. Chris Hedges, "Forty Years after Catonsville," *The Nation*, May 21, 2008.

14. "Daniel Berrigan on Terrorism and Its Cause," 22.

15. "A Conversation between Daniel Berrigan and Alan Fox," 142.

16. "Daniel Berrigan on Contemporary Developments in American Spirituality," 16.

17. Hedges, "Forty Years after Catonsville."

1

Credentials

CREDENTIALS

I would it were possible to state in so
few words my errand in the world: quite simply
forestalling all inquiry, the oak offers his leaves
largehandedly. And in winter his integral magnificent order
decrees, says solemnly who he is
in the great thrusting limbs that are all finally
one: a return, a permanent riverandsea.

So the rose is its own credential, a certain
unattainable effortless form: wearing its heart
visibly, it gives us heart too: bud, fullness and fall.

EACH DAY WRITES

in my heart's core
ineradicably, what it is to be human.

Hours and hours, no sun rises, night sits
kenneled in me: or spring, spring's
flowering seizes me in an hour.

I tread my heart amazed: what land,
what skies are these, whose shifting weather

now shrink my harvest to a stack of bones;
now weigh my life with glory?

Christ, to whose eyes flew,
whose human heart know, or furious or low,
the dark wing beat of time: your presence give
light to my eyeless mind, reason to my heart's rhyme.

INSIGHT

When I look, I see
I've spent my life seeing—
under that flat stone, what?
Why that star off kilter?

Turn, Turn! I intoned, and
out of the stone there stood
What-Not in a white garment.

Jacob's ladder descended
(the angels holding steady)—
I mounted and I
saw
what   *—ARB,* 3, 389

THESE MANY BEAUTIFUL YEARS

My brother Philip and I were two of six brothers. We were
depression babies, all of us. My father used to say that in the
1930s he had lost everything but his shirt. If that was so, we must
also recall with a certain wry humor that he only had one or two
shirts to lose.

We lived most of our lives in a sixty-year-old house on the top
of a hill, surrounded by ten not very fruitful acres. I remember
vividly that we housed and fed a continuing number of homeless
men during those dark years of loss. Even those neighbors who

would not themselves feed or clothe or house the poor would always tell them that they could find something at our place.

Our schooling was mediocre at best. But it was augmented by constant reading. My mother deserves an eternal reward for the constant tonnage of books she carried home by streetcar from the city library.

Our life was frugal and untidy, with regular cleanups on my father's part to reassert his iron brand of authority. But it was always something like a roundup of colts. The fact is that he was not home a great deal of the time, and we generally ran free.

I entered the Society of Jesus in 1939. I was acquainted with no Jesuits, so it was a matter of an act of faith on both sides. Not a bad arrangement.

As with any young person of eighteen entering upon an entirely new form of life, the memories of my first years are particularly vivid. With regard to present convictions, I think they gave me a deep sense of the presence of God in the world, and most especially in human community. I must say too that I fell in love immediately and incurably with the Jesuit style, although prior to my entrance I had practically no knowledge of it firsthand. But it appealed to me immediately as a ground for boundless idealism; and I found in the talents and youth and drive around me a constant spur to make my own life count.

When I entered upon my studies it became clear that I had a great deal of ground to catch up and win. Practically all of my classmates had graduated from Jesuit schools in the New York or Buffalo areas. They were invariably far ahead of me on almost every criterion that counted for achievement in our Bruderhauf.

I passed three miserable years at Woodstock College studying philosophy. It was simply not my dish. So I languished like an unhappy three-year freshman trying with varying degrees of desperation and moodiness to find myself in a thicket of logic and metaphysics. I finished that period with enormous relief and almost entire lack of distinction.

I taught high school for three years, 1946–49, in St. Peter's Preparatory School, Jersey City, New Jersey. As I recall, I taught French, Latin, English, and what was fondly called, at that time, "religion." Everything I had believed or hoped about myself, by way of being a contributory creature in the real world, began to come true. I struck out in every direction, like a belated flower child. And this at the hands of some three hundred rough and tough Jersey kids. It was indeed the first of many miracles.

With some misgivings, I undertook theological studies at Weston College, at Weston, Massachusetts, in the autumn of 1949. I was then twenty-eight years old, years away from my initial decision to enter the order; three years awaited me until ordination, five years until the completion of the ordinary Jesuit regime of studies. So it was as a kind of ageless elephant that I lumbered into this other phase and began anew. There is nothing of distinction to report of those next years. The courses were in the main mediocre, with some exceptions in scriptural studies.

I was finally (and from my point of view miraculously) ordained to the priesthood on June 19, 1952. Another year of theology and rustication in the same green acres. And a year later, in July of 1953, I departed for a year of studies in France.

Although I did not realize it for the space of several months, my real mind was being implanted; the future was being furiously sown. It was a tumultuous and even catastrophic year for French society and the French church. Pius XII was bearing down heavily upon the worker priests; he finally suppressed the movement entirely in February of 1954. The French were living through the dying spasms of Dienbienphu. The end of the Indo-Chinese colonial adventure was at hand, and the republic was stricken at the heart, to a degree it had not known since the crisis of occupation and Vichy. It was a year of national humiliation and turmoil.

Our house of studies near Lyons was as poor as any church mouse dwelling. But we had a sense of sharing in something extraordinarily painful in France at large. Many of my compatriots were survivors of German exploitation and had worked in labor camps and factories under the occupier. Almost everything I experienced was being experienced for the first time. I felt in many cases as though I had landed upon a new planet, and was being asked to operate in an entirely new way, to rebuild my senses, my very soul. It was not merely a matter of fumbling about with a new language and slowly gaining confidence in it. The truth was that the language offered new ways into the world of other human beings — and that these others, penetrated and formed by a thousand-year history expressed in their lucid and vivid language, were also new beings, into whose community I was invited to enter. The invitation was austere but irresistible.

What I discovered in France for the first time in my long experience of Catholic community was so simple a thing as personal freedom. It was an invitation to become a human being by way of others, immersed as we all were during that year in the tradition of our scripture, as well as the experience and history of our order.

I returned to New York in the autumn of 1954 and began to teach at Brooklyn Preparatory School. For three years, I undertook work with teams of students among the Puerto Ricans of Brooklyn, and on the Lower East Side of Manhattan. We also instituted an honors system of studies in the school, which later won some distinction as the students went on to university work.

In the autumn of 1957 I reported for teaching at Le Moyne College in Syracuse, New York. In a sense I felt that now my life was beginning on an entirely fresh and exciting basis. I was teaching college classes for the first time; the college was only eleven years old, and we were, in a rather innovating way, making go as we went. I was assigned to teach New Testament classes.

The following six years were an intense, even incandescent continuum — between the classroom on campus and the communities in rural Mexico, between my work in Syracuse and the work of my brother Philip in New Orleans. I cannot remember when I was more hardily tested or more blessedly renewed in spirit. For six long years I was riding the crest of a wave toward a shore that continually receded and expanded, showing now its reefs, now its populated and noisy centers, now the human faces upon its shore, inviting or threatening.

I think I had the reputation of being a very demanding teacher. I think too that my mind was still in a kind of mind-set. I know I always resented being referred to as a teacher of "dogmatic" theology. But the fact was that I was still, in many aspects, quite dogmatic. And that is the one regret that I have when I ponder those years. For the rest, I continued to grow, still very much in my own nest, with all possibilities both of befouling and of building it.

In 1957 I won the Lamont Prize for my first book of poetry. This was an enormous stimulus upon work that up to then had been wrought mainly in darkness. With the publication of my first book my mind exploded. The poems went into three printings, were a nominee for the National Book Award, and established me in the publishing world. Publishers would now take almost anything I chose to compile; the question of quality was largely in my own hands and my own sense of things.

I come now to the discussion of another watershed in my life. According to all plans, I was to lead a rather stereotyped year abroad in a Jesuit house, reportedly finishing a book and undertaking another. Those well-laid plans!

After some two weeks of searching for housing in Paris, I finally was able to find a student hostel and a job as chaplain. But by Christmas 1963, I had decided that Western Europe was no longer my cup of tea, and that if I had was to get anything out of the year I had better launch southward and eastward. And so I did. At Christmastime I visited Czechoslovakia and Hungary for periods of about one week each. It was my baptism in Marxist society. I was particularly moved by the evidence that the churches in those countries, especially the Protestant communities, were finding ways of survival in most difficult circumstances. I returned to Paris by way of Rome, in order to report to the Vatican on what I had discovered in Eastern Europe. It amounted to a very strong recommendation on the part of the Protestant communities that the Vatican begin to take a more practical interest in the religious and social situation in Marxist Central Europe. I reported to Cardinal Bea's assistant, a man who later became a bishop. He gave me a sympathetic hearing. I was trying to interest the church officials in the idea that I should be appointed a Vatican observer at the Christian Peace Conference to be held in the summer of 1964. Alas for those great hopes.

However, I did get to Prague in June of 1964 and proceeded with a group of American theologians into the Soviet Union, by invitation of the Orthodox and Baptist communities there. The impact of that trip is ineradicable upon my spirit. I was discovering for the first time, and at firsthand, the radically different social forms by which decent men and women were living. I was discovering peaceable communities of faith, surviving and even thriving in most difficult and trying circumstances. I was seeing at firsthand the damage wrought to the human spirit in the West as a result of the Cold War.

At Prague, I met with Christians from both Marxist and Western societies and gained some inkling of the role that the churches could play in the ongoing struggles for human peace and survival. Along with my American companions, I was also exposed to the full glare of world Christian opinion with regard to our part in the Vietnam War. From Japan to Cuba, Christians were assailing us, extremely embittered at the course that even then seemed to be written in our stars.

I returned to the United States in the autumn of 1964 convinced, as I now recall, of one simple thing. The war in Vietnam could only grow worse. The course we had set at the initiative of John Kennedy, and more remotely by Dulles's brinkmanship and by the nuclear fervor of Truman — all of this was about to turn in the direction of a war that we were in no mood to limit or to abandon. From one point of view, it struck me that we were about to repeat the already bankrupt experience of the French, with a new provocation and a new rhetoric. From another point of view, we were altogether masters of our own method. We had nothing like the colonial interest that France had had in Southeast Asia. But we were determined, justified as we were by the course and momentum of the war itself, to prove our manhood and to put to the test our formidable military machine. It is extraordinarily difficult, even years later, to attempt to unravel the tortuous symptoms and motivations that edged us even deeper into that remote morass. But the unraveling of that tangled and tightened skein is not my purpose here.

I am attempting merely to record that, for me, the course of
the future was made plain by everything I had experienced in
Europe and throughout other continents. That is to say, I began
after my return to the States in the autumn of 1964, as loudly as
I could, to say "no" to the war. I remember being afflicted with a
sense that my life was being truly launched — for the first time —
upon mortal and moral seas that might indeed overwhelm me,
as the tidal violence of world events churned them into an even
greater fury. I felt (and I believe I shared this conviction with my
brother Philip) that this war would be the making or breaking
of both of us. There would be simply no turning back upon the
initial serious moves we were making at that time.

I was even then signing statements of complicity and opening myself to the kind of prosecution that Benjamin Spock and
William Sloane Coffin were later to undergo.

Within a year's time, I had taken part in the forging of those
methods of protest against the war which, from our present vantage point, we perhaps are justified in calling conventional. We
fasted, marched, picketed, sat in, followed every step of escalation as well as we could with our halting methods and means; at
least we were digging the iron heel of Mars. We never succeeded,
and we never quite gave up. That is the best that can be said for
us. We must be content if it is to be our obituary.

Of course, the ground was shifting under my feet. My concep-
tion of history and of moral action was being altered, even as I
strove to act. The old, tidy, well-arranged box of the universe was
flying open, and the seven plagues were loosened upon the world.
There would be no closing that box again. There could only be an
attempt to follow the course of evil and the death with whatever
trail mercy and compassion might blaze.

Nor could I convey the electric and terrifying quality of the
times merely by saying that my relationship to my church and
my order were being profoundly reordered. The fact is, two cents
plain, that we were helping to create a new church, and a new
order. American Catholics had never before, in the history of
American wars, been found wanting. They were doubly patri-
otic because they were Catholic, and once had been commonly

branded as somewhat less than American. The epitome of the older Martian spirit was of course the cardinal archbishop of New York, then alive and flourishing. My "no" was being heard despite the sound of his immensely more powerful and permeating "yes." So it came to pass that only one year after my return to New York, I found myself faced with the most severe crisis of my life up to that time. It is almost impossible even at this date, to unravel the many threads that were weaving my shroud. The suffocating descent of that shroud about my head and body came about, I am certain, as a result of my peace activities. Among these, and evidently a source of great friction, was the fact that I had helped found Clergy and Laity Concerned about Vietnam during the previous summer.

Then there was the mysterious affair of the death of Roger LaPorte. He was a boy whose face I remember remotely at the edges of the crowd of young people on the Lower East Side who were resisting the war. He had recently left a monastery upstate and was seeking to discover his own soul among the young Catholic Workers. He had said to someone, as I recall, that he wished to get to know me better. But we had scarcely even spoken, apart from greeting one another on occasion. Then without warning, he immolated himself, in early November, before the United Nations buildings in New York early one morning. He lived for about three days. Within a week or two, the most atrocious rumors were linking his death to his friendship with me. It was not to be wondered that a time of growing national madness was also infecting us, on our own scene.

In any case, about a week before Thanksgiving, I was ordered out of New York and within a week was aboard a jet for Mexico City, bound for indefinite exile.

I spent about five months in Latin America. I traveled throughout ten countries, observing and writing. The story of those months is told in a later book, *Consequences: Truth and....* In the meantime, opinion in my behalf in the Catholic community had become so unified and pressing that my superiors were forced to recall me. An ad appeared in the *New York Times* challenging the archdiocese of New York and the Jesuit community as to their reasons for my hasty exit. The protest was effective. I was able to return, held a large press conference to announce the publication of two new books, and say that beyond doubt I would continue with my peace work as usual.

I finally was invited by Cornell University in the autumn of 1967 (the first Catholic priest in the history of the university) to take a position in the United Religious Work. I left New York with trepidation and many second thoughts. It appeared to me a choice of the utmost seriousness, to decide to leave the peace community, which was in perennial need of all kinds. But I decided to come, because Cornell was a new scene to me, and because the university had changed so rapidly in the previous two years. I must say that I have never had a serious regret for the choice I then made.

But the war was going from horrendous to intolerable; it was devouring more and more of the energies of our lives.

My brother Philip was working in the inner city of Baltimore; a community man, he drew the community around him like a magnet. The facts of life were his daily bread. He saw in his prophetic bones that our support of the student resisters was a game the government would tolerate indefinitely. So in November 1967 he and three friends decided to take their peaceable war into the enemy camp. As is by now well known, they poured blood into draft files in Baltimore.

I was at the time very far from their understanding of things. But I was shaken into reflectiveness. I had gone to Hanoi, I had experienced American bombings and brought home prisoners of war. So when Philip approached me in early May with a new action into which I was urgently invited, my immediate reaction was one of bewildered sympathy and shaken readiness. I was faced with the evidence of intransigent courage on the part of those who were already in legal trouble up to their very necks. Imagine Philip and Tom Lewis, men already under threat of several years of imprisonment, calmly repeating the same action that had brought them into jeopardy!

Like a shipwreck or a person sucked into quicksand or drowning, one to whom almost every resource of friendship and ingenuity is lacking, and yet who somehow emerges alive, I say simply that I was saved at the last moment.

In speaking analogically, I mean to speak no less rigorously. I was saved at the last moment. My brother and his friends were planning a new assault upon a new draft center. They visited me at Cornell toward the middle of May 1968. There, over a long evening of eating and discussion, they made their proposal to me. Would I join them? I was still wedded to the idea that in standing with the resisting students I was doing all that was possible, or indeed helpful. But after the others left, Philip opened before me the facts of the case, which he had so often outlined in correspondence with me. That is to say — it must be evident by now that the government would allow people like me to do what we were doing almost indefinitely; to sign statements, to picket, to support resisters in court. Even if people from the government did pick us up, it was they who were choosing the victim and the time and place of prosecution. The initiative was entirely in their hands. But in the plan under discussion, the situation was entirely reversed. A few people were declaring that the initiative of action and passion belonged to the peaceable and the resisting.

Toward dawn, I can remember seeing the light. I told Philip that I was with them. They should allow me some twenty-four hours to subject my decision to possible change of mood, but if they had not heard from me within that period, they could assume that I would be a member of the Catonsville group. And so, as the book of Genesis says laconically, it was done.

We nine invaded the draft office, took out hundreds of 1–A files, and burned them with homemade napalm in a macadam parking lot nearby. I remember so well the heat and fury of that afternoon, and the sense of almost crushing relief with which we faced one another after it was done.

I remember also, when we had been apprehended and put in temporary custody, the expressions on the faces of the FBI men as they entered and saw us clerics under arrest, the familiar face of Philip, previously apprehended in a like cause. How their jaws dropped! One of them turned in disgust to a companion and exclaimed, "I'm going to change my religion." Which was,

I would think, entirely to our point; we had invited men and women to a change of heart, so that in the case of this officer, to have changed from a conventional Catholic to a Christian, might portend the first success of our efforts.

We spent eight days in Baltimore County jail in Towson, Maryland. We fasted and prayed and rejoiced — and waited.

I remember that on the final day we decided to break our fast with a Eucharist. Someone had brought us in a loaf of freshly baked bread. We asked the warden if we might have a bottle of wine. He acceded on condition that he himself might be present for our Eucharist. Of course he might. Whereupon, around that board table, began one of simplest and most moving of communal actions. "Do this in memory of me." Which is to say: "In remembering me, re-member yourselves. Put your lives and your souls together again."

The unpredictable savagery of a federal marshal is also vivid in my mind. One day, as we were being taken handcuffed from the jail for a court appearance, a young nun who was a dear friend reached out her hand to mine in solidarity as we issued from the jail. One of the marshals came forward in a swift, reptilian move. He crashed down between our hands with a karate blow. "Don't touch!" It was the epitome of the system; he had said it all.

Don't touch — make war. Don't touch — be abstract, about God and death and life and love. Don't touch — make war at a distance. Don't touch your enemies, except to destroy them. Don't touch, because in the touch of hand to hand is Michelangelo's electric moment of creation. Don't touch, because law and order have so decreed, limiting the touch of one person to another, to the touch of nightsticks upon flesh.

I am, in this autumn of 1969, under federal sentence of three years, for destruction of draft files in May of 1968. So my life enters upon its middle course. These many beautiful years cannot be lived again. But they are compounded in my own flesh and spirit, and I take them, in true measure, with me toward whatever lies ahead.   —NBM, 11–26

LESS THAN

The trouble was not excellence.
I carried that secret,
a laugh up my sleeve
all the public years
all the lonely years
(one and the same)
years that battered like a wind tunnel
years
like a yawn at an auction
(all the same)

Courage was not the fault
years they carried me shoulder high
years they ate me like a sandwich
(one and the same)

the fault was — dearth of courage
the bread only so-so
the beer near beer

I kept the secret under my shirt
like a fox's lively tooth, called
self knowledge.

That way
the fox eats me
before I rot.

That way I keep measure —
neither Pascal's emanation
naked, appalled
"under the infinite starry spaces"
nor a stumblebum

havocking
in Alice's doll house.

Never the less!
Summon
courage, excellence!
The two, I reflect
could snatch us from ruin.

A fairly modest urging —
Don't kill, whatever pretext.
Leave the world undefiled.
Don't hoard.
Stand somewhere.

And up to this hour
(Don't tell a soul)
here I am.   — ARB, 393

2

Peacemaking Is Hard

PEACEMAKING IS HARD

hard almost as war.

The difference being one
we can stake life upon
and limb and thought and love.

I stake this poem out
dead man to a dead stick
to tempt an Easter change —
if faith may be
truth, our evil chance
penultimate at last,

not last. We are not lost.

When these lines gathered
of no resource at all
serenity and strength,
it dawned on me

a man stood on his nails.

an ash like dew, a sweat
smelling of death and life.
our evil Friday fled,

the blind face gently turned
another way. Toward life.

A man walks in his shroud.
                                        —ARB, 100

MIRACLES

Were I God almighty, I would ordain
rain fall lightly where old men trod,
no death in childbirth, neither infant nor mother,
ditches firm fenced against the errant blind,
aircraft come to ground like any feather.

No mischance, malice, knives.
Tears dried. Would resolve all
flaw and blockage of mind
that makes us mad, sets lives awry.

So I pray, under
the sign of the world's murder, the ruined son;
why are you silent?
Feverish as lions,
hear us in the world,
caged, devoid of hope.

Still, some redress and healing.
The hand of an old woman
turns gospel page;
it flares up gently, the sudden tears of Christ.
                                        —ARB, 60

FROM SHARPEVILLE TO SELMA

*In March 1965 Daniel Berrigan joined the civil rights march
from Montgomery to Selma led by Dr. Martin Luther King Jr.
The experience reminded him of his 1964 visit to Sharpeville,*

*South Africa, where in 1960 pro-apartheid white police officers
killed scores of anti-apartheid black protesters.*

One had the sense, rightly or no, of having landed here before.
It was not merely the red ground underfoot, swirling in the hot
wind, kicking up a red cloud around cattle and people and cars.
Nor the earth coming to life again, after winter in July, or winter
in January. Nor the plain that ran flat to the Spanish moss on the
buttonwood and scrub pine. One had seen all this before; but one
had seen something more, something that clung to the heart and
almost defied the reach of words.

It was in the air. It held the eyes of people to a stranger's
eye — too long or too briefly for comfort. It was in the air; it
was in the shuffle of the blacks, it clung to the unpaved streets,
the open garbage, the children playing in the dirt. It could almost
be touched; it was pervasive as memory; something terrifying and
obscene. It lingered around the troopers, played and played back
from faces too alike to be entirely human. It was death, and
violence, and years of terror.

It was the memory of Sharpeville. More than eighty had died
in a burst of vicious, pure unpremeditated violence. It was in the
air of Selma; the air bore it like a groan — memories of some
twenty years. Through these town roads, the body of a black
man, roped like a venison to the sheriff's car, had been driven
into the black area. Go slow — slow. Let them see who's in charge
here. It was in the air. Fifteen years ago a black man, arrested
"for talkin' back" on the word of a cranky white woman, had
been murdered in Selma jail. "An unknown policeman" had
entered his cell and shot him. His body was dumped off on
his family. No verdict, no investigation. But the town has not
forgotten.

It is still in the air. Jimmy Lee Jackson, shot in Marion for
defending his mother against a trooper's club, died in Good
Samaritan Hospital here. He had powder burns on the skin of
his belly. The barrel had been pushed to its closest range and
fired twice. The blacks remembered that night. When they tried
to send hearses from Selma to Marion to pick up the wounded,

lying untended in the streets, their answer had come from the sheriff's office: Come in here, you'll get what the rest got; I'll dump you in the river.

Could the whites forget, in Selma, or in Johannesburg? In Johannesburg they can, or almost. Once, Sharpeville had been a bitter memory; in '61, the economy was on the verge of a panic. Investors had taken their money elsewhere. There was talk that blood and revolution would follow on the deaths of the blacks. Small countries had begun a boycott; the British Commonwealth had expelled South Africa. But the great powers, and especially the United States, came to the rescue. In one year, 1961, we contributed almost the entire amount needed in foreign exchange to push the trend up once more; some 150 millions poured in to stop the crisis.

The slump was not only eased, it was entirely reversed. By June of 1963, with continued U.S. help, South African gold and foreign exchange reserves had more than tripled, to reach a record high. The boom was on. And no one, not even the hard-headed, cares to say where it will stop.

Time, they say, is a slow healer. Money, one thinks, works faster. One American businessman calls South Africa "tantalizing" to investors. "We know the people and the government, and we back our conviction with our reputation and our dollars."

But money has not come into beleaguered Selma. In the short weeks since blacks and northern whites declared nonviolent war, business has dropped by 50 percent. And time the healer has not arrived yet, is kept at bay; the false peace is interdicted. The blacks have seen to that; from Martin Luther King Jr. to the farmhand who shows up to march on Tuesday with Monday's bandage still bloody on his head. Indeed, the trooper is right when he cries, zooming like a tortured gadfly on his motorcycle from end to end of the marchers: "I've never seen anything like this in all my * * * life!"

Neither has the nation. Neither has the church. Whoever heard of a church, North or South, that has rung, day after day, week after week, with unending songs, prayers, sermons; a church that

spilled into the streets; a people ready for whatever hell the troopers are ready to bring down on them: dogs, horses, whips, tear
gas, billies? What liturgy prepares men and women and children for Lingo and Clark and Connor? What faith arms them
by forbidding them arms, tells them to march when they can, to
kneel when they cannot, to face the oppressors — maybe even
to convert them? The questions are fierce, and for the moment
(for white Americans), unanswerable. But the point is clear: the
questions are real questions, as real as the broken bones and the
blood, as real as the new hope.

Monday, March 15, 1965. We came in, thirty-five strong from
New York, in time for the memorial service for Reverend James
Reeb. We were from Harlem and Manhattan and Brooklyn,
blacks and whites, laypeople and priests. Selma was quiet as a
millpond; but the quiet was ominous; the pin had been pulled, the
depth charge dropped. Children wandered in the sun, the stores
were open, the fresh tourist signs were out: WELCOME TO SELMA.
Then we approached Brown Chapel, and the reality of Selma hit
like a tight fist.

The church was ringed with Clark's troopers. They lounged
in the open cars, feet hung out of doors and windows, eyes half
closed in the sunlight; helmets, billy clubs, a stereotype of sleepy
brutal power; the day of the iguana. Our car circled the church
for blocks — no way in. Finally, we parked and walked through.
The church was packed.

Light by light, individual purpose was fused in the incandescent air of black courage and black passion. Free-e-e-dom.
Free-e-e-dom. They sang it together, the skilled and the ignorant,
the neophyte and the victim. Some of them know what they sang.
But the others were learning.

The speeches began. Walter Reuther, an Orthodox bishop,
a Catholic bishop, two ministers, and, finally, Martin Luther
King Jr. The words range from noble to bathetic, and back again.
King's voice was ragged with exhaustion, the strain of vigils and
decisions, the killing round of the weeks, from courts to streets
to meetings and back again, with the responsibility of sending
the crowds out to face Jim Clark.

One thing was clear. This was the blacks' day. We were, at long last, at their side. But even the newsmen were not sure why we were there. They were not even convinced that we knew why. One of them asked us, in words that were not especially flattering: Why have the Catholics gotten into the act? We were not sure either, in a way that could easily be formulated. But it was something like an ethic of the guts.

In any case, it was the black people's day, their week; one might say, their week of creation. They had been conceived and born at Bloody Bridge, at all the bloody crossroads of the nation, weeks and years before Selma. Could they, this week, bring us over that Bridge, to birth? They might. Love is a marvelous midwife.

Johannesburg, the black township, Good Friday, 1964. The Gospel of Saint John was read in Zulu. And they crucified Him there; it was about the third hour. . . . The sea of color, the immobile, intent faces, men, women, children, hundreds strong, seated on the earthen floor. What could a white man say to them: what could a white priest say? He could say something surely; he might even say a new thing. He might say that Christ had died for all men and women, even for whites. He could take up his cross, hammered together by fate, propped up, waiting, visible to all. In South Africa, his cross was simply the fact of being a white man with some remnant of conscience. He could say in public, while the Special Branch Police lounged against the wall taking notes, that he was unworthy of his black brothers and sisters; that some day the whites might conceivably leave off being their executioners.

Monday, March 15, 1965, Selma. The long memorial service is almost over. Hardly any discomfort is evident; blacks are used to standing, kneeling, waiting; and the whites are learning. The weather outside is Alabama springtime, a frayed and dusty glory. Dogwood and magnolia are coming to flower. The benediction has been pronounced over the memory of Reeb. Flowers bank the speakers' stand. Someone has pinned to the front of the pulpit a drawing from a northern newspaper. It shows a wreath of thorns fastened to a gravestone, the tomb of James Reeb. Martin

King has spoken. And then the announcement comes; the march is permitted by court order. Three by three, in silence, we are allowed by the courts of Alabama to march on the courthouse of Selma. It is to be a memorial march for James Jackson and James Reeb. Prayers at the courthouse are permitted; we can even sing.

The Gospel of Saint John, in the Zulu tongue, so strange to American ears; sibilants and the clicking of tongues, with only the names Jesus, Mary, Peter, John, coming through. And about the third hour, they crucified Him. At the end, the veneration of the Cross. A great wave starts forward: mothers with children, young men, the very old. Three priests move among them, holding the crucifix to their lips. And spontaneously, as is the way with Africans, the chant starts: first, as one voice, hardly rising above the sough of bare feet, that sound which above all sounds is like sea, on a mild evening. The song is the Zulu dirge for a fallen warrior. They are bearing Him homeward to his village after battle. His name is Jesus, Great King, Black Warrior. Easily, with infinite delicacy and naturalness, the song breaks into harmony; two parts, then four, then eight. Jesus, Great Warrior, we mourn you.

The Zulus have a saying: those who are behind must run faster than those who are in front. Even to the Cross. Even when the Cross is held in white hands. Shall the whites time us, even to the Cross? Do they any longer even know the way?

The strangest thing about the march to the Selma courthouse was the utter silence throughout town. That, and the faces of the troopers. There was a trooper for every marcher, someone said. Almost, but not quite. The three hundred who left the church were joined, like streams to a great river, by those who had arrived outside, and were waiting; some two thousand in all. The town had gone silent, as though a great hand were clapped to its mouth, at five o'clock on a workday evening. Traffic was lined up at corners, storekeepers in their doorways; the troopers' cameras were clicking in the faces of the clergy. (Good to know we'll be in Jim Clark's scrapbook!) But mostly silence. Except that, all along the route, the transistors kept telling us and the nation what it was like, what it could never be like again, in Selma on a spring evening.

The breakthrough had come, irresistible as spring. You could see it, whoever you were, trooper or housewife, white or black. You could hate it like the approach of death, or feel it in your bones like the nudge of Christ on Lazarus — but it was there, for all the world to see. In the dusk around Courthouse Square (that's Jim Clark's courthouse — but no more, no more) the big TV lights went on in a wink, punctual as dawn, the lights no black had dared hoped to see. The prayers began: for the dead, for the living, for the persecutors. Martin King laid at the glass doorway a purple wreath: "For James Reeb," it said. At that moment, the worried, porcine face of Sheriff Jim Clark was peering through the glass. Jim Clark, framed in a burial wreath; beyond the mild ghost of James Reeb, the death of southern power and conscienceless law. For the blacks, it was a moment delicious beyond words.   — CT, 63–73

YOU FINISH IT; I CAN'T

The work is somewhere visibly round,
perfectly lighted, firm, free in space,

but why we die like kings or
sick animals, why tears stand
in living faces, why one forgets

the color of the eyes of the dead —
                                  — ARB, 58

THE ALTERNATIVE OF NONVIOLENCE

We were talking about the meaning of nonviolence in history and the relevance of the Sermon on the Mount. We tried to be real about the real state of humanity with regard to violence and then to suggest the hope that underlies a history of violence in a prophetic movement which does not declare this history is final, or is fully human, in spite of all the evidence to the contrary. We tried also to admit, as we think an ingredient of realism would, that the church has a history of violence, that the church at certain periods has consecrated violence, especially in the Middle Ages, during the periods of the Crusades.

So the hope here perhaps is two-fold from the point of view of the church, that her progressive emergence as a spiritual force and her separation from the powers of war have allowed her to emerge also as a force toward love and nonviolence. And then secondly, that the conscience of humanity, even as violence escalates, is also emerging in a profound counter-movement of Love, which expresses itself, let us say, not narrowly in opposition to war, but in works of compassion all over the world, which is of course the largest and most positive sense in which this idea of nonviolence can be taken.

Then we went on to the idea that the nonviolent understanding includes both a mystique and a tactic. This is a celebrated distinction of Péguy, not with regard to nonviolence, but with regard to all the central movements of life, that is, the inwardness and then the political and public consequences of this inward movement. As mystique, we claim that this is always and everywhere a way of looking at life and that the second question of political effectiveness is really secondary, even though extraordinarily important. And that the first aspect of all of this comes to us from many sources, we might say in the widest sense from the spirit of humanity itself. We can't claim it solely as a Gospel possession, though it is of course very strong in the Gospel, beginning with the teachings and the nonviolent work and ending with the nonviolent self-oblation of Christ our Lord.

The history of all religions shows that this nonviolent mystique is a constant, and perhaps we could say in proportion as history claims universality, it also claims this kind of compassionate inwardness. For instance, the writings of Buddha speak simply of the compassion of the Buddha and the possibilities of redemptive suffering. The deepest humanism of Confucius shows the same idea, though it's much more worldly and concentrates more on the second aspect here. The Taoist way is also rooted in a sense and reverence for humanity.

Gandhi is the first great figure of modern times to seize upon a viable idea — *satyagraha,* which someone translated, "the deathless embrace of the truth." It was his vision of life, that discipline for being human, that total metanoia, that change of heart toward God and neighbor which included, he said, the great virtues of scorn of death, abnegation, purity, single-mindedness. Through the long course of his struggle, both in South Africa and in India, he kept insisting, with the simplest of people and the most sophisticated of political opposition, that the means and ends are so closely joined that the purity of the end can only be measured by the purity of means.

This was the marvelous undercurrent of the whole movement: the means were never allowed to foreshorten the end or to bring the end closer by themselves becoming impure. There were no shortcuts to Gandhi's spiritual goal. The whole wearying and troublesome and anguished way must be undergone, step by step, because the purity of the means was so closely related to the purity of the goal that one built the purity of the end by undergoing the journey. He went on to say that anything is possible to a people if they kept this in mind. And that nothing was possible, that the whole idea of a pure end could be destroyed with very great speed, once the means became unimportant or ambiguous or impure.

The aim of violence always claims to be the suppression of violence and the achievement of the human community, and says that by using violence one removes the need for violence. Gandhi saw this as a tremendous historical illusion, that a pure end could be kept pure in the face of such means. During the years of the nonviolent struggle for freedom in India, this seems to have been his key insight. He played upon it in many ways in his letters and his addresses, both to the people, to his own leadership, and before the British courts. Claiming no immunity from suffering himself or on the part of his followers and, as Camus would say, placing his "body where his words were," he saw his life as a process that was continually reinvigorating his sources, continually keeping means in mind, so that the end did not become progressively abstract and vague, and allow for a growing kind of violent current within it. This is of course always a danger, as we know from our own movements here, that the violent means will be seized on as a way of foreshortening the human struggle.

Maybe in a few statements we can sum up what we've been trying to say so far. First of all, a nonviolent movement proceeds from a personal conversion. Martin Luther King Jr. has certainly adopted this. Many others have undergone profound personal conversions, either in the beginning or during the course of the struggle.

Second, nonviolence proceeds from an inspired faith of refusal into a positive stance in the world. So it insists on being within history, and will not allow itself to be shunted off into some sort of sectarianism or extremism before others. So it is constantly trying to keep its roots in the actual community even though it must in a certain sense stand apart by its refusal.

Third, this nonviolence sees itself at its best, as indivisible, and at its least, as potentially universal; that is, as a way of life that is simply human. In the nuclear age, it is the only alternative to the escalation of genocide and universal incineration. So you always note among responsible people both a profound spiritual root and a profound political responsibility.

Fourth, a difficult point. A nonviolent movement must be content with long-range vindication and be conceived of as a long-range hope for change. Thus in the past we can see it identifying itself with the end of feudalism or with the hope of the workers in Europe or with the anti-colonial movement in Africa and the East. So we are speaking here of the mystique in action, a mystique which has become a public technique. We have to look not merely to the quality of the men and women involved, but to the realization that an idea has met its hour. This is the glory of nonviolent history, that it has had this kind of visionary sense of "The times they are a-changin,' " as the song goes, and what the change means, where it is leading, and where it can be invaded. Thus an individual, or a small group, must be seen, not so much in negative terms as people in jail or people on picket lines or people under the censure of society. They must be seen as a positive offering to history, as connected with the most profound political and social change, the amelioration of humanity's despair.

Fifth, in societies founded on or dedicated to violence, the technique of nonviolence becomes extremely difficult, if not impossible. And I suppose that that's a judgment that has to be worked through by the people involved. I couldn't find any of the younger people of South Africa, for instance, encouraged about any aspect of nonviolent witness. This was completely obliterated by the political system. Perhaps ten or fifteen years ago it would have been quite possible but things have worsened horribly since.

So we could define the nonviolent person, in biblical language, as a prophetic nucleus of political movement. Such a person sees himself or herself not precisely as the person inserted into a crisis alone, but a person of history and a person within history, the person who believes that history has a future. That's not the easiest thing to believe in these days. She doesn't see herself as a sort of firefighter being rushed up to the point of disaster, and then becoming immediately ineffectual and irrelevant as soon as normal times resume. This is not the point at all. This person is actually the one who can give the possibility of a resolution to the crisis.

The nonviolent person is the one who within normal times can save normal times from their idolatries — neglect of the poor, growing bourgeois selfishness, weapons of war, and the other realities around us. So the nonviolent person is a person there. Period. In normal times, in crucial times. The faith is in the person and in history. In fact, over the long run, the nonviolent person is the one who appears as the realist, as what Camus loved to call "the modest Utopian," the one whose vision is implemented and is here and now for others. The nonviolent person does not seek an impossible compromise with the times, nor a prior, intemperate synthesis for the times. The nonviolent person sees life in terms of a choice toward change, involving a re-ordering of life.

— *Unpublished notes from a lecture on nonviolence, 1965*

THE FACE OF CHRIST

The tragic beauty of the face of Christ
shines in our faces;

the abandoned old live on
in shabby rooms, far from comfort.
Outside,
din and purpose, the world, a fiery animal
reined in by youth. Within
a pallid tiring heart
shuffles about its dwelling.

Nothing, so little, comes of life's promise.
Of broken, despised minds
what does one make —
a roadside show, a graveyard of the heart?

Christ, fowler of street and hedgerow
cripples, the distempered old
— eyes blind as woodknots,
tongues right as immigrants' — all
taken in His gospel net,
the hue and cry of existence.

Heaven, of such imperfection,
wary, ravaged, wild?

Yes. Compel them in.   — ARB, 45

DEATH DOES NOT GET THE LAST WORD

On November 9, 1965, Roger LaPorte, a young activist associated with the New York Catholic Worker, poured gasoline over himself in front of the United Nations and burned himself to death, in protest over the Vietnam War. Daniel Berrigan offered this homily at a memorial Mass for him on November 11, 1965, and because of it, was immediately ordered by his Jesuit superiors to leave the United States and go to Latin America for an

*indefinite period. His exile led to widespread outrage, including
a full-page ad in protest in the* New York Times. *He returned to
the United States in the spring of 1967. This homily has never
before been published.*

The immolation of Roger LaPorte has shaken us to our very
souls. It is part of our grief that he took this terrible action in
the midst of our community, that he was one of us. He was
our brother, not in a generalized sense which can be kept at distance — a brother across the world, or a brother who worshiped
in another form of Christianity than ours.

On a morning of this week, the flames have touched us. They
have ignited our own dwelling; have destroyed the flesh of a
brother, who was also a Catholic. There is no more immunity,
there is no more distance. Our hearts are without defense before
an act which is surely without precedent in our lifetime.

An event is striving to speak to us in a way no tragedy has spoken before. A man has allowed the history of violence to enter his
own flesh. One of the household of the faith has worked violence
against his life. Let us have the courage to reflect on these things,
to strive for some measure of understanding.

It is a time, indeed, to reflect on our history and on ourselves.

A community of Christians has been doing the works of mercy
for many years, in New York City and elsewhere. They have
worked out of the mainstream, counter to the tide of selfishness
and fear and mutual rejection which has stained our century in
America, which has stained the church as well. They found in
one another, and in the poor they served, a beloved community
which neither neighborhood nor parish, nor seminary nor school
nor family had offered them.

And what were they like, these men and women of service? Let
us speak openly of them; they are our brothers and sisters, they
are ourselves, often beset and perplexed and inarticulate, as each
of them would admit. They did their service clumsily, they were
often maladroit toward one another, they claimed no monopoly
on virtue or long sufferance or discipline. If any definition served

them, it was that of a community at the edge of Providence, tolerated by the church, unsure in its resources of mind and heart, unskilled in love, unschooled in theology; men and women whose vocation was neither a clarion call nor a clear mandate, but a tough-hearted daily measure of discouragement, fear, ennui, even of mutual betrayal and failure.

All this is freely admitted. And yet when it is all conceded, not one-tenth of the truth has been told. The psychology of the Catholic Worker family reveals only its problems; it leaves untouched its mystery. And the mystery is our concern; for it is that mystery of thirty years' duration, which alone can shed light on the encompassing tragedy of November 9.

The mystery I speak of is one of love, consecrated in the New Testament by the words, the action, and the death of Jesus. "A new command I give you; that you love one another, as I have loved you."

In a sense, of course, the commandment is not a new one at all. In Israel it was as old as the revelation to Moses. Our Savior paid tribute to it as the first and greatest of commandments. And in the cosmic religious experience of humanity, the commandment is as old as Buddhism and Hinduism. It marks men and women of conscience wherever they take their lives seriously, no matter what their idea of God.

And yet the commandment is new. Its newness lies in the unparalleled character of the One who proclaimed it. The Savior who makes all things new makes love new by incarnating it in his own person. The command of love issues from human lips which are also the lips of God. And the full rigor and glory of the command can be understood only in the measure in which we can follow his life, its gentleness and strength, its rigor and availability, its beauty and sorrow, and finally the form of death he submitted to.

The command of love was also new, because it marked a break with the dead past. Men and women had grown weary of love, neglectful of the occasions of love. They had been victimized by a most pernicious untruth, which corrupted the springs of their existence, their relations to their brothers and sisters and to God.

The untruth was in fact an attempt to announce a new definition of God. It started with all the force of a false tradition, that God was not love; that he was a lawgiver, an expert of observance, a master of the jot and tittle. According to such a God, it followed with a kind of baleful logic that an ox could be drawn from the ditch on a Sabbath, but that a person could not be healed on the Sabbath. It followed that priests could leave a person wounded in the ditch, to await the merciful hands of an outcast. For mercy was not the business of religion; compassion was outlawed from the sterile sanctuary, service to humanity was an anachronism.

It was in this breach that the Savior stood. His lucid, fearless conscience, his power of imagining the real world, his passion for the truth — all these stood outraged before the dishonor paid the Father by men who presumed to be sons of the Father. To restore the center of things, to bless and approve our instincts, to defend the neglected and outraged and forgotten — this was the task of his life. It was a task for which death itself was not too heavy a price.

And so he put his body where his words were. He submitted to death at the hands of violent men. And the energies of that life were so pure, the force of that love so encompassing, that a few defeated persons took heart once more. A great wave had gathered force; it could never again be stilled. It was a rising tide of love and of sacrifice. And the wave has at length reached us; we must now taste its bitter waters, of which the psalmist spoke: "Your waters have passed over me; I am utterly overwhelmed."

To be faithful to the death of Roger LaPorte, it is necessary to be extremely honest and exact in seeking to understand the struggle of one youth with the realities of the Gospel, as its truth is faced by modern life. He came to the Catholic Worker family at a time of bitter and cruel war. He sought and moved closer to a community of mercy and peace. Long before the Vietnam War, the Worker had grown through the works of mercy into the works of peace. The members came to understand that the two are in fact one. They are joined by the single blessing conferred on them by the Savior in his Sermon on the Mount. It could not be thought strange that before most Catholics could see the juncture, the Catholic Worker saw it, and spoke of it, and explored it, with that prophetic charity which is granted in greatest measure to the merciful heart. So when the war was unleashed, the peacemakers were ready. They confounded their society and won the respect of the press by exploding all the cruel stereotypes with which the public tried to brand their work. They fitted no one's caricatures; they were measured of speech, tentative in thought, conscious of the darkness in which they moved. They claimed no headlines; they acted without fear and took the consequences. And they found themselves in possession of a kind of knowledge, a grasp of history, a sense of humor, a rightness of direction, which were explainable only in light of the lives they were leading. Which is to say, service of the poor — immediate, anonymous, authentic, and single-minded — had conferred on these a balance of spirit which made them ready for times most were powerless to discern and helpless to interpret.

They were dealing with their times, and in so doing they were creating a future for humanity. And in the work of creating a future, and of themselves becoming men and women who were worthy of a future, the Catholic Worker found it was not alone on the scene. It was what Helder Camara has called one voice among many voices speaking for humanity. It shared with SNCC and CORE and the SDS and SANE a revolutionary and healing task in society. Its service to humanity now extended; the bread line, the soup line, the giving of clothing and shelter and hope, became symbols of the healing of the nation. The illness of that society is so nearly fatal that men and women rage against their healers, feverishly blinded to the truth of their condition. Futility and despair, triviality and waste of life, insensitivity to suffering, instinctive recourse to violence to protect the guarded playground — this is the prognosis of our American illness. Damaged consciences react in a damaged way. Men and women who dignify their fear of reality into a way of life, react murderously to the presence of reality. Men and women who claim no person for brother or sister turn with murderous wills on the brother or sister before them, whose presence and compassion and nonviolence are an overt invitation to violence. A lethal itch to have done with the burdens of adult life seizes feverishly on darkened minds — a murderous will to impose one version of life on others, to arm and implement and enforce one's obsessions at all cost. To stay history from summoning men and women to judgment, to silence the world of conscience and protest — these are dark forces which make war on the peacemakers, summon them to the tribunal, and condemn them.

But they cannot be entirely condemned. Their presence is within our bloodstream. People of peace are the other side of our baleful moon. They judge us. They are white and black, worker and intellectual, of faith and of no faith. They cannot be silenced while Western society still claims a tattered remnant of its own history and conscience.

And this judgment, ironically and tragically, is our hope. It is very nearly all our hope. The youth of the land are not buying the blueprint presented to them with all the pretensions of law and order, the misreading of history, the absurd military and political clichés. Against the armed might of its own nation, against the enslavement of loyalties a few are unlocking the forbidden door, are bracing it with their own bodies. The struggle is not new to them; they have had long experience in opening the alternatives to death; their lives have been a rigorous boot camp in the techniques of peace and unity. For some ten years they have traced in their blood and sweat and tears, their picket lines and jails, a thin line across the nation; a lifeline, a frontier of the spirit, a line drawn to mark the canceling of an evil history, a frontier of the only future we can claim. The line has not been drawn with bayonets; it is not a line of conflict. It declares war only on the enemies of humanity; its standard is one of service, its weapons are the tools of hope and compassion and competence.

I suggest that we have not seen such a thing before, in all our history. We have not seen the young so soon maturing, choosing for themselves the direction their lives will take, so fierce in their loves and hatreds, so clairvoyant in their grasp of essentials. We do not know how to deal with them. We come to them as teachers and find ourselves sitting at their feet, joining shamefacedly in a line already formed, a revolution already underway.

We speak in generalities about a gospel of peace and order, our gospel of cheap grace, our bland Rotarian texts; and they turn us off; our words and our lives. We talk with the false assurance of morticians about a great society; and they, from the rotting inner cities which are the truest monuments to our culture, have other news for us.

When life has taken violently contrasting forms, forms both of thoughtfulness and of betrayal, of responsibility and of abdication, it is not to be thought strange that tragedy will follow. It is not to be thought strange that the shape of death follows on the shape which life had taken. Men and women who live violently die by the sword, even though they die in their beds, secure in their possessions. Men and women who live the life of peacemakers die at peace, though they go up in the street like torches. For the unawakened and unconcerned are indeed at war — at war with history, at war with humanity's future, at war with the poor, at war with the majority of men and women, whom they have condemned to despair. And the men and women of concern die at peace though they die "spurned and ill-treated by a world too evil to see their worth" (Heb. 11: 38). Men and women bless the place of their sacrifice, their memory is seeded into the future; they breathe hope and courage upon us all.

Let us therefore not be deceived or dismayed by the death of Roger LaPorte. Beyond apparent violence, apparent tragedy, a great gift is offered to us. But the gift can be claimed only if our minds are open to it. The gift, I think, is this: an understanding that the death of a good man is always offered for the sake of life. More exactly, it is offered for the sake of the living. For those who understand, this horrendous final gesture of a young life, means exactly this. His death says, in a voice louder even than his life, "No more death! Death never again!" Death never again. The word is one with the great command: "Love one another, as I have loved you." But when we refuse one another, death again has dominion over us. When we meet the crises of other lives with indifference or temporizing or double talk, when we grow thoughtless and cruel in our security, death's dominion is asserted once more. When our communities of faith disintegrate into enclaves of the pious and the ineffectual, death is our master. Love has no dominion over us.

One man stepped outside the cruel and vicious circle in which humanity was trapped. "Love one another, as I have loved you," he said. Is not the death of Roger illumined by this Eucharist, by the meaning of the death of Christ?

In the deepest sense, what we remember here together is not a death at all, neither a dead Christian nor a dead Christ. It is a resurrection; it is a new hope, new steadfastness, new vision, new resources of joy and peace. Indeed, if Christ died, it was in order to rise again. It was to assert that death does not have the last word, or the loudest word. It means that we have the power of denying all tribute, all validity, all respect to the forces of death. It means that we have the power of putting death itself to death, of declaring war on war, of offering to others the pure and uncorrupted waters of their love.

At the news which reached us on Tuesday, we stood somewhat like the disciples before the sealed tomb. A great adventure had closed for them; death had asserted its brutal and absurd power. The Lord was struck down. A light had sunken in the heavens. Goodness and truth and joy were extinguished from the earth. But all this was only a darkness of a few hours, for them and for us. The scattered remnant, the watchers at the tomb, saw how "a great light has dawned on us." And they remembered his words: "In the world, you will have sorrow; but take heart, I have overcome the world. I shall see you once more; and your sorrow will be turned to joy, and your joy no one will take from you" (John 16:33, 22).

We submit to this young death, the death of our brother. About this table, we gather our scattered and distraught energies into wholeness and courage. We stand together once more at the Eucharist, celebrating the resurrection of Our Lord, as men and women restored in body and soul, men and women whose covenant with humanity is sealed and signed once more, as "witnesses to the resurrection," as the early men and women of faith proudly declared themselves, men and women ready to take up the burden of being sons and daughters of "the God, not of the dead, but of the living."

A NEW EXODUS UNDERWAY

These journal entries were written while Daniel Berrigan was in exile, traveling through Latin America, from November 1965 through the spring of 1966.

Cuernavaca, Mexico

The important thing was not that injustice had happened *to me*. The important thing was that injustice had occurred at all; that injustice was still possible — an evil of this kind, the defeat of good work, the silencing of truth. This bit deep. But the purification of evil was the most important thing of all; first of all in myself — neither bitterness nor vengeful thoughts, not even malingering around the idea of personal vindication. The desire for purification must advance into the possibility of creating purity in others, and especially in systems of authority which had become the persecutor, and in that measure were impure.

To turn others toward peace. One does not walk out of that vocation in walking across a border. Not even when one is forced across. For one cannot be forced out of his or her own peace, nor out of the making of peace. One can only be forced by the hand of God into another ambiance, another opportunity. In this sense, one is forced into the realization of what is always struggling to be born in the church, of what cannot be brought to birth without a struggle. The intelligence of Christ so often took up this theme: in death, in new birth, in a new age of humanity, in a new quality of life.

Unity is always cheap in the beginning. We are born into it; we inherit it. Such unity is a grace, a foothold. The falsity comes when we live off our inheritance without trading in it, without giving it away or starting anew. In such a case, the bloodline becomes a curse, the inheritance a slavery.

To the degree that life becomes conscious, it becomes charged with responsibilities. And becomes universalized. And yet more and more concrete. *Pax in parvis et in multis.* And conversely. The irresponsibility and regression implied in "leaving history to form itself" — or in leaving history to others, or assailing it with the stereotypes of one's own betrayals of truth.

We seek a morality which builds itself from a convergence of values. Lives press in on us and we are powerless to remain unconscious of them. They pour out on us their cries of lives betrayed, sold, neglected. To construct a conscience from such lives, from the living.

A time of war judges the time of peace that has gone before, and the quality of those who built the peace. Were they truly peaceful women and men, or were they sunning themselves along a wall they had not helped to raise? To go along with such a peace is very like going along with war.

The price of a false peace is as high as the price of a hot war. In fact, the cost of the first amounts to exactly the inevitability of the second.

A time of division, of misunderstanding, and of friction may well seem the least auspicious time of healing or of reconciliation. And yet, when love is in question, the opposite may also be true. The worst of times may be the best of times.

Those who have been evicted from their normal community may well be "the least of these" — the least qualified for peace and unity. And yet the opposite may be true: A testing of spirits may reveal that the worst have something in their favor, something to offer others.

A time of war may be the least favorable time in which to speak for peace. Much is against it: frenzy, conflicting loyalties, and newly inflamed fears drive passions forward with a boiling intensity. Who will have energy and staying power to confront the times, even to create a countercurrent, a kind of temperate Gulf Stream choosing its own mysterious direction, maintaining its own temperature?

One must accept the ironies of life and take up the tasks of life. Disgraced or not, foolish or wise, living in ill times or good, we are what we are, we are where we are. The actual world is our only world. We must go forward; we must accept all that people say to us, however painful or unfair it be. The times allow for no delay. Life grants us no space for idleness, regrets, the pursuit of illusions. The work of peace must go on, in hardiness and steadfast good humor. We must consent to being ourselves, to being the unworthy vessels of God's work, to working with others, to the slow inching forward of compassion and hope.

What is the task before us? It is as large as life itself, and remains so even when times of crisis or war narrow it to the compass of a needle's eye, to a simple *No* to war and violence. If we must pass through the needle's eye, must take an unfrequented road, still our journey must not be solitary or capricious. It must be a journey with others and for others. It must form the largest possible company which is commensurate with a good conscience. It must include those who agree with us wholly, those who disagree in part, those who confront us with unwelcome alternatives. All are our sisters and brothers: it is their task as well as our own. We journey toward humanity. We all hear the same cry in the darkness — the wounded and the violated, the neglected poor, the victims of our history, those in whose destruction we have had part.

The mystery of the Cross. It is the mystery of this war, which has destroyed so many lives, including the moral lives of those who destroy. A war that has now reached perilously into my own life and destroyed its former shape, deflected its energies, disrupted its friendships, made of my life an occasion of division instead of the sign of unity I had hoped for.

An acceptance of the presence of mystery implies a lucid understanding of one's self and of others. One cannot claim to master life so long as he or she is ignorant of life. The obsessive longing for peace at any price, the willingness to barter valuable men and women for the cheap grace of good order, the dread of responsibilities implicit in friendship — all these are germane to the mystery I speak of. They are the ingredients, since life is a rich vintage and offers but love and joy and heroism as well as other things. But we must speak of *this cup*, the taste of its contents presently on our lips. And the taste is that of gall, so extremely, so purely and outrageously bitter that one can perhaps conclude that no human ingenuity could have devised its essence. It is a vintage of God — or of Satan. Or, absurdly, of both.

So there is a problem of evil, and there is a mystery of evil. The first is a product of history, explainable to history, assuaged to a degree, within history. Its nature is not of formal interest to me. Or let me at least say: such evil could not create me as a human being any more than it could destroy me as a human being. It can awaken energies or render them lax and lazy. Its omnipresence can arouse compassion or despair. It can send my hand to my pocket or send me on a conventional religious mission. It can command gestures without content. But its power over me goes only so far, only so far into my eyes or skin or soul as to leave them intact, neither greatly offended nor painfully awakened. I remain what I am though a beggar is before me, though an accident occurs down the street. I sit in the sunlight; I continue with my dinner. My moral life takes food and drink, hears and sees and breathes the air of the world, evacuates its poisons. I remain a good intellectual animal, an approved domesticated specimen, a moral neutral. I deal inoffensively with the world; it offers me no reason for acting as anything but its colorless civil servant.

But the mystery of evil! Not a problem raised to the nth degree. Problems are made for us in order — through their largeness and scope and puzzle once confronted — to make us more fully ourselves. Through solutions we enter into wider, and richer, implications of our universe.

But mystery? A will exists, which declares itself in a Human Being like us, to be a Will of Love, of concern. This Will has its design in the world, is immanent in the world. But it is not subsumed, not seized on by the world. Indeed, this Will brings the world to a term that no confluence of history, no concentration of energy or genius or human love could imagine — much less bring about.

So the end of the problem is, at least in degree, an "arrival": a human being is in outer space; a disease is controlled; a theory is vindicated. But before mystery, we stand perpetually before an invitation so merciful, in fact, that our submission before it as well as our powerlessness to possess it is our greatest dignity. To stand under that waterfall whose music is the promise, "More, I will give more!"

It is cliché that history is always renewing with surprising events, that the truth is a matter to be lived, to be made present in persons and communities. One way of doing this — one among many — is to speak the truth. Which is not always possible, or even expedient. Or even, let it be added, valuable. One recalls the intemperate, insistent, all-disclosing kind of truth that leaves men and women unmoved, leaves them only more stubbornly where they were.

But to live the truth! Another matter entirely. So different a matter, in fact, of so different an order, that it raises questions of truth to another plane, sheds upon them an altogether unexpected radiance, grants them a new parabola of experience upon which to draw. To be concrete: Is it better, in defense of the truth, for us to be in community in New York exploring with others the questions that animate us, drawing on the resources concentrated there to protest evil, to uncover the alternatives of life? Or is it better to be thrown back upon one's self abroad, leaving our past like a diminishing wake, a memory that is freshened only by occasional flutters? It is hard to answer. Perhaps it is useless to attempt to answer. For if either activity is valid as a human contribution, it must be true that both the range of life is in fact being extended, and that we are living the truth for others. We are not wasting or violating life in either circumstance; nor are we turning selfishly or surreptitiously to our own ends.

The call to live the truth, rising from the pages of the Gospels as well as from one's own being, thus can act in two complementary ways. It can chasten and subordinate one's activity to the good of others, and it can act in order to interpret misfortune. The first is the task of conscience as reproof and limiting power of spirit upon egoism. The second is conscience as consoler. In both cases, we are speaking of the activity of the spirit of truth.

"It is sad not to see any good in goodness" (Gogol). It is at least equally sad not to see any evil in evil. In both cases we are speaking of a consciousness that is fearfully alienated from its proper world function. That function is the making of history, which "walks upon two legs" or falls flat. But which must go forward with humanity....

The truest joy of Christians is to know that their lives serve; to know even obscurely that something is building up within them; to sense that an obscure fidelity, moment by moment, act by act, has brought them to where they stand at present. In apparently haphazard or brutal circumstances, they can witness in their lives some larger creation than their lives had prepared for; a mysterious beginning of a race which is at length fit for the world — fit for here and now, and for eternity. Something larger than themselves! And exhilaration in all that is — in the midst of all that is apparently defeated and broken. An exhilaration, a gift to others, a life that shows when all is weighed in the balance, something left over, something available for others.

Suppose we were to disappear from the human landscape, in the sense that no merely inherited signs of our life on earth existed. To give up a history which is in so many aspects false, in what it is pretending to say, or persuading itself that it is saying. We must admit that a rather large percentage of what we are doing could disappear without any real damage to humankind. But force the same question further: What if the "Christian message" itself were silent for one generation? When the question is put in such a way, we perhaps come to the real point — which is that Christ might then have a chance to be heard, without the corruption of false signs offered by those who are irresponsible inheritors of the pure Word.

Human indignity attains another meaning here in Lima, Peru, and inevitable by way of contrast, men and women give another meaning to human dignity than we are used to. How can those who honor themselves allow others to be dishonored? We saw, coming in from the airport, the smoldering, stinking *favellas* — half garbage heap, half dump — where thousands of families live what may be called life. "And he fed the pigs, and would wish to have eaten the husks of pigs" (see Luke 15:15–16).

What happens to people who are condemned to live and die in the places we have seen? And, more to the point, what happens to the chiefs of society, who allow such conditions to prevail; indeed, whose power of place depends exactly on the existence of such places? To all appearances, the twenty First Families of Peru seem far indeed from the fate of Job. They are neither stricken by God, nor driven by frenzy to curse God. They exemplify what is in many cases a kind of blasphemy and a kind of judgment of God, for they are "good Catholics."

We have heard of a bishop in a poor diocese who asked $175 for a wedding in the cathedral. He wears a train some sixty feet long, never appears in the slum areas, and is known to live with a certain insistence upon personal comfort. We concelebrated this morning in a parish church where the pastor read the bishop's Lenten letter to his people. His words spoke much of heaven and more of hell, and urged, among other virtues, that Christians "be resigned to the social condition in which they were born." This in a diocese where Indians from the mountain areas live on less than five cents a day and chew coco leaves to immunize themselves from the cold and hunger. The people were also urged to fast and pray. For many of them, nature and feudalism had already conspired to ensure the first benefit. And no bishop could attach them the second, so long as the church itself invested in their misery.

We spent most of the day in the Monton slum. I suddenly came from great perplexity into a kind of peace. Sick at the stomach, eyes smarting from the smoke of spontaneous combustion arising here and there and settling in a pall upon the whole area. Was the peace a spurious one? In any case, it was as though God were trying to say:

Try to understand that these conditions are a biblical condition. They are joined to the life of Job and Jeremiah, to the death of Isaiah and Jesus. Try to understand further that my hidden mercy is never less hidden than here. Try also to understand that I have led my people as pioneers to this place, as a desert encampment, fortifying in them the fiber of heroes — steadfastness, freedom from illusion, isolation from the corrupt possession of the earth, love, and detachment. Understand also that you are led here for this purpose: to know in such a place as perhaps nowhere else that a future is being formed for you and others. In these people, in the few who share their fate, a new exodus is underway, a new form of death which always precedes birth.   — CT, 77–122

NOTES FROM THE D.C. JAIL

At midnight on October 22, 1967, Daniel Berrigan was arrested at the Pentagon for his participation in a massive anti–Vietnam War demonstration. It was his first arrest. He was charged with a misdemeanor for "refusing to move on when told." He was released on October 27, the day Philip Berrigan and the Baltimore Four acted.

The strangeness and inner difficulty at coming to terms with the new life thrust on one here. Last night, a lurid "confrontation," which seems more and more to me like the collision of two absurdities. One of them plate-armored like a clanking dinosaur. The other, the improvidence and absurdity of those who put their trust in "spirit and power."

Thousands of soldiers, air-lifted from distant points — an inconvenience that ensured their truculence in facing the "job": ourselves.

What a time, when theology is written on the run, in snatches and fits and starts. And yet I can say with all my heart's approval, we have come full circle and are back in the prison of Antiochus or Herod, speaking through the bars.

Five hours last night at the cold proscenium of a Greek state: the Pentagon, the lights, the stern tragic chorus of troops, the protagonists, the iron *anagke* of the White House, reaching even as far as our domestic distant lives, brought suddenly near at a point of mortal crisis.

So now I am forty-six, and at length in jail, and two reflections occur:

1. Why was I so long retarded from so crucially formative a happening?

2. What's the big joke, You there?

Today, things were not altogether easy; one feels pain and joy together in the same guts. When we were locked up last night, it seemed to me that we had been let out, for some brief time, of the horror and willful idiocy of the world into a place where goodness gathers by privilege, after long loneliness and struggle. Who is free anyway, and who is unfree, given the world, given the church?

I wish it were possible to write a poem. Everything, from the radiators, four-toned with rust, to the tympanum of the old heating valves, to the aggressive chaplain, to the phalanx of helmets and stern non-faces last night — everything so exceeds the prosaic that I am quite at a loss.

On the radio a senator denounces the Pentagon demonstrators: 99.99 percent of the American people, he pontificates, can never agree with such activity. And the President declares he will see the war through, in spite of such as us. It has not penetrated official consciousness that the Pentagon is itself the enemy. And who will remove or levitate or exorcise that one?

Transferred today from dormitories to cells, for various crimes; mine being the refusal to pay the fine. So here I am with about thirty others, the hard core resisters, fasters, limp-goers. This is going to be the simplest sort of housework I have every had — a john in the corner, a sink and a bed. Some light gets through the barred window. It is a narrower ambience than the gorges and skies of Cornell.

The court, quickly set up this morning to dispose of all the remaining cases, had the stale air of a kangaroo pouch. The presiding judge, quickly sworn in, was ill at ease before the hirsute, curious, intent faces. He seemed determined to conquer his greenness by administering the sternest and purest form of justice. So my punishment was the double of the man who appeared immediately before me, judged guilty of the same misdemeanor. I will evidently have some quiet hours ahead to figure this one out.

There is a great shouting at one another and cheering for one another, as some limp-goers are dragged in. Several are on water fasts. Many have refused to go before judges. There seem to be many styles of saying "no." Meantime, the chaplain addresses me soberly through the bars; he is quaffing a can of orange juice as he speaks. I think he would like to administer a Catholic loyalty oath. But it doesn't quite go over. A hard face, a hard manner. I suspect he has me catalogued for a heretic.

October 24. The third jail in three days. Now the D.C. jail. Arrived at 4:30 p.m. to face the humiliating public stripping and search for dope. All were in good spirits.

For the first time, I put on the prison blue jeans and denim shirt, a clerical attire I highly recommend for a new church.

Six and one-half hours later we were still without supper. Some twenty of us, with twenty of the prisoners who had returned from work crews, were locked in a forty-by-twenty-foot cage. Meantime, an unexplained "count" went on. One prisoner collapsed, vomiting on the floor, the temperature mounted. It was one of the few times that I knew fear. Perhaps I had bitten off too much "reality." But I made it after all.

"In framing an ideal, we may assume what we wish. But we should avoid impossibilities." (Aristotle)

The ideal here is manifestly a modest one, but presupposes reserves of good humor, balance of mind, and inner freedom — a modest utopia in fact. I hope my order can come to understand the workable limits of what I am trying to do. Perhaps through this and similar actions a few of the younger men might be impelled to get with human history in a more personal and imaginative way. What I do is certainly not done from obsession or a mental strait-jacket. Jail and fasting are by now well-worn tools of human change. . . .

I have not thought a great deal about the war. Strangely enough it seems that one comes to a center, by way of the war, whose fiery outer reaches protect the heart of the matter — community, the omnipresent possibility of love, waiting like an abandoned child for the moment of recognition.

"Why should you be stricken any more? You will revolt more and more. The whole head is sick and the whole heart faint" (Isa. 1:5). "Except the Lord of Hosts have left to us a very small remnant, we would have been as Sodom and Gemorrah" (1:9).

One of the least bearable of sights is the injury of the helpless, whether on the line Saturday when the paratroopers used rifle clubs to beat the linked arms of the protesters, or here, the sight of bodies being more or less deliberately struck against corners, walls, or dropped to the concrete floor when the prisoners are pulled or borne from place to place, refusing, as some of them do, to walk. At such a moment one knows both the gravity and the grace of flesh. What saves even worse things from happening is the continuous talk that goes up from the other prisoners, exhorting the guards to mercy, relieving the exasperation that attends on their hated burdens.

It is not so much that political solutions fall short of effecting social change. It is nearer the point to say that today politics itself is corrupted in its deepest intention. A chasm has opened between the meaning of the common good as public fact and spiritual change as a personal postulate. But to be a political man or woman implies openness to conversion of heart. The rest is vanity.

"*Attention! Attention!*" A quasi-military yell, based on the most inhuman assumptions about others, is also — strangely — a summons to freedom. Attention! Concentration! Intensity!

The sun comes up from afar, like a bearer of good news weary of his own burden. He arrives faint, with hardly the life left to breathe life into men. But he transfigures the faces, for a few moments. The young prisoners are at the barred door talking softly to the guards. The protesters have no objection, literally, not one, to conditions here. So they make peace in the unlikeliest places. The guards come to stare and glower and stay to talk.

Sometimes. Too much success would dull the fine edge of danger and change. . . .

There is news, and most of it bad, from the Hole. There, seven of our brothers spent the night naked on concrete, in near freezing cold, stretched next to an open non-flushing privy. At one point the guards attached wrist clamps to them, tightened them unbearably and dragged the men naked across the floors. They have no food or drink. Thus far the Great Society.

The only absolutes at work here are the extreme variables of love, in its sinuous, subtle, always exciting movement. One of the men does this, another does that, another a third thing. Each spins his own lifeline like a spider out of his guts. Result: a trembling daring web of great precision and strength — which we can all walk.

No need of organizing among us. Each acts spontaneously and truthfully, out of the heart and experience and the flesh, the concurrence on essentials is inevitable and right.

Variety! A two-edged sword. I think of how many in this room have the long-distance patience of Lincoln, the impassioned urgency of eighteenth-century nation-makers. And they are in jail, a commentary on a society that cannot bear with its own patriots. Springs in the desert, flowers in the barrels of rifles, life in the smoking breach of death. Am I really here? I will be asking myself in a few days — was I ever here?

One of the young prisoners comes at me like a red guard. He is puzzled, annoyed. "You're a believer, but you're a good man. Why do you need Jesus?"

To him, I drag along a series of tin cans, empty and noisy, the historical debris and waste of religion: inert ideas; warmaking cardinals; the hot, anti-human, anti-history, pure puritan, alienated "religious" community. My difficulty with him is not that I don't see his point. God knows I have struggled with it for years. But he is as intolerant as a barracuda, and won't admit of any good in a mixed scene. In spite of it all, what is the story of humanity, or religion, except the despised remnant, struggling in the toils of violence tightened by the world and by the world's religions? But on the other hand, where did God ever announce himself as a majoritarian anyway? The big text on consensus from Isaiah is, as one might have predicted, a corruption of the original.

Long discussions are provoked by the presence of men in the Hole. Yesterday three of them gave up and came back to us. Also to be dealt with are the immaturity of many, the settling pall of a routine. When is resistance a mature response to the systems and powers that claim our lives? And when does it become a petulant form of egoism? A hard line to draw — let alone hew to.

I wish it were possible to think noble thoughts or to write big words, or to have a sense of holiness or wholeness. But my pencil is drier than my mouth. What keeps me going is the sense, however obscure, of communion with the victims and the immediate presence of my friends here.

Friday. "Give honor to the Lord of Hosts, to God only. Let God be your fear, and let God be your dread" (Isa. 8:13). I thought of how this characterizes my friends here. Of course, there is a fine electrified line between fear as a death-dealer and fear as another human emotion, to be dealt with, walked with, as a man walks with his shadow. But walks.

Last night another Quaker meeting with long periods of silence. Then a discussion, the threads of which go into deeper meanings of these days — the community of poor around the world, religion, and especially Catholicism. A rather general and generally thoughtful critique of the church. A new style of belief, apparent in a different but analogous way, among students, too. The common note being — what keeps alive something that has stiffened and hardened beyond all serviceability? Is there a point at which one withdraws the tubes and bottles and expensive intensive care from the dying? Where would one go to today who wished to enter a mendicant order? The Little Brothers and Sisters of Jesus? I note in these young activists:

Interiority. They move skillfully and naturally through their own guts and heart. Honesty toward a corrupt and violent society makes for honesty with themselves. The air in lungs as pure as the outer air. They swim freely and totally in the here and now, like the mynah bird in Huxley's novel. The rhythm of days, so monotonous and enervating to monotonous men, thus comes a pitch of excitement and surprise that charges everything.

O Great Society, to what shall I compare thee? Shall the symbol of these days be our communal toothbrush or the beds sans sheets or the open-style johns or the affluent guards or the sun streaming like a stroke from Degas's brush, the great eye upon the blind, seeing us who cannot see him?

Intelligence. They are well read, they are capable of discipline as they are incapable of being pushed about. Dangerous, as a good mind is a danger to the mindless. A fine sword, a refusal to wound.

They should be in public office, in the Kingdom of the meek, the boroughs of the strong. They should be the Supreme Court and the Senate. They should be in the White House. They should be pope, with the College of Cardinals composed of say, the Beatles, Malcolm X (posthumously), Debray (on condition of nonviolence), Robert Lowell, Tom Merton (who would smile and refuse), Corita (to issue flowered press releases), two members of the *Phoenix* crew, an astronaut each from Russia and the U.S.A., Marianne Moore and one Brooklyn left fielder designated by her.

The sun makes it. Brilliant, conspiratorial, unfrenzied, uncozened, uncribbed, unbusted. We might make it, too.

—NFH, 3–16

THE CHURCH
AFTER THE BALTIMORE FOUR

The action of the Baltimore Four, as things evolved, proved not only a watershed moment in the antiwar community; it was also a reshuffling of the Catholic cards, stacked to the elbows with assured salvation and no losers.

For many reasons, the Catholics were the least equipped to grasp the import of that audacious action. A raid on a draft board, carried out with scrupulous care for the safety of all concerned, including the women who worked there! It was part of the moral grandeur of the act that it claimed to draw on a tradition, one nearly suppressed by second- and third-generation American Catholics, as they busily went about getting assimilated in this country. Who were we, anyway? And was the old just war morality of any point in the hideous Asian carnage?

The Catholics who ran the church said it was the only point. A cardinal said it constantly; other bishops said it by saying nothing. Then along came these upstarts, the so-called Baltimore Four. They tossed blood on the credentials of legitimate killing, the entrance cards into adulthood — if the truth were told, entrance into state and church alike.

Those draft files! They were, of course, more than they purported to be. They had an aura, they were secular-sacred documents of the highest import.

But who owned the tradition, anyway; and who was worthy to speak on its behalf? Was it the cardinal of New York, and his chauvinism? Was it the silent bishops and their uninstructed flocks, playing follow-the-leader, paying up, sent off to war?

Indeed, the issue was not simply that a tradition was traduced daily by those responsible for its purity and truth. The issue was a far more serious one. A tradition was something more than a moral fashion, to be laid aside when out of vogue, taken up again when the times dictated.

The tradition was a precious voice, a presence, a Person. The war had silenced the voice, outlawed the Person. Church and state had agreed, as they inevitably did in time of war, that the Person was out of fashion, "for the duration." He had nothing to offer in face of the guns. What indeed could He be thought to offer, with His utterly bizarre command — to lay down the guns?

He was a prisoner of war, this Jesus. He was in a species of protective custody. It was all done quietly, discreetly, out of sight and mind. Indeed, though the Embarrassment was removed, any hardheaded Christian could see that a veritable triumph had been achieved.

The subsequent game went something like this. It was as though He was still present: the church churned on, its wares were offered as usual, from font and table and pulpit. It all worked quite well; it was remarkable (no offense to Him intended), how His absence was scarcely noticed, or the derogation of the intent of His words, His healing, His reconciliation of enemies.

Priests spoke feelingly of this and that. His birth, public life, death, and resurrection were celebrated as usual. But these were rites held for the dead. They summoned nostalgia, not the hard force of presence. They touched on everything except the shame, the absence, the silence. So the sermons brought a mere ghost to bear, weightless, on every question but the real one. The faithful were exhorted to be moral, husbands to cherish wives, children to respect parents: it was all as usual. But the church had become a holy morgue, the dead were preaching morality to the dead.

Then, in the midst of this sorry charade, something happened. It was as though someone of infinite daring and courage, armed only with a rumor, a suspicion, had penetrated a castle keep, and found there alive, a fabled, beloved prisoner, long resumed dead.

He returned, this daring invader; he had a message. He could not free the Prisoner; but he brought back incontrovertible evidence: Jesus existed, His word held firm, He recanted nothing. The war was criminal; the guns were to be laid down. Likewise the bombers were to be grounded, and so on. Tell the people so, tell the bishops so, tell the pope so.

And further: blessed were the peacemakers, now as before; they were to be accounted true sisters and brothers of the Prisoner.

I suppose for the moment that a group of Mennonites or Quakers had performed the Baltimore draft action. In such communities, the act would touch on a history. Each of these communities has endured much trouble from the law, both in Europe and in the American Revolutionary period. Each has borne extraordinary spirits who risked their lives in quest of moral stance and statement; each has a history of martyrs and prisoners of conscience on our own soil.

I am not waxing romantic. Such an action as the Baltimore Four dared might indeed erupt in controversy within pacifist

communities. But the argument would be contained by the tradition; it would revolve around tactic rather than principle. And
on that score, it might be thought relatively easy of acceptance,
or, at the least, of tolerance.

Not so among Catholics. For a thousand years, the peacemaking Jesus has been out of fashion. In the matter of war, as
war became modernized and thereby totalized, the Catholics were
at sea; without leadership, at least among those ordained to such
office. And when, here and there, Catholics of courage arose and
risked repute and life itself, as happened during the Hitler years,
such would find themselves without sanction, friendship, support.

In consequence, no real debate ensued. Whether, for instance,
it was right or wrong, morally expedient or morally outrageous,
to enter a draft board and cast one's blood about: such questions were long ago answered. Or not so much answered as
superseded. So long ago had such questions been raised at all.
The moral questions, concerning government property and its
inviolability in time of war, the attitude of Christians toward
war itself — the American Catholic experience rendered the
questions void.

There remained only an assumption that cried to heaven for
redress; instead of the declared criminality of all wars, Catholics
were to assume the normalcy of war. The objectors against war
were thereby reduced to a suspect, isolated minority.

As a result, the war atmosphere among Catholics exhibited, in
the main, the same fear, hatred, ignorance, as were ravaging the
national community. The same and, for lagniappe, the example
of Cardinal Spellman, and a blessing once more traced over just
war theory and practice.

In sum, the church also declared war against Vietnam. A massive
cultural weight was brought to bear, shored up, rendered unassailable by a summons to loyalty and obedience, by that molding of
the common mind that Catholic practice brings to pass.

The war signaled the end of the questioning of war. What
emerged from audiences of Catholics after the Baltimore action
in 1967 were not questions at all, but accusations, indignation,
anger, moral conclusions cut and dried. The war was moral, it

was wrong to impede it, especially in such undignified, indeed hooligan, tactics, lawless, unclergylike. Priests belonged where priests had always been: in church sanctuaries and rectories; certainly not in draft boards and courts and jails, places where the faith could be held only in ridicule and scorn.

If indeed there were questions, they were not of the inquiring kind. They were rather in the nature of outcries concerning the unknown spaces where priests were venturing, slipping from moral foothold, freewheeling in the void.

No wonder. We Catholics were without landmarks in uncharted times. Our history has been narrowed, our heritage swamped. A nascent truth with regard to violence may have been clearly stated in scripture; but what leverage the origins could exert, given the long history of justified intervention and the rampageous present — the scriptural light was indeed meager. That light had been quenched, or nearly so.

As a community we were somewhat in the predicament of the seeker whose story is so movingly told in the Acts of the Apostles. A courtier of Queen Candace, alone, reads the book of Isaiah, and is lost in perplexity. What might it all mean, this story of a suffering Servant of the Lord? Luckily, the seeker encounters the disciple Philip, who questions him: Has he understood the Reading? The man answers, a perennial plaint: "And how am I to understand, with no one to aid me?"

No one to aid. We opened our scripture, on those formal occasions when it was read at all, in a way entirely American. For all liturgical solemnity and reverence, we read as though the book were opened only to be closed again. We read stories about Jesus and his friends, one among them the undoubted Son of God. We read exhortation to love enemies, to do good to those who assail us, to walk another mile with the opponent, to turn the other cheek to the persecutor.

But our country was at war! And the bloody matter of war, like the bloody hands of Mars, closed the book in our hands.

We were taught, not by Jesus and the apostles, but by churchmen, a circumstance that many would be inclined to call a different matter indeed.

The pope and bishops taught, up to the Vietnam War and its horrid course, that a given war could be called just, and therefore in degree godly, under certain conditions. By such teaching, and under the enormous pressure of wartime hegemony and propaganda, the Vietnam War too was rendered just, and to a degree godly. Thus went the bare bones of the case, the teaching. (Also the silence.)

What put flesh on the bones, and a gun in the hand, and a blessing on the gun, was something more mysterious and influential by far than mere doctrine. It was the enormous weight and import of a culture — being American. Being at war.

There was no place, no appropriateness, for argument. The argument was the war, and the war was just. The argument was flesh and blood: young lives displaced, armed, sent off. And then, inevitably, the argument took another, final form: the bodies, the ritual of return. And finally, the stern rhetoric of the survivors, who, it was presumed, spoke for the dead, demanding an ever greater expense of the living.

The war was an old story, refurbished. It was the sin named original — once more rendered original. There were new weapons in the hands of a new generation; there was a new enemy, whom distance and ignorance rendered a blank; and to a degree known only to ignorance and isolation, rendered expendable, hateful.

I recall this history, my own and my brother's perhaps at too great length, in order to put the Baltimore action into its place. It was not only a *defi* cast in the face of government. It reverberated also within the church: a moral explosion, a reaction, a casting off, or, in the words of one of the defendants at trial, "an exorcism, an anointing."

For the Catholics involved, it was in the nature of an adult baptism. A national history must be renounced, as the garments of adults were once discarded, before entering the water. "A way of thinking" is a mild way of putting it. Philip entered the draft board that November day, decent in clerical black, surrounded by the respect due "the cloth," his status and education and good looks and record of service to church and military — all intact. He might have been paying a routine pastoral call on one of the board employees, themselves untroubled Catholics keeping the licenses in good order. Was he there to reassure them, to indulge in the easy camaraderie typical between clerics and the flock? He entered the building a priest. He could rejoice in "good standing," as the expression goes — in the estimate of his community, his superiors, the law.

He departed in handcuffs: a prisoner, a felon, displaced and disgraced.

A friend said to me at the time, a modest man, not given to aphorism or prophecy, "You know, they'll have to kill your brother someday: he'll never change."

It was in the atmosphere charged with ominous event that I drove toward Washington that November day. I knew the draft board action was imminent. Legally, I suppose, I could be called an accessory: a demeaning phrase, denoting, as it does to me, the status of an appendage, a bystander more or less guilty — and this not by reason of foreknowledge or silence, as the law would have it. But as conscience would have it, an accessory by reason of moral inertness.

Let me be charitable toward myself. I was not ready, and Philip was. He had, of course, marked advantages, having worked and lived for several years among the urban poor. While I had rusticated at Cornell and, to a degree, been stymied there.

I traveled to Washington to support friends from the university and elsewhere, who were planning to surround the Pentagon. Support was all I was ready for; or so I thought. Misjudging, in my ignorance, the shove of moral pressure, more especially the pressure engendered by perils descending on my friends.

It was my first such demonstration. Indeed, nothing had prepared me for the spectacle of the Pentagon: the awesome pile of utterly characterless masonry, pretentious as a pharaoh's tomb and as morally void. It was also the first mesmerizing sight of a great throng, pressing against the river entrance, sitting, standing, singing, praying, exhorting, spilling upward like water defying gravity, up the lawn, up the steps, in face of the massed soldiery.

It was almost as though one species of creation were confronting another. On the one hand, improvisation, color, variety of clothing and hair and bodily gesture. And on the other, the human remolded, set in place, predefined, all but predigested. The uniforms not only clothed the frames, they veiled the eyes, silenced the tongues.

The young soldiers were by Pentagonal definition the complete humans, born from Holy Mother State. Complete, they confronted the incomplete, the gunless hordes of the univalent. Those who could not, or worse, would not, discharge a gun.

Evening approached; the massed floodlights were lit. We stood or sat or knelt in the glare of public knowledge and legal jeopardy. Eventually, it was announced with a great blare that "at midnight, the law will take effect: all who remain in place are liable then to arrest."

My friends, of course, chose to remain. And so, by force of example, did I. Again and again, in the heady Cornell days, we had applied to one another the word "friend." It seemed fitting that the word be tested here, in a place where, presumably, only weapons were to be tested — or humans, it might be, but only insofar as these were useful appendages to the weapons; accessory, and after the fact, so to speak.

Buses were at hand, out there in the rim of darkness. It was no great task for the military to move in and carry or lead us away.

We were brought to a disused military camp in Virginia. There, for a matter of some days, we were treated somewhat like wayward children in summer camp, temporarily restrained because of minor infractions.

Then one day, out of the blue, a squad of legal skulls descended on us. It was the first time, but by no means the last time, that a fairly closed community was disrupted by lawyers, dangling before the eyes of innocents the fast food of the culture: quick in, quick out, no questions asked.

The purveyors were wreckers of community, which in this case was tentative indeed, in its first stages, and extremely vulnerable to the dangling carrot: walking free.

Most of the formerly fervent seized the bait and departed on the instant. The remaining, who might be judged arbitrary spirits,

requested a trial. They were thereupon judged apt to benefit from
"a lesson."

We had begun an improvised fast, a way, we thought, drawn
from civil rights experience, of gaining a modicum of mental clarity. There came a moment of clarity indeed: the moment. when
the children's camp days were over. We survivors of the legal
eagles were placed in holding cells, to await transport to the
D.C. jail.

There, during a waiting period, I was visited by a young priest,
a chaplain. He had been flown in from Fort Benning, along with
transport guards, part of standard government equipment. He
leaned negligently against the bars of my cell and grinned into
my face, for all the world like a delighted child at a zoo. And all
the while, he was copiously refreshing himself from a container
of orange juice.

Hardly worth attention, the episode was yet instructive. I
remember the priest, the moment. Hilarious symbols: the priest
in concert, the priest in contest. The strange crossings-over that
occur: priests of the state, priests against the state.

We were taken off to Washington in cuffs and chains, and
there segregated from the prison populace in our own dormitory.
From thence we were led three times daily, after regular meal service, to a cafeteria area. A great rumble arose about our daring a
fast: such deviations would not be allowed, we were risking being
force fed, etcetera — none of which dire contingencies occurred.
The fast continued. And within a week or so, we were released.

A friend in the Washington area was waiting to transport me
to a Catholic Worker house nearby, where I was fortified by a
bowl of soup, and so in short order regained my land legs.

But it was in the car en route that we heard the news. The
derring-do of the Baltimore Four! The draft board raid, the
successful pouring of blood on the files, and the summary arrest.

It was a curious juxtaposition. I had taken part in a low-
intensity act, together with those who, shortly thereafter, would
vanish once more, into the tunnels and byways of college routine.

But when Philip and his friends walked through the door of
the draft board, there was no exit, not for years. They were seized

by the great Seizer. They were trespassers on his turf, had dared muck up the exquisite order of his necrophilic files, where the names of the soon to be killed, or the soon to kill, or both, were preserved against the Day of Great Summons.

First and foremost, the files bore witness to the absolute inviolability of legalized violence. The files were, as we were to describe them later, hunting licenses against humans. They declared an open season against the living — or as long a season as might be of advantage, in view of experimentation with use of new weaponry on unarmed populations, bombing of civilian centers, and so on.

The files were open to their subjects: they were open because no threat was to be construed by the young hands who would come seeking their status. A harmless legal privilege indeed, together with its fiction of open files, open society.

But now behold, on a November morning, the cabinet, a veritable sanctuary, stood void, violated. A photo shows Philip, his white poll and back overcoat: he is intently pouring blood into the dark maw. Tom Lewis stands by, calmly reading, presumably aloud, from the Bible. One of the employees, her face sulfurous with anger, presses forward. Her eyes and mouth are bulging, enlarged to a living O; she has a nightmarish look, like a figure out of Bosch.

The Baltimore Four were held in jail for some months, then released in view of a trial. The supposition was that being sufficiently chastened by their enforced stay, they could now be trusted to behave themselves. Henceforth the war would cease to trouble their minds. Common sense would take over. What should now occupy them, indeed vex them, was their precarious legal situation: the charges against them were sufficiently severe to deter all but the most foolhardy.

Indeed, in the view of the court, which was one with the view of the prosecutors of the war, the four had done their utmost. Misguided or otherwise, the trial would reveal.

So went the fond presumption: their wings and talons were clipped. And because two of the four were clerics, and all four first offenders, there were heavy implications of comparative leniency.

It would be difficult to conjure up a greater illusion than this: that the law, which was protecting the horrid war, would effectively put Philip in silence. Indeed, the law would hear more of him for years and years, and would I.   —TDIP, 201–10

NIGHT FLIGHT TO HANOI

In February 1968, Daniel Berrigan and Howard Zinn flew to Hanoi as representatives of the U.S. peace movement. In Hanoi, three captured American pilots were released to them by the North Vietnam peace committee. Afterward, U.S. Ambassador Sullivan ordered the three to return on a different plane without Berrigan and Zinn.

Friday, February 9, 1968

At long last, after a week of despair and hope and the cancellation of two planes, we took off for Hanoi. Our aircraft was described optimistically as a Boeing 707; we were told that it was about thirty years old. There survive only three of these marvels on our planet. A fourth crashed on the same run about one year before; no trace of it has ever been found. Our flight was half-filled; the complement included both children and civilians, Poles, Indians, and ourselves.

Five minutes after takeoff. The Mekong is below; a vast sprawl of water whose sleepy gods are placated by messy little shrines like pigeon cages along the banks. Like the Mississippi, the Mekong is capable of blindly breaking out in floods. Now, where it crooks an elbow in mid-Vientiane, there lies a great golden bar of sand, like the aftermath of a gesture of creation.

Below, the rice fields, the primitive villages. A misty tranquil day, in a country whose changes in light and temperature are never severe or sudden.

We have been circling the city for ten minutes, gaining our altitude. It is forbidden to move gradually into the air corridor. We must gain altitude and then take off like an arrow.

At ten thousand feet we can still see the huts at the center of the fields, the dikes going outward. Like cracks in a green crystal.

Cumulus clouds, a lonely sunset. "Nature is the imposition of consciousness on fact." The fact for us, as we go to Hanoi, is the maelstrom of violence and death that have strained the country, while we trudged our dusty vacuum and waited the nod of the powers. But a like scene, viewed from an airliner above the United States or Europe, might induce a reaction of an entirely different order: the contentment of the gods, empery from sea to sea.

The pilot came along the aisle to chat with us. He has flown the same planes, he said, back in '54. He has been back on this Saigon-Hanoi run the past two months. He explained that they had radio contact with Hanoi; that we had three hours from Vientiane to make it. Thereafter, the U.S. Navy, with its bombers, and the U.S. Air Force were free to bring us down. There would be a one-hour stop in Hanoi. He recalled how narrow a squeak they had before the bombers came in last October 27; it was announced over the radio that the supersonics were twenty miles away from Hanoi. He landed quickly, just made it.

We asked him about the difficulty of taking off from Saigon with the city in siege since the Tet uprising. He said that ours was the only civilian aircraft to have left; there was still heavy fighting at the airstrip.

The mountains rise to about nine thousand feet; the plane is at about eleven thousand feet. The crew wants DC's introduced; there is no pressurization in the cabins of these crates.

Every day, before the bombing sorties, the pilot said, the American flyers are shown the design of this plane and its markings. Yet, he reflected dispassionately, one of these planes was shot down and no remains ever found.

It is now 5:30 p.m. We have crossed the border and are in North Vietnam. Congratulations Zinn, Peacenik, Soul Brother!

There is great interest in us on the part of the French crewmen and stewardesses.

Not yet death. This is a wait longer than Godot, longer than Beckett.

Darkness. The lights are flashing from the ground outside. Howard (my cherished brother and friend, and Old Testament man of heart and guts) is deep in converse, in his delicious fractured French, with a passenger up ahead.

The old craft is shaking in every rivet, like a clay duck before the trap shooters, the war game experts.

How long have I wished to share the common life, to be compassionate with men and women, within the same fear, the same skin, the same trembling and fire and ice, to mourn with the men and women who die and do not wish to die; to weep for the children.

The first lights of Hanoi, 7:15 p.m., the runway. Easy down. The lights of the antiaircraft nest shine full upon us: "Just checking, bud."

How to convey the atmosphere, that long dolorous entrance into the destroyed city; the endless pontoons of the bridge replacing the bombed span; the desolation and patience and cold; the convoys, the endless lines of military vehicles and cars.

As usual the loveliest fact of all was the most elusive and insignificant; we had been received with flowers.

We were ushered at about 9:30 p.m. into the austere Napoleonic deluxe of the "Hotel of Reunification." Supper. We are instructed, "Sleep well...."

An air-raid alarm. We went to sleep like children and awakened like adults to the Boom! Boom! The guns of an Indian summer, courtesy of our Air Force. Howard appeared at my door, disheveled in the half light, like a runner awaiting the shot, without his socks forsooth. In a few moments we had crossed the garden and ducked into the shelter. Howard was decently covered by a German who placed his own rubber coat over those extensive and defenseless lower limbs.

Later that day, and throughout the week, I could hear the chambermaids in the corridor, singing; the plaintive atonal music with which the meek of heart console themselves for life in the cave of ravening lions.

Friday, February 16, 1968

[With the three captured U.S. pilots, Berrigan and Zinn returned to Laos.] The two-hour flight into Laos was uneventful in a way in which every ride of that sort is without issue; or rather, has at its outcome only the issue of survival.

So, too, the entrance on the scene of U.S. Ambassador Sullivan, accredited to the United States Embassy in Laos, a man at once ruthless and fascinating.

My words with regard to the conduct of the ambassador may be of no great import in the larger question of the brutal progress of the war itself. Zinn and I were but one instance in a larger betrayal, whose field of action is the bodies of the Vietnamese people. And yet because a betrayal was wrought upon us, and because both the military, represented by the fliers, and ourselves of the peace movement, were involved in an extended and even dangerous episode, it seems worthwhile to recall the event, and to reflect upon it here.

We should perhaps be grateful that the outcome was not worse than it was. Treated as we had been by American officials with minimal courtesy, and with a rather obvious effort to remain out of our way, should we not remain content with that? No. Like all resisters, we are afflicted beyond remedy with the idealism of which we read so often in our history, and the history of political protest in the West. We have not grown used to knavery, and to that species of untruth which lies so near to the truth as to be able to wear its clothing, and to turn upon the idealist its seductive and silencing countenance.

Still, against the ambassador we had, I would think, one great advantage. Men and women of the truth, who constantly search their own motivation and hearts, are perhaps equipped to deal also with that fine art of untruth known to our world as diplomacy. And this may be a clue as to why Sullivan found himself

in a much more difficult situation than he could have anticipated. He mounted our plane like a buccaneer; he was governed,
I would think, by the expectation of holding us captive to the
grandeur of his office and the charm of his personal qualities. No
such thing transpired. The five minutes he had perhaps granted
himself to hold the press at bay outside and to win over a rather
absent-minded cleric, extended into forty and then to fifty minutes of heated and close discussion. In that hour all of us knew
that our mettle was being tested to the utmost. The meaning and
momentum of our voyage were at stake — the presence of the
three released men in our midst, a prey worthy of steel and will,
the clamor of that eagle on the embassy insignia, and even now
loosing its thunderbolts upon the northern nights, the promise
so recently concluded by us, fliers and men of peace, pledges so
charged with implication for the future of other men and women,
lying so heavy upon the prisoners of the North, that their import
must yet ring in our ears. All this and more charged the stale air
of the grounded craft with drama and danger. And through it all,
we could see outside, like the eyes of jungle night, the lights of the
television cameras, a closure of fire and anger and expectation.

What was it to be obedient, what indeed to disobey? This may
be the deepest question of the war; it played like a wayward lightning between the fliers, the ambassador, and ourselves on that
night. It was a question as old as aerial warfare itself, and much
older. But it seemed to us entirely and exactly fitting that the
question should be raised in a grounded aircraft, at the edge of
an airstrip, itself at the edge of that world which some delighted
in calling free — without even questioning their own unfreedom.
"I am an army career man," finally said the ranking officer, the
major. "Any least indication of the will of my superiors is a command to me." It was the most ominous sentence I had yet heard
in a war whose daily currency was groundless rhetoric, duplicity, body counts, and murderous ideology. Yet I must confess that
the sentence also had a kind of untouchable platonic perfection.
As an expression of the system from which it issued, the senti-
ment was virtuous beyond praise. The word was spoken. There

remained only what we of the West call, with a clumsy instrumental neologism, its implementation. *Verum caro.* We issued from the cave of Plato, where all words are indeed an emptiness, to face the world, the times, the purpose. We issued from the cave and stood in the glare of humanity's eyes and instruments, under judgment, under the yoke of the law.

The fliers finished with the press, there on the oil-stained macadam, after a short general statement, delivered in the exhausted monotone of the major. Zinn and I lingered in the background. We were of no interest; the peace had lost its prey. We knew nothing of what was to come; we were desperately in need of sleep and wanted only to get apart and reflect upon the sudden explosion of all our hopes. An attaché offered us an embassy car; they wanted us off the scene, once and for all; and I refused, discourteously, as I recall. The pilots rode across the airstrip to the waiting plane. The sleek door of the jet closed upon its burden, as in the children's story the door of a mountain closes upon a piper and the village children. Farewell to the children, farewell!

The newsmen turned about, in our direction.

—NFH, 34–39, 136–38

CHILDREN IN THE SHELTER

Imagine; three of them.

As though survival
were a rat's word
and a rat's death
waited there at the end

and I must have
in the century's bone yard
heft of flesh and bone in my arms

I picked up the littlest
a boy, his face

breaded with rice (his sister calmly feeding him
as we climbed down)

In my arms fathered
in a moment's grace, the messiah
of all my tears I bore, reborn
a Hiroshima child from hell.

MY NAME

If I were Pablo Neruda
Or William Blake
I could bear, and be eloquent

an American name in the world
where men perish
in our two murderous hands

Alas Berrigan
you must open those hands
and see, stigmatized in their palms,
the broken faces
you yearn toward

you cannot offer
being powerless as a woman
under the rain of fire —
life, the cover of your body.

Only the innocent die.
Take up, take up
the bloody map of the century.
The long trek homeward begins
into the land of unknowing.
                    —ARB, 114, 117

OUR APOLOGIES, GOOD FRIENDS

It seemed to me, as the war went on and on, that one had to try and operate on two fronts. The war itself had, in a sense, given away the secrets of war; the war had suggested to us, sotto voce, the methods of peace. Those methods went something like this: one war was to be fought on two grounds, Vietnam and the American ghettos. So it was crucial, in spite of all roadblocks, to be present in both places.

In order to make peace, at least a few Americans had to share, at least in some measure, the life and hard times of Hanoi; the terror, the death from the air. One would have to crouch in a concrete bunker, like a mole with an eagle's microscopic eye gyring overhead. He would have to know death firsthand; the presence of death, the end of rhetoric, the beginning of wisdom.

And in the course of such a war, one had to go to jail. It was an irreplaceable need, a gift not to be refused. You got arrested, were stripped, your body was searched and poked for drugs. You stood in public showers, were issued the denims, were herded about, segregated, counted at odd hours, yelled at.

All to the good, and after all, the scene was no Dachau; you would come out the other side intact, a few pounds lighter, the skin of your soul darkened with insight — the fate of the poor, the blacks. Knowing white justice for what it is, to the poor; knowing that the D.C. jail is one roof and fabric with the D.C. ghetto, a single architecture and intent, the logical "other room" in the haunted house. There were no priest holes any more, you were not riding circuit in tony Elizabethan England, hiding out, moving on. No; you were American adventuring — pacification-cum-napalm, racism-cum-Bible, the churchgoing military and the militant churchmen.

Man, you'd better save your soul, no one else could do it for you now. It was midnight at the Pentagon, late as literal hell. Move when told, or sit there on your hunkers and take what would come; the vans were rolling up, the lights were on, fierce as bared teeth, the exterminator had turned about, there was a tiger in your flank.

The teeth hurt, but the hurt was superficial. The tiger bit mortally elsewhere. After all, you were white and middling, *sacerdos in aeternum,* it wouldn't do to make overkill here and now. Besides, the ring of soldiers was uncertain, they had been marched out of the military temple on a dirty errand; they weren't mercenaries, this was a new scene. It wasn't Hanoi, not by a long shot.

Hanoi! At home the jail was joined to the ghetto; more, the American ghetto and the Hanoi "operation" were a single enterprise. Both were conceived by military minds; pararacist and plenary, total, a total war, war in both cases, in both places. A racist cleanup, a segregation triumph, a zoo under fire, a condemned playground for the war game, an ordinance proving ground.

Proving — what? Why, that we're the great, the pure, the best, the unique and chosen, deciders and destructors. We separated, by divine right, wheat from chaff, gooks from whites, the living from the dead.

I thought, in both places, of unity, community, communication. The old, good words, bathed in a fresh light. Human beings were a unity; we were not a nation of county coroners, the world was not a morgue, we had no right to dismember the living, to read our future in their bared guts. Community; put people together! The military nation state was not a community; it was a walking zombie, stitched together out of obscene rags and tags, a rifle for a backbone, sawdust for a heart, a cadaver programmed to the jargon of realpolitik, a horror stalking by night, flapping the skies, dropping hot fasces in the eyes of sleeping children. No, Say no. Communicate. Get to Hanoi, the action was there, you had to see it, to tell it like it was.

Hanoi; that ancient eastern icon decked out in French robes, the artist's stroke lingering along eye and hand, long and contemplative, the lotus in the fingers. We were there toward the end of January, we got in by the skin of our teeth, while the hottest horror of three years blazed away to the south. The Vietnamese were celebrating the Tet holiday, with a new twist. We were Guy Fawkes, and the scarecrow, and the hidden and sought; they tricked and we retreated.

In the peace movement, you got used to being without power; that was your name. Then the invitation from Hanoi — suddenly, what power! Howard Zinn and I grinned at one another across three continents, like carved pumpkins lit in the night. Why, we were doing what all the king's armies and all the king's men couldn't do. We were going where Mr. Rusk couldn't go, or Bundy, or the president himself.

D.C. jail, North Vietnam. Mobility, inwardness; tumult, travel; incarceration, incineration. Take it, eat it up. You couldn't die where you'd been born. The earth was shedding its skin with every new season; it was pulling out from under you like a rug. You had to keep running to keep living, a moving target had more chance. Or, you had to go under, to hibernate, to live like a dreaming animal, off the fat and marrow of your mind. To say, here, there and everywhere, like Mrs. Rooney; Christ, what a planet!

Next week nine of us will, if all goes well (ill?) take our religious bodies during this week to a draft enter near Baltimore. There we shall, of purpose and forethought, remove the A-1 files, sprinkle them in the public street with homemade napalm and set them afire. For which act we shall, beyond doubt, be placed behind bars for some portion of our natural lives, in consequence of our inability to live and die content in the plagued city, to say peace peace when there is no peace, to keep the poor poor, the homeless homeless, the thirsty and hungry thirsty and hungry.

Our apologies, good friends, for the fracture of good order, the burning of paper instead of children, the angering of the orderlies in the front parlor of the charnel house. We could not, so help us God, do otherwise.

For we are sick at heart, our hearts give us no rest for thinking of the Land of Burning Children. And for thinking of that other Child, of whom the poet Luke speaks. The infant was taken up in the arms of an old man, whose tongue grew resonant and vatic at the touch of that beauty. And the old man spoke: this child is set for the fall and rise of many in Israel, a sign that is spoken against.

Small consolation; a child born to make trouble, and to die for it, the first Jew (not the last) to be subject of a "definitive solution." He sets up the cross and dies on it; in the Rose Garden of the executive mansion, on the D.C. Mall, in the courtyard of the Pentagon. We see the sign, we read the direction; you must bear with us, for His sake. Or if you will not, the consequences are our own.

For it will be easy, after all, to discredit us. Our record is bad: troublemakers in church and state, a priest married despite his vows, two convicted felons. We have jail records, we have been turbulent, uncharitable, we have failed in love for the brethren, have yielded to fear and despair and pride, often in our lives. Forgive us.

We are no more, when the truth is told, than ignorant beset men, jockeying against all chance, at the hour of death, for a place at the right hand of the dying One.

We act against the law at a time of the Poor People's March; at a time, moreover, when the government is announcing even more massive paramilitary means to confront disorder in the cities. The implications of all this must strike horror in the mind of the thinking person. The war in Vietnam is more and more literally being brought home to us. Its inmost meaning strikes the American ghettos: one war, one crime against the poor, waged (largely) by the poor, in servitude to the affluent. We resist and protest this crime.

Finally, we stretch out our hands to our brothers and sisters throughout the world. We who are priests, to our fellow priests. All of us who act against the law, turn to the poor of the world, to the Vietnamese, to the victims, to the soldiers who kill and die; for the wrong reasons, for no reason at all, because they were so ordered — by the authorities of that public order which is in effect a massive institutionalized disorder.

We say killing is disorder. Life and gentleness and community and unselfishness is the only order we recognize. For the sake of that order, we risk our liberty, our good name. The time is past when good people can remain silent, when obedience can segregate people from public risk, when the poor can die without defense.

We ask our fellow Christians to consider in their hearts a question that has tortured us, night and day, since the war began:

How many must die before our voices are heard, how many must be tortured, dislocated, starved, maddened? How long must the world's resources be raped in the service of legalized murder? When, at what point, will you say no to this war?

We wish also to place in question by this act all suppositions about normal times, longings for an untroubled life in a somnolent church, that neat timetable of ecclesiastical renewal, which in respect to the needs of people, amounts to another form of time serving.

Redeem the times! The times are inexpressibly evil. Christians pay conscious — indeed religious — tribute to Caesar and Mars; by approval of overkill tactics, by brinkmanship, by nuclear liturgies, by racism, by support of genocide. They embrace their society with all their heart, and abandon the cross. They pay lip service to Christ and military service to the powers of death.

And yet, and yet, the times are inexhaustibly good, solaced by the courage and hope of many. The truth rules, Christ is not forsaken. In a time of death, some men and women — the resisters, those who work hardily for social change, those who preach and embrace the unpalatable truth — such men and women overcome death, their lives are bathed in the light of the resurrection, the truth has set them free. In the jaws of death, of contumely, of good and ill report, they proclaim their love of the people.

We think of such men and women in the world, in our nation, in the churches, and the stone in our breast is dissolved. We take heart once more. —NFH, xiii–xix

3

The Burning of Paper
instead of Children

THE PRICE OF PEACE

Christians do not search the scriptures for the sake of justifying their life or law of conduct, for even the devil, we are told, finds comfort in God's word. The saying is a salutary one. The motive that drives us back to our sources is a far different one from that of pride. We go to this Word in fear and trembling, knowing that the Word itself is a judgment, a two-edged sword, as Paul declares. The *logos* is still a crisis; that is, the Word is not meant to offer comfort to the slovenly, to blur the edge of life, to set up a no-man's-land in which we are free to wander at will, pursing our pagan adventures unhindered.

The Word of God is one of crisis. It confronts us putting their acts under the scrutiny of the God of history, there to be judged. We are familiar with this. We know, too, that out of submission to God's Word issues the deepest stream of joy, that this Word liberates us from pharisaic fear, dread of life, the multiple power of death in this world.

But even this is not the deepest meaning of God's Word to us. That meaning, I take it, is bound up with history and this world, to the degree that God's Word becomes our own — that we recognize in the Bible our own people, speaking our own tongue, prophets and saints, men and women who lived to the depths the common life of humanity, with all that implies for our own darkest hours. And finally: The Word that comes to us is the mysterious voice of a brother and friend, God's Son, living our life, beckoning to us from the common condition — marketplace, family, courtroom, garden, agony, and death itself.

God's Word thus urges forward and extends the range of our human experience. In its light, moreover, all suppositions about what it is to be religious, all self-justification and self-reliance, all obscene Olympianism based on technology, race, and religion itself, are confronted and defeated.

One of these invitations of God's word — into exodus, into freedom, into death — one scarcely knows how to characterize it — comes to us toward the end of John's Gospel. The Lord is summoned into a courtroom, as he declares, to give testimony to the truth. The truth itself is on trial. It must not be presumed, before the fact, that God is speaking the truth; so men say, so the human powers decree. God must submit to the probing of humanity. It is for God to render account of God's self. So God answers the summons; the docket of Jesus is opened before his fellows.

And this is no mock trial. Its outcome may possibly grant him new prestige, a new and cleansed people, grateful for the truth he has vindicated in the breach. Or the trial may hand him over to death.

We know that in fact the second outcome occurred. The Lord was convicted and died the death of a malefactor. But more to our point, I would think, is the extraordinary self-conscious and deliberate manner in which the Lord entered upon the courtroom scene, and made it his own scene. He steeled himself for the crisis, he added a cubit to his stature. So that out of Pilate's court come some of the most profound and disturbing of his self-revelations. Consider, for instance: *For this have I been born, for this have I come into the world: to bear witness to the truth.* I suggest to you that the life of Jesus would have lacked something of its majesty and strength had he not stood in the court of Pilate and endured the proceedings there. I suggest, moreover, that we are offered during the trial of Jesus an example that reappears constantly and mysteriously throughout history, at the edge of life and death where the martyrs walk and let their blood. That is to say, the truth is never fully itself apart from the conditions of witness; to be itself, the truth must be summoned to accounting by the powers and dominations. It must endure crisis, it must be purified in the furnace of this world. It is not enough to declare, "I embody the truth," or "I speak the truth." Indeed, such claims are historically very nearly useless. They fall together with innumerable other such claims into the common wastebin of time. Every malcontent and charlatan and quack has claimed the truth. But the range of risk is narrowed. The issue is met, when one testifies under pressure, amid danger, to the sovereignty of a truth that he does not claim or preempt but that literally possesses him.

It is necessary above all to be concrete when we speak of these things. People, even good people, are commonly disposed to submit to the slavery of the actual; they literally cannot imagine themselves in any life situation other than the one in which they live. They inherit a style, a culture, a religion, and they prolong such forms — because they are there; useful, comfortable, logical, venerable. Their minds wear the costumes of their ancestors, a clothing that was once befitting, literally, but is now a simple folklore or a fakeout. So they call a folklore a religion and a fakeout an adult life. And, alas, who shall disenchant them? But let it at least be said, as the Lord implies from his Roman courtroom, such lives as these must not make large claims to the truth.

We can think, for example, of the differing styles of truth offered by Pope Pius XI and Gandhi. They were contemporaries; both were deeply troubled by the course of events; both urged peace on the world. But one knew at firsthand prison and fasts and marches, the immediate anguish of the masses. When he spoke, he spoke from the villages, the impoverished home, the prisons — which are conditions of the common life of men in struggle. The other spoke from a baroque palace in the Eternal City. Today, though his words remain unimpeachable, and his tomb is honored, he is all but forgotten. Gandhi's ashes are scattered to the sea, but his words and examples are among the few spiritual legacies that survive the horrors of the past decades.

You may recall (we are speaking of witness and the truth) that in 1934, Gandhi was voyaging to England to plead the cause of the freedom of the Indian masses. Pius XI refused to receive him in audience, and Winston Churchill referred to Gandhi contemptuously in Commons as "that half-naked savage." But Gandhi went on to Britain to live among the very people whom his boycott in India was threatening — the mill workers of Liverpool and Birmingham. He moved through their streets, explaining to the people in the simplest possible terms that the cause of Indian weavers and of the British factory workers was the same cause. And they understood, and gave him a tumultuous welcome, though their own livelihood had been placed in jeopardy by Gandhi's boycott.

Now, when someone consents to live and die for the truth, he sets in motion spiritual rhythms whose outward influences are, in the nature of things, simply immeasurable. I take the courts as one symbol of Gandhi's method. What indeed did he hope for, from that vantage point? He hoped to say to others something that had come to have the deepest meaning for himself. Out of a virile disregard for personal danger and stress, he wished to make it possible for others to live — to be conscious, to be freed of demons, to welcome their brothers and sisters. The point, I would think, for Gandhi and Jesus, is not that people would agree with them, or do the same things they did. The point is that others would come to a deepened consciousness; that their sense of existence and human issues would be sharpened to the point where they would "do their thing" — a good thing, a human thing, as they were doing theirs.

The eminent scholar C. H. Dodd, writing of Christ before Pilate, says: "It is significant that the words we are considering, on witnessing to the truth, are placed in the context of a trial scene. Where the truth is, *there* men are judged, and it is only the 'one who does the truth' who can stand the scrutiny of the light. So here, John treats the question of judgment on the claims of Jesus and in the end found the tables turned on them. So here

Pilate believes himself to be sitting in judgment on Jesus, yet it is himself who is revealed as judged."

Americans who can bear equally with the sight of burning children are enraged and baffled by the sight of burning draft files. Moreover, Americans are unable to create new forms of civilized political power to express our tardy sense that a bad war is being waged with our money, in our name, by our sons. We have declared a moratorium on radical or disobedient protest, and have placed our hopes, with a certain despair, in the promise of three successive presidents to control, mitigate, and end the war. Meantime, peace talks opened in Paris; but Americans and Vietnamese in enormous numbers continued to lose their lives. Our political future is clouded, to say the least; it may well be that the next years will rest in the hands of those who believe that Vietnam has established a virtuous norm of international conduct, that despite its cost, it justifies further military adventuring.

After more than four years of struggle, perplexity, and doubt, my own course is at last clear. In a sense, I claim a certain sorry advantage over most of those who have yet to choose the place and time of their response to American violence, a response that will embody their existence and carry their lives captive, in bonds to a choice, in a direction they cannot yet know. Such an hour as Catonsville may still come to them — we have every reason to believe that the price of peace will escalate grievously in the months ahead. And nothing in our history makes such a prospect easily bearable.

We have assumed the name of peacemakers, but we have been, by and large, unwilling to pay any significant price. And because we want the peace with half a heart and half a life and will, the war, of course, continues, because the waging of war, by its nature, is total — but the waging of peace, by our own cowardice, is partial. So a whole will and a whole heart and a whole national life bent toward war prevail over the velleities of peace. In every national war since the founding of the republic we have taken for granted that war shall exact the most rigorous cost, and that the cost shall be paid with cheerful heart. We take it for granted that in wartime families will be separated for long periods, that men will be imprisoned, wounded, driven insane, killed on foreign shores. In favor of such wars, we declare a moratorium on every normal human hope — for marriage, for community, for friendship, for moral conduct toward strangers and the innocent. We are instructed that deprivation and discipline, private grief and public obedience are to be our lot. And we obey. And we bear with it — because bear we must — because war is war, and good war or bad, we are stuck with it and its cost.

But what of the price of peace? I think of the good, decent, peace-loving people I have known by the thousands, and I wonder. How many of them are so afflicted with the wasting disease of normalcy that, even as they declare for the peace, their hands reach out with an instinctive spasm in the direction of their loved ones, in the direction of their comforts, their home, their security, their income, their future, their plans — that twenty-year plan of family growth and unity, that fifty-year plan of decent life and honorable natural demise.

"Of course, let us have the peace," we cry, "but at the same time let us have normalcy, let us lose nothing, let our lives stand intact, let us know neither prison nor ill repute nor disruption of ties." And because we must encompass this and protect that, and because at all costs — at all costs — our hopes must march on schedule, and because it is unheard of that in the name of peace a sword should fall, disjoining that fine and cunning web that our lives have woven, because it is unheard of that good men and women should suffer injustice or families be sundered or good repute be lost — because of this we cry peace, peace, and there is no peace. There is no peace because the making of peace is at least as costly as the making of war — at least as exigent, at least as disruptive, at least as liable to bring disgrace and prison and death in its wake.

Consider, then, the words of our Savior — who speaks to us gravely, with the burden of his destiny heavy upon him, perplexed as we are, solicitous of heart, anxious with a kind of merciless compassion — that we comprehend lucidly, joyously, the cost of discipleship:

*You have heard it said, "You shall not kill; whoever kills
will be liable to judgment." But I say to you, whoever is
angry with his brother or sister shall be liable to judgment.*

*You have heard it said, "An eye for an eye and a tooth
for a tooth." But I say to you, do not [violently] resist one
who does evil. But if any one strikes you on the right cheek,
turn to him the other also.*

*Blessed are you when they revile you and persecute you
and utter all kinds of evil against you falsely on my account.
Rejoice and be glad, for your reward is great in heaven, for
so they persecuted the prophets who were before you.*

*And finally, Pilate said to him, "You are a king, then?"
Jesus answered, "You say that I am a king. For this was
I born, and for this have I come into the world, to bear
witness to the truth. Everyone who is of the truth hears my
voice."*   —NBM, 53–59

THE TROUBLE WITH OUR STATE

The trouble with our state
was not civil disobedience
which in any case was hesitant and rare

Civil disobedience was rare as kidney stone
No, rarer; it was disappearing like immigrant's disease

You've heard of a war on cancer?
There is no war like the plague of media
There is no war like routine
There is no war like 3 square meals
There is no war like a prevailing wind

It flows softly; whispers
don't rock the boat!
The sails obey, the ship of state rolls on.

The trouble with our state
— we learned only afterward

when the dead resembled the living who resembled the dead
and civil virtue shone like paint on tin
and tin citizens and tin soldiers marched to the common whip

> — our trouble
> the trouble with our state
> with our state of soul
> our state of siege —
> was
>
> Civil
> Obedience.   — ARB, 239

THE PENTECOSTAL FIRE
OF CATONSVILLE

The spring of '68 dawned over Cornell. No lovelier change of season could be imagined. I must have been one of very few mortals who walked to work each morning through a woodland, the sound of birds and released waters gushing in the early sunshine. I was, for a time, an early bird in more senses than one: the first campus member to visit North Vietnam, and much in demand to recount and reflect, not only locally, but across the nation.

More serious events were gathering steam. I was working to complete a diary I had sketched out in the course of my unprecedented voyage. But there were difficulties: too much happening, too quickly. The recent past, with present realities pressing hard, was receding into a kind of pluperfect. Only two months previous and I "had been" in Hanoi. But now was now; and a new question arose, jostling and tumbling the past. Where might such an experience lead, and when?

Where and when. The question was not to remain unanswered for long. Philip came to campus for a quiet visit, overnight. He was again free, in no sense quelled, either by months in jail, or by the prospect of impending trial and sentence. He came with a proffer.

His visits, rare as they were, were invariably a joy: occasions of grace. He, his visits and letters, were slowly extricating me from an impasse.

My "Cornell conclusion" for what it was worth (not much), stood firm. It stood hardly weakened by the exemplary action of the Baltimore Four. To wit: We, the good antiwar clergy, had gone as far as could be. We had counseled the young in their quest for a peaceable kingdom. We had even approached law-breaking and conspiracy, in our support of the campus ministers who renounced their draft cards.

We had not yet come on the moral equivalent of the resisters: we were far removed from their legal risks.

How is an impasse broken? Only a startling discovery, an epiphany, a dawning, could reveal my ignorance for what it was. Short of that, in the Socratic sense, I did not know that I knew next to nothing.

Into our sublime, serene island, our El Dorado, came Philip. He is not to be thought of as a portent: nothing so pretentious. He was a friend, and he came bearing a gift.

Such a gift as stops the heart short. He and others, he stated simply, were not content that the action at the Baltimore draft center should rest there, a flash in the pan, a gesture. For it was more than that, and government lenience or sternness in the coming trial must not steal the thunder of the peaceable.

The action, in short, must be repeated elsewhere; and he, for one, and Tom Lewis, for another, were prepared to repeat it, in Catonsville, Maryland. Would I join them?

Well, would I? The idea was immensely attractive; it was also a shocker. But it was less frightening than it would have been months before. I was freshly returned from Hanoi, where I had cowered under American bombings. That helped wonderfully to clear the mind. I told Philip I would give the proposal twenty-four hours, monitoring meantime the course of emotion and mood. And if my purpose held for that period, I was in.

Which in due time I was, up to my chin.

A sense, as I recall, of immense freedom. As though in choosing, I could now breathe deep, and call my life my own.

A sense, also, of the end of a road, or a fork, or a sudden turn; and no telling what lay beyond. At the same time, a certainty deeper than logic: what lay behind was best placed behind, once and for all, and no looking back.

Who was to tell me all this? There was no telling. There was only the force of a friendship, and an offer. And suddenly, my hands and heart lifted, and I know. What had stood at center stage, the focus and heart of things (Cornell, and all I loved there, perhaps intemperately) — this receded quietly, in an hour, to the wings. At the center stood — darkness, myself, my friends. And what would come of it all, no one of us could tell.

There was shortly to be a spotlight on us: it was thin as a pencil slate, and would pierce us through and through; a testing light that touched on the very soul, and illumined and burned. The light of the adversary, light of the church, light of the eye of God? Light, perhaps, of self-knowledge: of all these together. But for a start, there was that opposite element, that darkness. I was in it, body and soul, blind, feeling my way, humiliated; but strangely exalted, freed.

The foregoing could now be called hindsight. At the time, there was no such thing; something closer to hindsightlessness, if the term can be credited. In place of eyes, or sight, I had only faith to go on or trust, which perhaps comes to the same thing. I know my brother, I know his testing and coming through, and the travail he was inviting on his own head. I know also his love for me. So there was no such element as pure darkness. How could there be? Instead of sight, or evidence, or logic, there was something better to go by — a hand in mine, someone to walk with. Enough, and more.

I was becalmed for a brief time. The new calm was different indeed from a metaphysical stalemate, a resigned self-satisfaction in the Cornell manner. It was a kind of clearing in the jungle. I had reached it at considerable labor. I knew the image for what it was: a sign of respite, after which I must move on once more.

My reading of the times was both tragic and energetic: the war; and something to be done. Mine, I know, was a most unacademic sense. On campus, the ruling metaphor was tenure.

Some had tenure, others set their timepieces by that clock of privilege, and trailed along behind the pack, picking up the scant largesse.

The metaphor went further: presumably the very stars of the heavens were tenured; firm set in place. It followed that mortals took their lead from the fixed nature of things above.

I was fixed nowhere, except in the lives of those I loved. I had determined to move on, out of the Platonic state of Cornellian beatitude. In view of the war, its cost, its call — to linger would be to lose.

Indeed, it might be argued that my decision was presumptuous in the extreme. Philip was well tested as to physical deprivation, living as he did. And more: he had been tried in lockup, and survived. In comparison with him, I was a coddled egg indeed: an academic who only of late proposed shedding his shell.

Would I survive? Was my purpose sound? Or was I indicated in the Gospel parable: the king who went out to wage war, with vastly inferior numbers of troops, a peculiar metaphor of war, but apt in raising the question — good sense versus nonsense.

It was only after the Catonsville action that I came on a precious insight. The knowledge thus came hardly, as perhaps real knowledge does. Something like this: presupposing integrity and discipline, one is justified in entering upon a large risk; not indeed because the outcome is assured, but because the integrity and value of the act have spoken loud.

When such has occurred, matters of success or efficiency are placed where they belong: in the background. They are not irrelevant, but they are far from central.

I was in need of such reflections as we faced the public after our crime. The revulsion could only be called ecumenical. All sides agreed — we were fools or renegades or plain crazy.

The supporting arguments were wonderfully diverse and inventive. The action was useless: it "spoke to no one." It was violent: it involved an assault on property, which the government had made sacrosanct. It was scandalous, including, as it did, two priests, who should have known better. And so on, and so on.

I tried, in response, to put matters biblically. That there was a history of such acts as ours. In such biblical acts, results, outcome, benefits, are unknown, totally obscure. The acts are at variance with good manners and behavior. Worse, they are plainly illegal. More yet: everything of prudence and good sense points to the uselessness, ineffectiveness of such acts. And finally, immediate and perhaps plenary punishment is bound to follow.

So, despite all, a history of sorts was launched on a May morning in 1968. Also, a tradition was vindicated, at least to a degree. Or so I believe to this day.

The night before that fateful May morning, we assembled at a friend's house and made a rite, preparing the napalm. Kerosene and soap chips. A simple formula, out of a Green Beret handbook, ignited the hell.

Next morning, with fast-beating hearts, we drove to Catonsville. The draft board was on the second floor of a tacky frame building, above an office of the Knights of Columbus.

On Catholic ground! We entered, armed with our resolve and symbol: the container of home-brewed napalm.

We reassured, as best we might, the transfixed employees, withdrew the A-1 files, carried them outside, to a parking lot. And shortly a fire flared.

The act was pitiful, a tiny flare amid the consuming fires of war. But Catonsville was like a firebreak, a small fire lit, to contain and conquer a greater. The time, the place, were weirdly right. They spoke for passion, symbol, reprisal. Catonsville seemed to light up the dark places of the heart, where courage and risk and hope were awaiting a signal, a dawn.

For the remainder of our lives, the fires would burn and burn, in hearts and minds, in draft boards, in prisons and courts. A new fire, new as a Pentecost, flared up in eyes deadened and hopeless, the noble powers of soul given over to the "powers of the upper air."

"Nothing can be done!" How often we had heard that gasp: the last of the human, of soul, of freedom. Indeed, something could be done; and was. And would be.

We had removed an abomination from the Earth. It was as though, across the land, a series of signal fires had been lighted. The first was no larger than a gleam of an eye. But hill to hill, slowly at first, then like a wildfire, leaping interstices and valleys, the fires flared. As though by instinct, fire found its combustibles, beyond and beyond.

In the following years, some seventy draft boards were entered across the land. Their contents variously shredded, sacked, hidden out of sight, burned, scattered to the winds. In one case, the files were mailed back to their owners, with a note urging that the inductee refuse to serve.

That morning! We stood in the breach of birth. We could know nothing. Would something follow, would our act speak to others, awaken their resolve? We knew only the bare bones of consequence.

Consequence indeed. It was shortly made clear that our action was taken with utmost seriousness. There was, first of all, the unbelievable matter of Tom Lewis and Philip. Had they actually the effrontery to commit a second crime in the teeth of the first?

The act was done. We sat in custody in the back room of the Catonsville Post Office, weak with relief, grinning like virtuous gargoyles. Three or four FBI honchos entered portentously. Their leader, a jut-jawed paradigm, surveyed us from the doorway. His eagle eye lit on Philip. He roared out: "Him again! Good God, I'm changing my religion!" I could think of no greater tribute to my brother.

Faith brought us to Catonsville, and a vagrant hope. In my case, it was faith seeking understanding. I went ahead on the basis of intuition and instinct, a smell, a sense of things, a right-ness. But intuitions, as I know (I was, after all, a Jesuit), are notoriously unreliable, all but incommunicable. I must set out to tell our story; first of all to myself.

And in public interplay and critique, I would also learn that "other side" of the action. What did it mean to others? Did they see it as a blessing or curse? Only time would tell; meantime, we must tell the story.

I was released, and returned to Cornell to await trial. Philip and Tom Lewis, now considered recidivists and virtually unrehabilitatable were, of course, kept fast.

Shortly, standing before audiences, I discovered something unexpected. The closer my explanation drew upon biblical instruction and source, the less palatable it became; and this to Catholics. It was as though in so speaking, one was by no means building bridges of understanding. One was putting up a wall, stone by stone, and mortising it tight.

It was quite acceptable to talk "politics." There was at least a nascent sense that the war was intolerable, granted the American system and its "normal" workings. One gained this small leverage. But the fact that the war might be inconsistent with the words and example of Christ, that killing others was repugnant to the letter and spirit of the Sermon on the Mount — this was too much: it turned living ears to stone.

And not only the ears of lay Christians. The lay folk followed the lead of experts: theorists and ideologues and moral theologians. The vast majority of these eminences had backed up wars and armies, for centuries. It was they who had built up a common mentality among Christians: suppositions, solidarity of conscience, justifications, lesser evils, proclaimed limits. (Always the "lesser evils.")

In proclaiming that, under certain conditions, some wars were immoral, they had salvaged a great deal; or so it was said. They had saved humanity (and the church?) from the awful assumption that all wars were good. So we were told.

My ears itched at these sounds. A sense that something deeper, something unspoken, was implied here. A basis, a supposition: a somber view of the human, entirely at variance with Christ's view. What was a human being, anyway, or acceptable human conduct? According to a number of theologians, as far as I could understand, Christians and others were created so frail in decency and so prone to evil that it was continually necessary to allow violence, greed, license, some measure and movement. Thus salvaging (at least partially, at least now and then) some hint of a less than worst case.

The theory implied something else: a quite minimal faith in the Christ of the Testament. Was He to be taken literally, in this sorry, stressful business of loving one's enemies? The church and the emperor (better, the church of the emperor) and the church's experts decided, in effect, that He could not. He could not have meant His moral statements, commands of undeniable rigor and clarity, to apply, here and now everywhere and at all times. Apply moreover, to public and political conflict.

Thus, one thinks, the morality of a "me too" church was early born. Impeccable personal and sexual life, the family praying together and staying together. And born in the baptismal waters was the emperor into the church — and the church of the empire. And thus, at a stroke, was added a quality to the church; one hardly envisioned by our crucified Lord: the church compatible.

In consequence of these events, or in cause (it is almost impossible to disentangle), a certain critical light is cast on the moral teachings of popes, in my lifetime and formerly — teachings concerning the self-defense of nations; teachings that, willy-nilly, justify the guns, simultaneously discharged as they often are, in the frenzy of mutual murder.

One is led to think of actual war, any war, between "Christian nations." Each side grasps the holy doctrine, and mounts a charge. The war is manifestly just, "on our side." The universal pope has set the norms, the national bishops have applied them, each to its own case, like a powerful magical unguent, guaranteeing a healing victory. Each side proclaims: We are wounded or dishonored or invaded; our cause is just, and shall prevail.

It must all be enormously puzzling to thoughtful folk. Which side is in the right?

In such wise also, the universal church is broken in bits, like a body fallen on a grenade. The church is held up to shame among the nations, including warmaking nations, who contemn her even as they enlist her blessing. She is held to mockery before true history — which is the evidence not of self-contradicting teachings, contradicted in the act; but a history (her own, in spite of herself) of those who withstood, of the great, humiliated refusers.

What was to be done, what could be done? If the Nine of Catonsville had waited on the bishops or pope, our wait would have been long, and our consciences cooled. Until the hell of the war froze over.

In American chanceries during the terrible decade, if rumor of the war reached their occupants, it sounded as only a distant reverberation, a slight boom on the eardrum, no earthquake. Was the war beating at the door, like a despairing refugee? Did the war portend a kind of creeping catastrophe, a hair's crack in the flagstones of the floor? Nothing of the kind; or if something of the kind, unapprehended. As far as one could judge, all was business as usual. In more than a few dioceses, at the highest levels, there was political mutuality and stroking. And a supposition, suave on the air: the business of the American church is business.

One asked his soul, in near despair with such a church: what of the children of Vietnam, what of the victims of the merciless air raids, what of the Buddhist monks driven to self-immolation, and what of the destruction of peasants and land and streams? And equally to the point, what was one to make of a church that could live, in a kind of spurious peace, with such crimes? Did we deserve the name Christian?

In the strange twilight "meantime" of our appeal, the defendants not in jail traveled the land, speaking of our crime, its meaning and consequence. It shortly became clear: the scandal attending our action in both church and state was quite simply — nonviolence.

The discovery was capital in my mind, and bears scrutiny. State violence, when now and again it is found scandalous in the church, is commonly considered bearable, a matter of toleration, if not of lightheartedness. Almost any level of official violence is sanctioned. The gears hum and turn: how much violence, how tolerable. The answers emerge: in effect, almost any level. Or, at very least, the present level. Tolerable. Prosit.

The seven (or nine, or twelve) rules of justification of war lurch forth, for all the world like the classic figures of a steeple clock. The law, the law! It will tell the hour right!

Only let someone contradict the clock, dare cry "Murder!"

Alas, the scandal is the denial of violence, the interference with
violence, the interruption: the shocking symbols, the untidiness,
the blood, the fire — of nonviolence.   — TDIP, 215–25

ON TRIAL
WITH THE CATONSVILLE NINE

Defense

What was the impact of the act of your brother Philip Berrigan
when he poured blood on draft files in Baltimore?

Daniel Berrigan

I began to understand
one could not indefinitely obey the law
while social conditions deteriorated
structures of compassion breaking down
neighborhoods slowly rotting
the poor despairing   unrest
forever present in the land   especially among
the young people
who are our only hope, our only resource.
My brother's action helped me realize
from the beginning of our republic
good men and women had said no
acted outside the law
when conditions so demanded
And if they did this
Time might vindicate them   show their act to be lawful
A gift to society
A gift to history
and to the community
A few men and women
must have a long view
must leave history to itself

   to interpret their lives   their repute
   Someday
   these defendants may be summoned
   to the Rose Garden and decorated
   but not today

Defense

Could you state to the court what your intent was in burning the
draft files?

Daniel Berrigan

   I did not want the children
   or the grandchildren of the jury
   or the judge
   to be burned with napalm

Judge

You say your intention was to save these children, of the jury, of
myself, when you burned the records? That is what I heard you
say. I ask if you meant that.

Daniel Berrigan

   I meant that
   of course I meant that
   or I would not say it
   The great sinfulness
   of modern war is
   that it renders concrete things abstract
   I do not want to talk
   about Americans in general

Judge

You cannot think up arguments now that you would like to have
had in your mind then.

Daniel Berrigan

My intention on that day
was
to save the innocent
from death by fire
I was trying to save the poor
who are mainly charged with
dying in this war
I poured napalm
on behalf of the prosecutor's
and the jury's children
It seems to me quite logical
If my way of putting the facts
is inadmissible
then so be it
but I was trying to be concrete
about the existence of God
who is not an abstraction
but is someone before me
for whom I am responsible

Defense

Was your action at Catonsville a way of carrying out your
religious beliefs?

Daniel Berrigan

Of course it was
May I say
if my religious belief is not accepted

as a substantial part of my action
then the action is eviscerated
of all meaning   and I should be
committed for insanity

Defense

How did your views on the Vietnam War take shape?

Daniel Berrigan

My views on war and peace
arose in me slowly
as life itself
pushed hard and fast
I should like to speak of
5 or 6 states in my development
I was invited to South Africa
around Easter of 1964
there I had about two weeks
of intense exposure
to a segregationist police state
At one meeting in Durban
I remember the question being raised
What happens to our children
if things go so badly
that we have to go to jail?
I remember saying
I could not answer that question
not being a citizen of that country
but I could perhaps help
by reversing the question
What happens to us and our children
if we do *not* go to jail?
2   I visited Eastern Europe twice
in 1964
meeting with Christians

in Czechoslovakia   Hungary   Russia
This had bearing
on my development   I was coming to realize
what it might cost to be a Christian
what it might cost
even at home
if things were to change
in the direction I felt events were taking
In the summer of 1965   I went to Prague
to attend the Christian Peace Conference
This was a kind of breakthrough
For the first time   a Catholic priest
sat in that vast assembly of Christians
from all over the world from Marxist countries
from India   from Africa from the east and west
talking about things
that diplomacy and power and the military
were not talking about
That is to say
How can we survive as human beings
in a world
more and more officially given over
to violence and death
I think the imperceptible movement
of my conscience
was pushed forward by that experience
3   I returned in the summer of 1964
and was assigned as editor and writer
at a magazine in New York
named *Jesuit Missions*
I was quite convinced
that the war in Vietnam
would inevitably worsen
I felt that a cloud
no larger than a man's hand
would shortly cover the sky
In the autumn of 1964

I began to say no to the war
knowing
if I delayed too long
I would never find the courage to say no
In that year
I underwent a kind of boot camp
in the "new humanity" becoming a peaceable man
In a time of great turmoil
New York was not an auspicious place
to be a peaceable Catholic priest
Cardinal Spellman was living
He had always supported American wars
He believed I think this states his thought:
that the highest expression   of Christian faith
was to bless our military
By his Christmas visits
to our foreign legions
he placed official approval
on our military adventuring
I had to say no to that too
I had to say no to the church
4   Finally
in the autumn of 1965
I was exiled from the United States
to Latin America

Judge

What do you mean, "exiled"?

Daniel Berrigan

I was sent out   your honor
with no return ticket
As one of my friends expressed it
sending me to Latin America was a little like
tossing Br'er Rabbit into the briar patch

I visited ten countries in four and half months
from Mexico to Southern Chile and then
up the western coasts
I discussed American involvement
in the political and social scene of those countries
I spent time with the students   the slum dwellers
with whatever government officials would talk
as well as the church leaders
In Mexico   a student said to me
We hate you North Americans with all our hearts
but we know that if you do not make it
we all come down   we are all doomed
I arrived in Rio in January of 1966
in the midst of devastating floods
In the space of a single night
the rains came down with torrential force
whole towns collapsed
people and shacks fell into a stew of death
I remember the next morning
slogging through the mud
in the company of a slum dweller
who was also a community organizer
He looked at me and said
My friend   millions for war in Vietnam
and this for us.

Judge

What? Are you saying that the United States government caused
the flood?

Daniel Berrigan

I think the fact
was a bit more subtle than that
I think he was saying
the resources of America

which belong in justice
to the poor of the world
are squandered in war and war preparation

Defense

Now may I ask about your writings and publications?

Prosecution

What difference does it make how many books he has written?

Defense

I show you the book *Night Flight to Hanoi*. Will you outline the
circumstances out of which this book was written?

Daniel Berrigan

5   The book marks
The next stage of my development
In January of 1968   an invitation came
from the government of North Vietnam
Professor Howard Zinn and myself
were invited to Hanoi
to bring home 3 captive American airmen
For me to go to Hanoi
was a very serious decision
I believe   I have always believed
that the peace movement must not merely say no
to the war
It must also say
yes to life   yes to the possibility of a human future
We must go beyond frontiers
frontiers declared by our country or by the enemy
So I thought it would be important
to show Americans

that we were ready to risk our lives
to bring back American prisoners
because we did not believe
that in wartime
anyone should be in prison
or should suffer separation
from families
simply we did not believe in war
And so we went.
In Hanoi I think we were the first Americans
to undergo
an American bombing attack
When the burned draft files
were brought into court yesterday
as evidence
I could not but recall
that I had seen in Hanoi
evidence of a very different nature
I saw not boxes of burned papers
I saw parts of human bodies   preserved in alcohol
the bodies of children   the hearts and organs and limbs
of women   teachers   workers   peasants   bombed
in fields and churches and schools and hospitals
I examined our "improved weaponry"
it was quite clear to me
during three years of air war
America had been experimenting
upon the bodies of the innocent
We had improved our weapons
on their flesh

Judge

He did not see this first hand. He is telling of things he was told
in Hanoi, about some things that were preserved in alcohol.

Daniel Berrigan

French   English   Swedish experts   doctors
Testified
these were actually the bodies
whose pictures
accompanied the exhibits
The evidence was unassailable
The bombings
were a massive crime against humanity
The meaning of the air war in the North
was the deliberate systematic destruction
of a poor and developing people

Judge

We are not trying the air war in North Vietnam.

Daniel Berrigan

I must protest the effort
to discredit me on the stand
I am speaking of what I saw
There is a consistent effort
to say that I did not see it

Judge

The best evidence of what some "crime commission" found is
not a summary that you give.

Daniel Berrigan

So be it
In any case we brought the flyers home
I think as a result of the trip to Hanoi
I understood the limits

of what I had done before
and the next step that must come
On my return to America
another event
helped me understand
the way I must go
It was the self-immolation
of a high school student
in Syracuse New York
in the spring of 1968
This boy had come to a point of despair
about the war   He had gone
into the Catholic cathedral
drenched himself with kerosene
and immolated himself in the street
He was still living a month later
I was able to gain access to him
I smelled the odor
of burning flesh
And I understood anew
what I had seen in North Vietnam
The boy was dying in torment
his body like a piece of meat
cast upon a grille
He died shortly thereafter
I felt that my senses
had been invaded in a new way
I had understood
the power of death in the modern world
I know I must speak and act
against death
because this boy's death
was being multiplied
a thousand fold
in the Land of Burning Children
So I went to Catonsville
and burned some papers   because

the burning of children
is inhuman and unbearable
I went to Catonsville
because I had gone to Hanoi
because my brother was a man
and I must be a man
and because
I know at length
I could not announce the gospel
from a pedestal
I must act as a Christian
sharing the risks and burdens and anguish
of those whose lives were placed
in the breach by us
I saw suddenly   and it struck with the force of lightning
that my position was false
I was threatened with verbalizing
my moral substance out of existence
I was placing upon young shoulders
a filthy burden the original sins of war
I was asking them to enter a ceremony of death
Although I was too old
to carry a draft card   there were other ways
of getting in trouble with a state
that seemed determined upon multiplying the dead
totally intent upon a war
the meaning of which no sane man could tell
So I went to Hanoi
and then to Catonsville
and that is why I am here.   —TCN, 81–93

THE VERDICT

Everything before was a great lie.
Illusion, distemper, the judge's eye
Negro and Jew for rigorists,

spontaneous vengeance. The children die
singing in the furnace. They say in hell
heaven is a great lie.

    Years, years ago
my mother moves in youth. In her
I move too, to birth, to youth, to this.
The judge's *toc toc* is time's steel hand
summoning: *come priest from the priest hole. Risk!*
Everything else
Is a great lie. Four walls, home, love, youth,
truth untried, all, all is a great lie.
The truth the judge shuts in his two eyes.

Come Jesuit, the university cannot
no nor the universe, nor vatic Jesus
imagine. Imagine! Everything before
was a great lie.

    Philip, your freedom
stature, simplicity, the ghetto where the children
malinger, die —

    Judge Thomsen
strike, strike with a hot hammer
the hour, the truth. The truth has birth
all former truth must die. Everything
before; all faith and hope, and love itself
was a great lie.   —ARB, 125

PROPHECY

The way I see the world is strictly illegal
To wit, through my eyes

Is illegal, yes;
to wit, I live

like a pickpocket, like the sun
like the hand that writes this, by
my wits

This is not permitted
that I look on the world
and worse, insist that I see

what I see
— a conundrum, a fury, a burning bush

and with five fingers, where my eyes fail
trace —

with a blackened brush
on butcher sheets, black on white
(black for blood, white for death
where the light fails)

— that face which is not my own
(and my own)
that death which is not my own
(and my own)

This is strictly illegal
and will land me in trouble

as somewhere now, in a precinct
in a dock, the statues
thrash in fury, hear them
hear ye!
the majestic jaws

of crocodiles in black shrouds
the laws
forbidding me
the world, the truth
under blood oath

forbidding, row upon row

of razors, of statutes
of molars, of grinders —

those bloodshot eyes
legal, sleepless, man-eating

— not letting me
not
let blood   — ARB, 230

I WAS A FUGITIVE FROM THE FBI

May 7, 1970, marks exactly a month since I packed the small red
bag I had bought in Hanoi, and set out from Cornell, looking for
America. So far, it has been a tougher and longer voyage than the
one which set me down in North Vietnam some two years ago.

In the course of that month, I have changed domicile some six
times; this in strict accord with a rule of the Jesuit order, making
us, at least in principle, vagabonds on mission: "It is our vocation
to travel to any place in the world where the greater glory of God
and the need of the neighbor shall impel us." Amen, brothers.

It may be a time for a modest stock-taking. The gains sought
by such felonious vagrancy as mine are, in the nature of things,
modest to the point of imposing silence on the wise. The "nature
of things" being defined simply as: power. It is entirely possible
that any hour of any day may bring an end to the game; the wrong
chance meeting, a thoughtless word of a friend, a phone tip — the
possibilities are without end. But one takes this for granted, and
goes on, knowing that practically all of us are powerless, that the
line dividing the worth of one's work from inertia and discouragement is thin indeed. (What manner of person today exudes
confidence, moral spleen, righteousness, sense of messiahship at
once cocksure, and dead serious? God, who grants us very little
these days, at least keeps us from that.)

But what can I hope to accomplish, on the run as I am, having
to improvise and skimp and risk being ridiculous, or plain two-
cents wrong? How can I reject honored presumptions of conduct,

like "the good man is responsible for his actions," and he "pays up on demand"? Or the older Socratic dictum: "One owes the state restitution for broken law, violated order"?

The method of Martin King, violation of local or state law and submitting to jail, had a great deal going for it; circumstances supported the principle. Being in jail was invariably an appeal to a higher jurisdiction. It brought the attention of national authorities to the fact of local or state violations; it brought pressures from above. Such a tactic, apart from its mystique, was in fact a calculated political act. It dramatized in the fact of brutal local forces, purportedly of law and order, the captive state of the virtuous, at the mercy of lesser jurisdictions. And it seemed for a while to pay off. Both Kennedy and Johnson professed to be moved by innocence under fire; they pledged themselves to amelioration, not merely in freeing demonstrators, but in bringing legal redress of widespread wrong.

Alas and alas, how could such a tactic apply to me and my friends? What superior jurisdiction would rush to action on the occasion of our jailing? To whom could we appeal? To the International War Crimes Tribunal? To the United Nations? To the World Court? In our instance, straw figures all; the United States has pushed them flat, along with the other superpowers. No, those of us who are willing to go to jail must seek our analogies elsewhere than in the civil rights movement if we would seem to be politically serious (as indeed, Philip, David, John, Tom, and Marjorie are, and will be heard from).

But as far as national due process is concerned, the highest appeal courts duly swept aside the issues we tried to raise. That, of course, did not remove the issues; they grow hotter and more lethal every day. The war is mounting in fury. The Congress, the universities, the churches, bankers, workers, decent citizens of all stripes, separately or in concert, are talking to stone-deaf power. For at least the past six months, when jail was becoming a nearer and larger threat, the students with whom I worked for three years, and for whom my decision seemed to be of some import, said to me time and again, with imploring: "When they come for you, don't go in!"

The festival at Cornell offered a delicious opportunity, too good to let pass. Some ten thousand students had come together for a post-Woodstock festival of arts, politics, communal living, all in honor of nonviolence and Catonsville. Such a gathering, it seemed to me, must not be taken lying down, lost in wondering admiration. According to certain presumptions, mainly of university officials (whose relief was guarded, oblique, but in the air), I was indeed going to jail. But those to whom I was responsible, in the church and resistance, had other urgings, rarely expressed, often legible in faces and eyes. Would I be inventive on the night, open to other voices, other directions?

Irresistible. At 7:40 p.m. on Friday, April 17, I ended ten rustic days in hiding on the land, and entered the great Baron Hall, scene of last year's forty-eight-hour live-in after the black seizure of the Student Union. Scene, too, of ROTC reviews and maneuvers and confrontations; the only place on campus where gun-toting is "invisible" and legal to this day. I was decked out gorgeously, like an outer-space insect, in big goggles, motorcycle helmet and jacket, surrounded by a troupe of students, variously hirsute, hippy, fierce, and celebration. Rabbi Waskow was thundering away on stage, the Freedom Seder was in progress. The moment arrived when Elias the prophet is summoned, figure of providence for all those in legal jeopardy. Supposing that I qualified, I walked on stage.

The next hour and a half were stormy indeed. I recall a sense of weightlessness, almost of dislocation; the throng of young faces, singing, dancing, eating, the calls of support and resistance. Much love, many embraces, the usual press of journalists. Then, in a quiet moment, a friend whispered: "Do you want to split?"

It was all I needed. Why not indeed split? Why concede, by hanging around, that the wrong-headed powers owned me? Why play mouse, even sacred mouse, to their cat game? Why turn this scene into yet another sanctuary, so often done before, only delaying the inevitable, the hunters always walking off with their prize?

When the lights lowered for a rock group, I slipped off backstage. Students helped lower around me an enormous puppet of one of the twelve apostles, in use shortly before by a mime group. Inside the burlap, I had only to hold a stick that kept the papier-mâché head aloft, and follow the others, making for a panel truck in which we were to pack the costumes. The puppets were pitched aboard; I climbed in, blind as a bat, sure of my radar, spoiling for fun. It was guerrilla theater, a delight, just short of slapstick. An FBI agent ran for the phone, our license plate was recorded, the chase was on. But our trusty van, hot with destiny, galloped for the woods and we made it.

The rest is modest history, of sorts. My brother and David Eberhardt were picked up in New York the following Tuesday amid a hue and cry worthy of bigger game. I settled in, here and there, for the short or long haul, resigned to the fate of harmless creatures in the open hunting season of our society; neither hoof nor claw, only protective coloration. A kind of roadrunner, stopping here and there to gain breath and take soundings with friends, and then move on.

The first month has been an interesting experiment: the breaking of idols. That myth of omni-competence surrounds almost any large federal authority, a myth inflated despite all sorts of contrary available evidence: the successive CIA fiascos in Southeast Asia and elsewhere, the wrong Marines on the wrong beaches, the utter inability (a spiritual failure) to touch the sources of unrest at home. Was there something to be dramatized? The FBI is quite possibly composed of earnest, stern, honorable Romans. (I am always made to feel secure when meeting them, there are so many Catholics; even when they stoop to conquer, poking under beds for priests, they never forget their folklore; it is always: "Are you there, Father Dan?")

Grant them all that. Still I suggest my case offers interesting evidence of a striking failure of power, beginning with the FBI and extending even to Vietnam. It is a failure of overkill technology, of pacification, of search-and-destroy missions, of indiscriminate trampling of national boundaries.

I am prepared even, subject to acts of God, to set down a tentative principle, a kind of translation from the sayings of Chairman Jesus: "Where the fish travel in schools, it is useless to work with even the most sophisticated reel. The only solution: metamorphose into a fish." Also to our point, is a warning drawn from strict textual scrutiny of the New Testament. To wit, there is only the barest internal evidence that Luke 5:10 ("Fear not, I shall make you fishers of men and women") has literal reference to the FBI.

I could go on, but perhaps a point is made. A dizzying thought occurs to me, shaking my hand as I write. Could it be that your humble servant, without script of staff, might be an instrument for demythologizing Big Bro Justice? I like the idea, even as a voice reminds me it is fraught with presumption.

But in the face of all that power, all that legitimacy, all those hunters and hounds — what can I count on when the chips are down?

Attorney General Mitchell, it is reported, was recently presented with a shiny night stick by a local police department. It was inscribed: "To the Top Cop." He carried it home under his arm, grim with satisfaction. Now the head of the Justice Department has at his disposal, directly or through others, some hundreds of thousands of night sticks and assorted other hardware, goods and services, plus the hands itching to wield them on command. I contemplate all this vast panoply of power; and I am not shaken, any more than Buddha under his tree. For I have other armaments, resources, and visions, of which Mr. Mitchell can know little....

The question burns like a night flare. The night sticks come running. But the night sticks can do nothing; they do not signify. In the deepest sense (forever lost to top cops), they are ersatz, wooden limbs in place of living ones. They substitute woodenly and hardly at all, for lost friendship, lost communion, contemplatives and activists, for friends and dreamers, open minds, closed mouth, the network of men and women who at need can be counted on to "harbor, aid, and abet," to interrupt the works and agents of power.

Finally, if they do run me down, I will claim a win anyway. I will go off to jail in better spirits than my captors.

A clue for Americans. There are some of us who claim to own this land. We do not hold current lien or title or mortgage, or want to. We have no political power. Our claims are based finally on the strength of our intuitions — on a sense of history generally lost sight of, despised, or suppressed. To wit: human beings have an inalienable right, in Kent State as in Song My, in a resister's jail or a resister's underground, to life, liberty, and the pursuit of happiness.

That "pursuit" is indeed something more. It draws blood — a chase, a hunt, an FBI-wanted list, jeopardy, dislocation, the poverty of someone on the move. Those who pursue happiness must endure unhappiness, the dark night of resistance, doubt, delusion, nightmare, because they pursue decency and a human future, for the despised and expendable, the wretched of the earth.

The first month is over, the future is charged with surprise, Come, Holy Spirit. The time will shortly be upon us, if it is not already here, when the pursuit of contemplation becomes a strictly subversive activity. This is the deepest and at the same time, I think, the most sensible way of expressing the trouble into which my brother and I have fallen. What else have we been up to these several years? We have been trying mightily to avoid the distraction from reality which is almost a stigma of the modern mind. We have been practicing with very mixed success so simple a thing as concentration; we have been sticking with the pertinacity of bloodhounds to the trail — to the blood of Christ, another name for history in process, in movement.

We have been trying to remember humanity; to re-member humanity in the rigorous liturgical sense — to exercise anamnesis, the heart of the Eucharistic command and privilege: When you do this, remember me. Which is to say, Stay with history, Make something of it, by falling within its main line of action, the breaking of bread, the sharing of wine. Make a community whose life will also be available to history.

We have been trying not to forget, not to forget either by way of amnesia or distraction. We have had very little time or patience for celebrations which we took to be merely another form of induced forgetfulness. We could not celebrate something which we were perhaps refusing to let happen — which might possibly be our own death; or short of that, the will to embrace, in however fragmented a way, the insecurity and loss we were being called to.

I am quite sure of what I mean, however badly it comes out. I am convinced that contemplation, including the common worship of the believing, is a political act of the highest value, implying the riskiest of consequences for those taking part. Union with the Divine leads us, in a sense charged with legal jeopardy, to resistance against false, corrupting, coercive, imperialist policy. We have been living a recorded history long enough for the evidence now to be in. The saints were right: their best moments were on the run, in jail, at the edge of social acceptability. Tactics, modes of response, vocabulary, the public uses (and misuses) of mysticism — all were entirely secondary. They might win or not in the short run. They might or might not succeed — in Bonhoeffer's phrase — in putting a stick in the wheel of power; they would try for that modest disruption. But the heart of the matter lay elsewhere. It lay in irreducible content of a memory that could not finally suffer brainwashing; some event to "remember" (and therefore to reproduce — an image, an action captive to choice), some reality to call into unity and peace, to bind up and heal our broken estate.

We are back with our image of life at the edge. That edge turns against the one who chooses to live and die without weapons. His freedom has made it possible for him to choose another way of life than the death of his brother. But this does not mean — when pseudo-history moves up close with its massed demands on body and soul — that a person will not suffer death himself. Quite the contrary. Have you ever heard of death by solitude, by ostracism? Of the "extramural" activities of Christ? (He was born, says the author of the Letter to the Hebrews outside the walls, *extra muros*, to die; extradited, we would say — a man without a people, cut off from the privileges of community and citizenship.)

Deep waters indeed. One startling sign of the rightness of a course of action may be the initial sharp outcry against it, in church and state alike.   — AIHF, 60–66, 77–79

THE DARK NIGHT OF RESISTANCE

April 1970. I start these notes quite literally on the run. In town, spring is breaking out in a cataclysm — unexpected! As though in midwinter, dark and pandemic, a healing had been found. I walk down streets like a shadow or a cardboard man, invisible as the mild air, observing, smiling, anonymous, apart from the big march of gain and loss, violence, speed, defeat. The forsythias crowd about, a cloud of witnesses, every person's forgiveness, a promise kept. I think of the far end of the lane, yearn toward it, in hope it may sow the faces of Phil, David, John. What might not happen, if one believes?

I want to do an unfashionable thing, in a time which is not so much fashionable — as simply mad. So mad that it has become a wearying stereotype to speak of its madness. Since the admission hangs choking on the air, is part of the daily burden. You young resister, what of the madness to which we have delivered you, like a sour ration at the cell door? You fervent apostles of war normalcy, you hunted Panthers, you police, you political bigstick wielders, you few men and women faithful to suffering and the long haul, you, my friends, concocting ways of keeping me uncaged, you students pondering a future in the shadow of Dame Liberty violated (your future closing like a vise). For all of you; resisting, resisting resistance, keeping it heated, keeping it cool, you great self spawning disease, you nation, you of the nation within the nation, still unrecognized, still in bondage — for you. Something unfashionable; one man's spiritual journey. The delayed journey, into light; or more exactly into a light forever quenched, delayed, snuffed out.

To offer a proposition: the state of resistance as a state of life itself. Since like it or not, this is the shape of things. We will not again know sweet normalcy in our lifetime. What seems *outré* now, outrageous, disruptive of routine and pattern, is simply the obscure shape of things unknown, as far as we can discern any shape at all. (We can.) Shapes we can no longer cringe from, run from (very far), bribe out of sight (for very long). All of which it seems to me, once the admission is made, clears the air. When the future need no longer be resisted, the true form of resistance can be spread out before us, analyzed, dealt, losing hands and winning. All to the good. It being pernicious and lethal and against the right order of things that we should cling to the past, sanctify what we have known, give our hearts to it, sell our souls. No.

Everything begins with that no, spoken with the heart's full energies, a suffering and prophetic word, a word issuing from the nature and direction of things. No. A time to tear and pull down and root out. A time for burning out the accumulated debris of history, the dark noisome corners of our shrines, a universal spring-cleaning. So that the symbolism of Catonsville may become a permanent method and symbol. Of what?

Of moral process. Not of escalated ethical improvement, or social engineering of American dreams, or exportation of techniques. We have had enough of that. We must speak of something other, closer to the dark roots of our existence, to beginnings, to the heart of things.

I wanted to do something foolish, in a bad time. Those students and resisters and priests and nuns (and blacks and Chicanos) who perhaps rejoiced and understood what I had done in going underground — I want above all to avoid offering merely a new kind of captivity, a stasis, food for romantic fascination with what I had done. I want to help others come over into freedom, in the very effort to free myself. I want to suggest a strong note of reserve, of pessimism, of the ambiguous which it seems to me are of the very nature of life today. (Not so much to introduce these qualities, as though from outside, but to point to them as already there, part of the makeup of this, or indeed of any such course of responsible action.) And then to ask: In spite of all, what are we to do with our lives? A question which seems to me a peerless source of freedom to the one who dares pose it with seriousness.

It seems clear by now, anything short of confronting this question ends up sooner or later in a suffocating dead end. We have had a history in recent years, both in the movement and in its expression in the church, of the inadequacy and emptiness of just such shortcuts. We have taken up, one after another, almost every question except the one which would liberate us: the question of humanity. How is a human being to live today? Is it possible for us to do something other than kill a brother or sister — the practically universal demand laid upon us by the state, approved by a silent church? Is there another way, which will allow humanity to live here and now, will allow the unborn to get born, and to live their lives in a way different from the (one) way sanctioned today?

How shall we live our lives today? It is scarcely possible, it will be less and less possible, to live them at the center of the web, without being cursed in our humanity, metamorphosed finally into the beast whose activity we take up as our own. The beast who eats human beings.

It seems to me that two eventualities are in the air, and one of the two will certainly occur, as a fact of history — and soon. Americans, a certain number of them, will struggle to keep alive a human style and method, to enhance it, to make it possible for human beings to be born of human beings. Or a genetic (which is to say spiritual) catastrophe will be born of us. I do not know of a more truthful way of putting the question — our destiny, what is to become of us.

Shunting from city to city, dependent on the goodness and ingenuity and risk of a few friends, one comes to a better sense of these things. How are we to live our lives today? We are in the dark preliminary stages of a new humanity, together. Imagine! My brother in prison, myself on the run, our friends here and there (in prison, on the run), and in every city between. Thus, all of us are enabled, in an utterly new way, to probe and ponder the new forms of community, the questions about the future, the usefulness and joy and hope that may arise from this. From physical stasis, and from a slippery, even absurd mobility (in prison, underground) — in both conditions, to explore our spiritual freedom. Am I suffering delusions, or can others see with me the stunning opportunity that opens like a grace before us?

Meantime, I would like to do something unfashionable, in the sense not of mystification, but facing the fact that everything or nearly everything of worth today is despised or devalued. Except to a few. I should like to raise the questions whose very posing implies one is not seeking a more bearable form of insanity or illness in the Imperial Madhouse.

Instead, one seeks sanity and health; which is to say, one is at least initially and in principle, on a subversive errand, determined with whatever energy and courage he can summon, to persevere in it.   —DNR, 1–7

THEY CALL US DEAD MEN

I remember Thomas Merton writing me about a year before his death, with his own mix of the playful and grotesquerie. I am already dead, dead, he declared. I am already dead, only they haven't discovered it yet. When they do, they will undoubtedly bury me with honors; for the present, I go around with all the business of living, playing a part. But everything is gone.

I think I know what he was driving at. With regard to most of our fellows in church and state, both my brother and I are really dead men. It makes no sense not to start with that fact. We have no stake in church or state, as currently in evidence; their aims, their values, their mutual transfusions of comfort. We have said no to it all. And more than this; for our "no" has been taken at its word. What else can I conclude, when he sweats out a felon's day in high-security prison, when the sedulous hounds are hot on my trail? No, we can never complain that we have not been taken seriously.

And what of the church? There, we are taken seriously too. *Aus mit.* Even if we are tolerated, the tolerance has little virtue about it; in a time of public irrational upheaval, we are simply another instance of those who fly the coop, kick over traces, or antic wise, hang around to make trouble. In any case, we are never to be taken seriously, never to become the occasion of rebirth, renunciation of wealth, conversion of heart. We are never invited to be heard from; we never count for much. This is the sentence, passed *in absentia*. It is the reduction of the living to the remote acre of the dead.

Did we once think we would count for something; or that suffering repression, the threat or actuality of personal harm, we would win the attention of our fellow Christians, of our fellow priests? Alas and alas. When Philip was cast into solitary confinement and began his fast, we could not think (as one would instinctively think), now they will listen, now they will protest, now they will speak up for him! No such thing. Our hope was extinguished. We must appeal, across all lines, to the good sense and compassion of all our friends, including of course, a few fellow Catholics, a few priests. But the attention of the Great Church was as usual, fixated on the Great Society. We are dead to all that.

Someday, wrote Merton, they will discover that I am already dead.

When one comes to this truth, as to a still center of existence, he quite possibly has become a person of prayer. What is certain, is that such a realization gives me an inkling, however fleeting and mazed, of the fate of human goodness in a bad time.

We normally win the kind of eternity for which our lives prepare us, Socrates said to his friends. Indeed.

—DNR, 180–81

CERTAIN OCCULT UTTERANCES FROM THE UNDERGROUND AND ITS GUARDIAN SPHINX

If you seek pleasure in everything
you must seek pleasure in nothing

if you wish to possess everything
you must desire to possess nothing

if you wish to become all
you must desire to be nothing

if you wish to know all
you must desire to know nothing

if you wish to arrive where you know not
you must go by way you know not

if you wish to possess what you do not
you must dispossess

if you wish to become new
you must become as dead   —ARB, 137

WE ARE FORBIDDEN
TO SERVE IN THEIR WARS

In times such as we are enduring, it seems necessary above all
else, I think, to allow the Word of God full play in our lives and
our minds. For myself, I know beyond any doubt that I must sink
or swim by virtue of a very simple act of faith, drawn from our
Testament. For my present, as you must know, is obscure to the
point of darkness. I have no real idea of what my Underground
state may mean for others, where it is meant to lead me, or what
contribution it may be supposed to make for peace, for justice.
As far as the future is concerned, that is all too clear. It means for
me the fate of my brother Philip, already entered upon, as well
as the fate of so many friends who are paying a very heavy price
for an equivalent witness.

If I bring all of this up before you, it is not, dear friends, in
order to wage an assault upon your compassion. It is merely to
share with you one Christian's understanding of what faith is
exacting in these times. For I think this is always the burden of
such times as we are enduring — the faith which is at once dark,
and yet undeniable and clear in its demands; which is costly, and
yet is generous in its return upon us; which is the call of a jealous
God upon his sons and daughters, and yet a love of that prodigal
Father returned to us a hundredfold.

I began by suggesting that it is in the Word of God one finds the resources to keep going in such times as these. I have been asking myself in prayer, asking the Lord for a clue as to the meaning of this strange existence I am leading. I would like to share with you a few insights that the past months have granted me.

It seems to me that we start with a literal fact. The "Underground" is a kind of rehearsal, a metaphor I think, for Death itself. It is in that Underground that humanity is literally ground under. Dust to dust, we are told. Prison, of course, is another such image. So is illness, serious incapacity, so is poverty, so is race in a racist state.

But I think what makes this metaphor of particular interest to me is that nonviolent life outside the law — a definition of the Underground as I see it — is a kind of life outside the law of Death itself. I hope this sentence is not too complicated. We can put the same thing another way. By becoming an outlaw, I am seeking to outlaw Death. This, I think, is an insight our Testament grants us. I think this is one way of putting the Savior's view of his own life. That reign of Death he saw as all but universal, all but omnipotent, all but omnivorous, carnivorous in its intention and method, claiming all flesh for itself. No one, but no one, could stand aside from those claims or show cause for exemption from Death: no one, not in all our history.

Now suppose for a moment, as indeed I think our Savior supposed, that one finds the presumptions of Death presumptuous. Suppose one wishes to play another game. Suppose the implications of the Death game stink in one's nostrils, with all their assorted smells and whiffs of duplicity, of political corruption, or promises broken, and life destroyed, and property misused, and racism encouraged, the poor benignly neglected, and the rich seated unassailably in places of power. And religion in the midst of this game ambiguous in its own voice, and the spiritual goods of the people diminished beyond recognition.

Supposing all this to be true, what is the tactic of the believer? Of a human being? Quite simply, I think, reading the New Testament, one says *No*. Quite simply, one puts his life where the Gospel tells him it should be, if indeed the Gospel has something to say at all.

One submits in a very true way to Death, in order to destroy the power of Death from within.

There are, of course, as many ways of doing this as there are people capable of opening the book of Jesus and reading what it says there. What our Savior says to us, it seems to me, may be translated in many ways: as jail, as exile, as Underground, as tax-resistance, as courageous public action of any kind which costs, which diminishes one's freedom of movement or place or action. But as the Savior reminds us, with a certain vigor, based upon a certain unkillable vision of his own, our reaction had better be *something* — something of this sort. That is where you saw, as we say in the ancient creed, "He was crucified, died, and was buried" — which is to say he submitted before the imperial power that claimed his life. He preferred to suffer violence in his person rather than to inflict it on others. He died a criminal, his body placed in a tomb. He was shoveled into the inert grave. Or as we say in the Resistance, he acted and went underground, and some days later when it was expedient for others, he surfaced again, and with great pains identified himself as the One of the Friday we call Good.

I am struck by all this as an exemplary action and passion for ourselves. That is to say that Jesus, by a method that was breathtakingly realistic and right, sought to break the universal dominion of Death over humanity. Which, translated to his times and ours, has something to do with the claims of the militaristic and imperial state, the stigma placed upon the forehead, the slaveries forged by the powerful of this world, the notion that the lives and deaths of men and women are the crude properties and chattels of whatever Caesar.

To confront all this, Jesus refused again and again to confront the sword with his own sword. No, he drew back from that method — that mirror game — in a gesture of ineffaceable dignity. "My kingdom," he said, "is not of this world." And to illustrate, by way of contrast, his own dynamic, he offered a figure of speech: "Unless the grain of wheat, falling to the ground, die, it remains alone; but if it dies, it brings forth much fruit." Here, his tactic and method are reconciled to the organic world

itself in its cyclic cheating of death. Let the one who would live —
die! Let him go underground if he would rise to the life of God
and of humankind....

Dear friends, I would not have any child born into this world,
into this nation, into this church, in order to bear arms, in order
to belong to the stratagems of death, in order to obey the Pentagon, in order to raven the poor in distant lands, to die there,
to kill there, in any sense, in any case, to perish there. Neither
would I have any parent approve of such disposition of the lives
of others. Nor would I have the churches support it, nor clerics remain silent before it, nor congregations argue on its behalf.
Nor would I have such a tearing apart of the right order of things
as condemns the poor here and throughout the world to lives of
utter degradation and hopelessness while we stand idly by, our
ill-gotten goods turned to weapons turned against others. And all
this despite our Gospel and the stern claim of Christ upon us, in
life and in death.

Both my brother and myself, Philip in prison and myself in
hiding, wish that our resistance, narrowed as it is to the issue of
the war, be seen as a service for all our brothers and sisters in
the world. Indeed, we could not but wish that that service could
have taken a less obscure and anguished and ambiguous form.
We would infinitely prefer to be free, about our Father's business,
in what one might call the ordinary errands of the Gospel: feeding the hungry, clothing the naked, housing the homeless. Alas,
the times are twisted. In the kingdom of Death we could not but
resist Death with all our means and might. Thus are we outlawed,
forbidden free access to the community of decent people.

In such a time the perverse logic of power dictates that people
such as us must be hunted down and locked away. We who are
without weapons or riches or a stake in this world have become
a danger to the masters of the kingdom of death.

But, dear friends, if the keepers of that kingdom have their
logic, so do we. We may be hunted and locked away. We will
be, according to their plan. But we will also break their locks,
which are the very bolts and rivets of death, for the wielders of
such power are as dead to history and to humankind and to the

future as any Caesar. Their claim is declared null and void by Christ himself. We are forbidden to serve in their wars. We are forbidden, that is to say, in biblical language, "to worship their gods." And as far as Philip and I are concerned, we shall never do so, so help us Christ. May that Lord of History grant you also a measure of courage and light in perplexed and anguished times.

—ST, 3–10

LETTER TO THE WEATHERMEN

In early 1970, while underground, Daniel Berrigan was asked by leaders of the Weathermen, a violent antiwar group that operated illegally and underground, and occasionally blew up military installations, to write a few words of advice for them. His open letter helped end their violence.

No principle is worth the sacrifice of a single human being.

That's a very hard statement. At various stages of the movement, some have acted as if almost the opposite were true, as people got purer and purer. People have been kicked out for less and less reason. At one remote period of the past, the result of such thinking was the religious wars, the wars of extinction. At another time it was Hitler; he wanted a ton of purity too. Still another is still with us in the war against the Panthers and the Vietnamese. I think I'm in the underground because I want part in none of this inhumanity, whatever name it goes by, whatever rhetoric with which it justifies itself.

When madness is the acceptable public state of mind, we're all in danger, for madness is an infection in the air. And I submit that we all breathe the infection and that the movement has at times been sickened by it too.

The madness has to do with the disposition of human conflict by forms of violence. In or out of the military, in or out of the movement, it seems to me that we had best call things by their name, and the name of this thing, it seems to me, is the death game, no matter where it appears. And as for myself, I would as soon be under the heel of former masters as under the heel of new ones.

Some of your actions are going to involve inciting and conflict and trashing, and these actions are very difficult for thoughtful people. But I came upon a rule of thumb somewhere which might be of some help to us: Do only that which one cannot not do. Maybe it isn't very helpful, and of course it's going to be applied differently by the Joint Chiefs of Staff and an underground group of sane men and women. In the former, hypocritical expressions of sympathy will always be sown along the path of the latest rampage. Such grief is like that of a mortician in a year of plague.

But our realization is that a movement has historic meaning only insofar as it puts itself on the side of human dignity and the protection of life, even of the lives most unworthy of such respect. A revolution is interesting insofar as it avoids like the plague the plague it promised to heal. Ultimately if we want to define the plague as death (a good definition), a prohuman movement will neither put people to death nor fill the prisons nor inhibit freedoms nor brainwash nor torture enemies nor be mendacious nor exploit women, children, blacks, the poor. It will have a certain respect for the power of the truth, a power which created the revolution in the first place.

We may take it, I think, as a simple rule of thumb that the revolution will be no better and no more truthful and no more populist and no more attractive than those who brought it into being. Which is to say we are not killers, as America would stigmatize us, and indeed as America perversely longs us to be. We are something far different. We are teachers of the people who have come on a new vision of things. We struggle to embody that vision day after day, to make it a reality among those we live with, so that people are literally disarmed by knowing us; so that their fear of change, their dread of life are exorcised, and their dread of human differences slowly expunged.

Instead of thinking of the underground as temporary, exotic, abnormal, perhaps we should start thinking of its implication as an entirely self-sufficient, mobile, internal revival community — the underground as a definition of our future. What does it mean literally to have nowhere to go in America, to be kicked out of America? It must mean — let us go somewhere in America, let us stay here and play here and love here and build here, and in this way join not only those who like us are also kicked out, but those who have never been inside at all — the blacks, the Puerto Ricans, the Chicanos, the Native Americans.

Next, we are to strive to become such men and women as may, in a new world, be nonviolent. If there's any definition of the new man and woman, the man or woman of the future, it seems to me that they are persons who do violence unwillingly, by exceptions. They know that destruction of property is only a means; they keep the end as vivid and urgent and as alive as the means, so that the means are judged in every instance by their relation to the ends. Violence as legitimate means: I have a great fear of American violence, not only in the military and diplomacy, in economics, in industry and advertising; but also in here, in me, up close, among us.

On the other hand, I must say, I have very little fear, from firsthand experience, of the violence of the Vietcong or Panthers (I hesitate to use the word "violence"), for their acts come from the proximate threat of extinction, from being invariably put on the line of self-defense. But the same cannot be said of us and our history. We stand outside the culture of these others, no matter what admiration or fraternity we feel with them; we are unlike them, we have other demons to battle.

But the history of the movement, in the last years, it seems to me, shows how constantly and easily we are seduced by violence, not only as method but as end itself. Very little new politics, very little ethics, very little direction, and only a minimum moral sense, if any at all. Indeed one might conclude in despair: the movement is debased beyond recognition, I can't be a part of it. Far from giving birth to the new human, it has only prolif-erated the armed, bellicose, and inflated spirit of the army, the plantation, the corporation, the diplomat.

Yet it seems to me good, in public as well as in our own house, to turn the question of violence back on its true creators and pur-veyors working as we must from a very different ethos and for very different ends. I remember being on a television program recently and having the question of violence thrown at me and responding — look, ask the question in the seats of power, don't ask it of me, don't ask me why I broke the law, ask Nixon why he breaks the law constantly, ask the Justice Department, ask the racists. Obviously, but for Johnson and Nixon and their fetching ways, Catonsville would never have taken place and you and I would not be where we are today; just as but for the same people SDS would never have grown into the Weathermen or the Weathermen have gone underground. In a decent society, functioning on behalf of its people, all of us would be doing the things that decent people do for one another. That we are forbidden so to act, forced to meet so secretly and with so few, is a tragedy we must live with. We have been forbidden a future by the forms of power, which include death as the ordinary social method. We have rejected the future they drafted us into, having refused, on the other hand, to be kicked out of America, either by aping their methods or leaving the country.

The question now is what we can create. I feel at your side across the miles, and I hope that sometime, sometime in this mad world, in this mad time, it will be possible for us to sit down face to face, as brothers and sisters, and find that our hopes and our sweat, and the hopes and sweat and death and tears and blood of our brothers and sisters throughout the world, have brought to birth that for which we began. Shalom to you.   — AIHF, 95–98

I WILL SIGN MY NAME

Now what the hell sort of dog's life is left to limp?
I may not mean what I see.
The FBI has devised for this emergency a poetry censor
whose eyes flame like an alcoholic's,
　　smoke like Beelzebub's dry ice or dry armpit
when the bubonic smell of a poetic name-place
　　falls under its snub snout.
I may not name river.

No, nor mountain, street, alley nor valley.
At least I will sign my name.
Now hold your nose, eyes, ears,
    in a one-mile perimeter of infernal headquarters,
All hell will shortly like dull scissors and sirens
    gouge, saw, at the inner ear.
Ready? Set? Then.
Daniel Berrigan.   —ARB, 144

WE HAVE CHOSEN
TO BE POWERLESS CRIMINALS
IN A TIME OF CRIMINAL POWER

On Sunday morning, August 2, 1970, while underground, Daniel Berrigan appeared at a church in suburban Philadelphia and preached this sermon to the surprised congregation. He was arrested a week later on Block Island, Rhode Island.

Dear friends, I come to you in the name of all those who have said No to this war, from prison, from the underground, from exile, from the law courts, from death itself. I do not hesitate to say, in the light of the readings we have heard from scripture, that I come to you also in the name of the unborn.

To present on an ordinary Sunday morning to fellow Christians the scandal of one who lives outside the law. The added scandal of one whose brother, also a priest, is in federal prison, the first political prisoner in our history who was a priest. To present you with the further scandal that I have refused to submit before the law and to go to prison myself and that I am hunted and underground for the duration of the war, at least. To suggest to you that my life may open questions also for yours — for your families, for your work, for your attitude to human life and deaths, especially the death of children and the innocent.

We heard this morning that tale of the great men and women of old who suffered persecution in their time. Who, in the Old and New Testament, were such witnesses to the truth as to become part of that truth itself, so that we may now hear their lives and deaths as God's word. To such men and women, it seems to me, again and again the truth of human life was made flesh. And the flesh which declared that truth was the flesh of Humanity, often violated, exiled, despised, ostracized by the powers, unable to come to terms with the Caesars of church and state. Men and women who endured life and who endured deaths because they believed.

Dear friends, I believe we are in such times as make such demands upon us also. I believe we are in such times as make it increasingly impossible for Christians to obey the law of the land and to remain true to Christ. And this is the simple word that I bring to you as a brother in Christ. I bring it with the full consciousness that in so doing I increase my own jeopardy. But I bring it, as I stated before, from my brother in prison, from all my brothers in prison, from all of those who suffer because children and the innocent die.

We are told that, some thirty years ago, when the Nazis had occupied Denmark, the ministers of religion made an agreement among themselves that, week by week, they would mount their pulpits with a common project in mind. That is to say, they would go before the people with the Word of God, in order to translate the lies of the times. All of that hideous language of blood purity and of the liberation of people through death and of the thousand-year kingdom of the racist Führer and of Jews who must be eliminated in order to attain or to keep that purity and of the cult of violence and blood and death and the captivation of the churches as good civil servants of the state. All of this, week after week, people found translated to the vital truth that saves. Week after week, the liars were unmasked. Week after week, the Jews were protected. Week after week, men, women, and children went on living, supported in hiding, gotten out of the country, saved from the executioners.

Dear friends, how do we translate in *our* lives the bombing of helpless cities? How do we translate in our lives the millionth Vietnamese peasant perishing? How do we translate into the truth of our lives the one hundred thousandth village burned?

How do we translate to our lives, in the light of our Bible, the millionth refugee rounded up? How translate into the truth of this morning's text [Heb. 11:1–40] the fifty thousand children napalmed? How translate on this summer morning the fifty thousand American dead? How translate the perfidy of the Gulf of Tonkin Resolution or the tiger cages at Song My?

Perhaps we have no translation. Perhaps our lives are meant to go on as usual. Perhaps, for us, there will be no suffering. Perhaps our moral equipment allows no limit to the death of the innocent. Perhaps we will continue to link our lives, not with the great men and women whose lives are commended to us today, but with the obedient American Christians, with the good obedient German Christians under the Nazis, with the good obedient South African Christians under the racist state, with the good obedient Brazilian Christians, with the good obedient police state of Greece. I do not know.

But for my brother and myself the choice is already made. We have chosen to be powerless criminals in a time of criminal power. We have chosen to be branded as peace criminals by war criminals. This is how we have tried to read the simple words that you heard this morning. This is how we have tried to read and translate and embody in our own lives the will of God. To respond to the voices of those great men and women who speak to us out of Eternity, out of the past, but, most of all, out of today, out of today's prisons and exile and underground and death itself.

Good men and women are increasingly perplexed. They listen and their hearts are sore with the continual ill news of the daily press and television. They find themselves cornered by life with fewer and fewer decisions to take in regard to conscience. They ask again and again, night and day: what can we do?

A Christian can confront the law of the land, that law which protects the warmakers, even as it prosecutes the peacemakers. The Christians can refuse to pay taxes. They can aid and abet and harbor people like myself who are in legal jeopardy for resistance, along with AWOLs. They can work with GI's on their bases, helping those young men to awaken to the truth of their condition and their society, in coffee houses or in hospitality in their own homes. They can organize within their profession and neighborhood and churches so that a solid wall of conscience confronts the death-makers. They can make it increasingly difficult for local draft boards to function.

There are a hundred nonviolent means of resisting those who would inflict death as the ordinary way of life. There are a hundred ways of nonviolent resistance up to now untried, or half-tried, or badly tried. But the peace will not be won without such serious and constant and sacrificial and courageous actions on the part of large numbers of good men and women. The peace will not be won without the moral equivalent of the loss and suffering and separation that the war itself is exacting.

Dear friends, I thank you for being patient. I thank you for accepting me in this very brief span. I ask your prayers for all those who are in deep trouble with the law, who have had to face separation from families and friends and to forge new lives for themselves in such times — a very small price indeed to prevent the death of a single child.

May the peace of Christ, which is promised to the courageous and the patient and the cheerful of heart, be yours also.

— WB, 140–43

4

Lights On
in the House of the Dead

SEPTEMBER 27, 1971

A Chinese ideogram
shows someone
standing
by his word.
Fidelity. Freedom
consequent
on the accepted
necessity of
walking where
one's word
leads.
Wherever.
Hebrew prophets and
singers also
struck the theme;
bodies belong
where words
lead
though the com-
mon run of exper-
ience be

that stature
shrinks as
the word
inflates.
The synthesis;
no matter what (or
better) *never*
the less.
— ARB, 222

DIARY FROM PRISON

There is no answer I know of, except to live by faith day after day and leave the future in the hands of God. It is hard in middle age to be crushed between the two millstones of days and nights in captivity. Is it too hard to bear, or not yet hard enough to be human? It would be easier if one could see some light on the horizon, some larger horizon opening before one which would allow the year to act as a mere interlude, a chastening of self toward a "normal" future in a civilized society. But the truth is something darker and more ominous. No dawn is in sight — in fact the night itself is deepening, to the point where one is constantly being pushed further to the edge of personal extinction, as the price of bringing any change at all.

There is this to be faced: that any action possible to us will bring little change worth mentioning. So one is reduced, not to impotence, but to something like a deeper gesture — fraternity with those who, here as elsewhere, are far more consistently and purposefully brutalized than I am.

Thus the refusal "to adore the gods of the state." Which would mean, in the context, refusing to place one's well-being, good time, good name, expectations (slight enough, God knows) of shortened imprisonment ahead of the iron course of injustice toward others. The gods of the state are, after all, the inflated ego of power, technology, money in their rake's progress, dragging all before into the abyss.

If I can lighten the burden of one or another of the men. A simple exercise in the truth that "God is love." Thus one's life is simplified to the point that it may be worthy of God, worthy of being human.

I lose heart so easily. Long periods when I can only hang on, and hope — for the best against the worst. This must be true of the majority here — especially of those terribly silent and broken men for whom prison is no mere interlude in a life that has gotten somewhere, but a dreary chapter in an infinitely dreary story — with more of the same ahead.

I am growing content to be silent, psychologically, to function at some 50 percent of my native strength, without those passionate moments of insight and relief which elsewhere would issue in poetry. Nothing of this. The common prose, the filthy cramped enclosure which is the common life of humanity in the world. How exempt I have been from all this for half century — the whole of my life up to now!

A man ought not to consider his chance of living or dying; he ought only to consider on a given occasion whether he is doing right or wrong. (Socrates)

To allow such a principle to rule one's life, how many other considerations have to be swept aside; and how few are ready for such extraordinary detachment of heart. We think we are living for God, for an ideal, for our brothers and sisters, for principle; and we end up at Mass on Sundays, and beget children, and love them, and keep our jobs, in despite of what we are doing in public. How cruelly such a life weaves its net. A rabbi tells of the Catholics in Poland who ran an extermination camp near his home and bused to Mass on Sundays. The horrors that a single life can "make sense of" are almost beyond belief, given the stupefying effect of habit, inheritance, routine.

To break through the net. To be the occasion of a fresh start for humanity, because one has made it for himself. To stand with others even while he consciously walks a few paces ahead of them.

In Jesus: tenderness, majesty, and above all personalism. The certainty of one who is familiar not only with the human scene and its range of experience, but with the transcendent life as well: "We testify to what we have seen. I give my life, as the Father commands me...." It is this double life, hypostatically joined, marrow, mind, fiber, heart — the infinite One, radiant and humiliated in our flesh. Prison is a new chance to test that faith: as one would seek, not added "evidence" of truth, but that apparent counter to truth which lends the truth substance in conflict.

They say so often here: it makes no difference whether he is God or not, we find him a real man. One rejoins *sotto voce*, his spirit: it makes all the difference, as a clue leads to hidden truth. Why this probed and approved manhood, whose stature even the worst sins of Christianity has been unable to diminish? Because He is God, he can command such constant historic respect, even from enemies, even from Christians.

I know for certain that deprived of this faith I could not for a single day endure the rigors of this jungle, keep myself from a destructive, exhausting, corrosive hatred. With him, I endure, I believe; help my unbelief.

It seems to me our presence here has to take into account the suffering servanthood of Isaiah. Seriously into account. Much of what that oracle speaks of is simply built into the humiliating daily spectacle — as it touches us, and tests our fiber, and shears away so much of the cultural accretion that in life outside obscures the priesthood — or positively defaces it. We stand in the same garb, subject to the same capricious discipline as the other prisoners — live in the same crowded, noisy conditions, feel the sharp file of the days and hours scraping at our bones. From the majority of the prisoners we receive the "institutionalized indifference": which is the approved attitude, since men are advised to do their time, mind their own business, make no friendships, keep relationships at a distance to forbid the organization of "common fronts."

If jail is the great seizure of humanity by the death force of the state, then every assertion of life, goodness, cheerfulness, friendship is glue in the locks. No key may enter and claim. If the state is a death mechanism, it is up to us to live here, and to give life, and to measure the passage of days, as well as our failure and growth, by the life we lead. If "free men" make war, it is up to caged men to disclaim war, in their immediate dealings, and thus deal another hand. Our sin is to parrot the state by our murderous treatment of one another, or to cherish like a death wish, a cancer in the bowels, our return to the "normalcy" of the state — which is to say, the society in which murder is the daily round of activity.

If religion is to be a leavening power, it is up to us to be religious — i.e., to give immediate palpable evidence that (1) we come here in conflict with the state, and (2) we so live here that the state suffers defeat at our hands — even though it is "winning" elsewhere, in its ordinary body counts.

One is not commanded to be on the winning side, but to be in the right place — when the Lord returns. Even to order one's immediate life in such a place as this, with some measure of sanity and compassion.

That what we do, that what we endure, will have meaning for others.

That our lives are not wasted, in the measure in which we give them.

That the giving of our lives is a concrete, simple task; at center eye, the men we live with and suffer among and strive to serve.

That life in jail, in proportion to one's awareness, has powerful analogies with "life outside" to the inquiring mind and the contemplative heart.

That to be fools for Christ's sake is a responsible political position, given the rampant death society, its irresponsibility and horror of life.

That we are called, as prisoners, to be disciplined, prayerful, constant, vigilant over sense and appetite, cheerful and of good heart.

That relief of inequity, inhumanity, and injustice are present and pressing tasks. The struggle goes on here, too.

That powerlessness is a way which offers solidarity and concurrent action with all those who struggle and endure in the world.

That in prison we are in communion not only with suffering men and women of our world, but in communion with the saints in every time and place.

That our jailers also lie under the scrutiny as well as the saving will of God, and stand in great need of our compassion and our courtesy — especially the large number of Catholics among them.

That we are called to live the mystery of the cross and to sweat through the mystery of the resurrection.

That we accept first, in body and spirit, our conviction that human conditions must worsen, that there is more to be endured than we have so far endured, before amelioration comes.

That good humor and riding easy are the saving salt of our condition. We may win big, we may win small, we may lose everything. We can take whichever outcome. Important: stand where you must stand, be human there.

The Sermon on the Mount (Matt. 5–7) has been called the charter of the kingdom of God. It is a summation of human conduct based on the most exalted altruism. It demands virtue and constancy of a high, even a heroic order. The chapters, to be understood in context, should be placed against Matthew's account of Christ's passion and death. It will be seen how it all comes together in an act of love for his brothers and sisters.

This seems to be the crux of things, as Christ came to realize and to invite his friends in his direction, to live and love and die responsibly, to include others.

There is no guarantee of political or personal success. There is rather a sense of "rightness," of standing within history, in a way that confers health and creates spiritual continuity.

One is called to live nonviolently, even if the social or political change one worked for is in fact unlikely or even impossible. It may or may not be possible to turn the United States around through nonviolent revolution. But one thing is in favor of such an attempt: the total inability of violence as a social or personal method to change anything. On the other hand, one notes how a violent society justifies itself by forbidding its people to explore alternatives. So violence proliferates, captivates consciousness with the myth that it is the sole savior, and thus multiplies wars and victims, the boundless litany of human misery.

The best gift of such a tradition as the New Testament is what Gandhi called "soul force" and the New Testament calls "grace." This often takes a modest and humiliated form, but its presence cannot but be felt. We might translate it today as the presence in individuals of their groupings, of inner consistency, peaceableness, courage, good humor. In any case, there is now and then the felt presence of the Spirit.

Such a gift enables us not to give up. It keeps us at a distance from the tottering brinkmanship of spirit spoken of by Camus — to whom the first question of modern life was that of suicide. For us, the question must be quite different: how to keep going; how to minimize human damage and destruction; how to love the enemy even while one's life stands in opposition to him.

The presence of grace. We cannot know in any given age whether we are going to "make it" or not; i.e., to achieve even on a modest local scale a viable and beloved community. The question grows enormously more painful today, since of necessity such communities must culminate in a world order of goods, services, communication, and governance. Moreover, the urgency of the question and the changes it entails in our thinking and structures create a virus of fear and dread and violence. All of which delays the real question and the search for solutions.

In such an atmosphere, the individual feels trapped between upper and lower millstones, conflict and counterclaim. Control of one's own life and destiny is ground to bits by the machine.

One must, at such times, calmly evaluate events and his part in them. Modesty. The times are so evil and winds so contrary that survival itself is a kind of triumph, the survival of even the smallest communities. It may be that one's hopes for the world stop short; that they include only himself and a few friends; that this will be one's total contribution toward peaceableness. It may be that one will die stripped of all accomplishment, dignity and hopefulness as his only contribution. So Bonhoeffer, Gandhi, Jägerstätter. Yet their "soul force" lives and lives on, in communities everywhere.

It remains important that prison be regarded as a boot camp for spiritual change, at least on the part of some. For prisoners to get reborn (for anyone to get reborn), someone must pay. The payment for birth is blood; the cost of rebirth cannot be cheap. The question is not how to evade payment, but how to pay up like a human being. How to reckon coolly on one's resources, muster them, cherish and love and deepen them; in view of life that refuses to live off the misery of others, and that takes death seriously.

It is time to take death into account — seriously. Jesus did; so did Socrates, King, Gandhi, Malcolm X. Nonviolence demands that we do; the public facts of life make the issue real, bloodstained, up close, daily.

How does one take death seriously? He disciplines himself, daily, hourly. This touches on every aspect of life here: use of time, reading, study, meditation, talk, food, and drink. It demands that we reject interpersonal violence, even when provocation is great.

One makes *love for others* his chief concern. He is not perpetually caught in a net of personal turmoil, frustration, despair. He creates a space of sanity and cheerfulness, in which others can find relief. He does not exploit those who are powerless as himself. He knows the difference between daydreams, delusions, dread — and reality. He is more interested in the fate of others than in his own, knowing that the fate of others *is* his own. It goes without saying that one who so lives is continually dying to his selfishness, ego, childish dreams and whims. He is taking death into account because he takes life seriously. He is doing that measure of violence to his violent self that is the requisite for living nonviolently for others.

In a true sense it can be said of Philip and me that we have nothing to do but stand firm in these months: to survive, to act as a silent prick to the consciousness of those outside — whether of friend or opponent, church or state. "Here we stand." On the other hand — there are the prisoners, the task of understanding, the discipline required to be men for the men, to grow in love, to use time as though time were indeed "tinged with the blood of Christ." To be here in a certain way — which is, to believe. We are writers and spokesmen for Catholics and must ponder deeply the state of the church, love her, keep far from us the corrosive hatred which is infecting the church everywhere. Not to be dupes or children, but neither to give up on the accumulated wisdom and prayer of the church — which, in the earthen vessels of present life, are still available to us.

It is fifty years since You fashioned me through my father and mother and brothers and school and the Jesuits and books and photos and universities and cities around the world — tramping, flying, reading, arguing, and yes praying, everywhere on this globe. You have not been a stranger to me; I have been no stranger to men and women. I have been literally everywhere — usually, I hope, on Your errands. The things I have seen, the faces I have looked into! I have skulked underground for months, before I was flushed by the bird watchers, a most exotic survival, and brought here, and caged — for the duration. And here, with Philip and the others I have not ceased to cry out to You — quite the contrary. I have had daily to exorcise from my bones the constricting horror of the lockup, the seamy underside of creation, the little plot of earth hardly bigger than a mass grave, with its tattered vegetation and dripping webs — a limbo of the heart if ever there was one.

No stranger, Brother. Philip and I have held our scalded hearts in our hands, for You to see. We have stood at the improvised table in the chaplain's office, summoned "up front" over the loudspeakers — those faceless iron throats that call men to meals, to lockup, to justice within justice. They might as easily summon

*them to the furnaces. Remember us. Out of the depths, for we
are brought very low.*

*It is terrible to be powerless. It is doubly terrible to witness
powerlessly the mutilation of the Word, the death of a living,
beautiful, and truthful Word, by the slovenly retailers of religion
whose vestment might in truth be a butcher's apron.*

*Out of the depths. Monday Tuesday Wednesday Thursday Fri-
day depths. Saturday you are free to wander the yard, to talk
or read, to roll the stone out of the depths. Sunday, out of the
depths, a "religious" hell for a secular. You may sleep in, you
may rise early for a bad sermon, a stale Eucharist. The choices
are not large. Mauriac spoke of them: you do not come to this
God as to a great one of this world holding court in a pentagon.
No, you assemble broken men to break bread.*

I have never found You an easy Master.

*Undoubtedly, said a friend, you have a cave of dark pessimism
at your heart. What I wonder at is that you function so well, in
spite of all. So be it. And yet there are moments even in prison
when the dark caul lifts from one's eyes, and in knowing You,
Your presence, Your love, one may breathe more deeply the air
of another land.*

*I wanted You to be Lord of the imagination, to help me imag-
ine ways of living in the world which would be both true to the
values I loved and an endlessly rich and spontaneous variation
upon them.*

I cannot "act as though" and still retain any semblance of sanity
or selfhood. It is a fact too that I sweat blood and give up and call
out, like the psalmist. And You do not intervene. You are absent,
like the dead. You have nothing to offer my fate — no palliative,
no open door. As though You were not.

It is staggering and humiliating to be brought so low. So low
one does not know if he will ever stand again, or see the other
end of this night. One had thought it would end more gracefully,
more honorably. It may not. Then the past, or others, will have
to stand surrogate for what is in fact destroyed — without rhyme

or reason. Except that one has been willing to go so far — and the journey was for the sake of others.

Most days I am stupefied by the fact that locks are turned on me, by the noisy days and nights around me, by the atmosphere of distraction and abandonment to iron fate, by sleeplessness, by the uncertain future which casts so thick a shadow. Most of all by the sufferings of Philip which I share to the hilt.

We have Mass together and I cannot scrape together a single thought — whether of acceptance, aversion, hope, response. Stand there like a vertical corpse, take the bread and wine, empty as a plank, dry as a stone. My whole being, the open throat of a man who has died of thirst, who has no succor in this world — whose only justification for existing at all is that he believes, and so stands there. Let the Lord make of it what he will — nothing at all, or someday, a human being. After such days and nights, one must surely count death as dearest friend. Except that I could not die without Philip, or apart from his fate.

One resolves in face of this to continue his diet of prayer, reflections, and reading and let the chips fall where they may. Someone sent me a poem by Neruda written while he was on the lam; he lived to be an old man, now is ambassador to France — but what will our future be like? The clouds are inexpressibly dark for us and our friends — and we know nothing of the other side of what we must simply suffer through, trusting in God that we are standing where men and women must stand — if there are to be any left in the world.

Sometimes the requirements of nonviolent love seem so picayune and suffocating (e.g., here, now) as to allow very little through as a greatness of resolve or horizon. How to *believe* that our being here is making a difference for others? We are truly in Lent, truly in a desert. The truth applied not only to the daily grind, which seems trivial and enervating, but to the vast horizons offered by our former life, and if the plain truth is told, by our talents.

Can one be destroyed in the role of suffering servant? Here we are; we are to believe, as I do most firmly, that being here is the natural crown of everything that went before, not merely in a humanistic sense that good people inevitably come to ill, but in the sense of the crowning of a journey of faith, by the opening of a wider vista of faith. The reward of faith, that is to say, is not a vision. It is life which both requires and bestows a greater measure of faith, the ability to see the journey through, stage by stage, so that the promise, still withheld, remains itself pristine, never canceled. "Come, into a land which I will show you." Epiphany: it is the journey, its continuance, the adhesion of mind and heart to what was first offered and is never rescinded. Thus our discipline continues.

If for Gandhi this was fairly clear, the reason must lie, first, in his unmatched purity of spirit, which kept him moving headlong into the heart of social chaos, clear of heart and mind and lucid in word, and second, in the comparative clarity of his social struggle. He could count on a measure of humanity from the oppressor. They were willing to weigh the nonviolent forces he was vitalizing and to yield before them in measure, with a certain respect both for Gandhi and for human life. We can count on very little of this latter. and our distance from the grandeur of the Mahatma is, let me assure friends, foes, and my own soul, a source of constant humiliation. As well as of emulation — as witness our passionate reading of his autobiography in our weekly classes.

There is one supreme motive for not allowing one's own spirit to be broken — it would not be useful for others.

What more fitting place to celebrate my fiftieth birthday. Ha! I feel in my bones and cranium thirty-five at the least. I want to start all over. I want to write one immortal line. I want to perform one good nonviolent act. I want to reactivate all the dead cells that cling to my skull like last year's honeycomb, sweet and musty. I want America to get reborn into gentleness. I want to survive, if I survive, as A. J. Muste did, or to go out tomorrow with grace. I want to die if I have to die (O my God) like Merton — in an unexpected way, with my saddlebags on. I want all jails to go up in smoke, like a kicked dry toadstool. I want to walk in the woods and kneel down in a sodden place and stretch out on pine needles and never get up. I want to metamorphose into a pine tree growing out of a rock wall on Champlain shore. I want everyone to have the above-mentioned gifts. All swordfish to be liberated from the mercury in their guts. To hang around sane and sound for a few years in which the above may be seen occurring.

(This being continued at the window after lights out. Strange sense of recognition here, as of taking notes under bombs in Hanoi.)

To say thank You for being in the right place, with the thanks a flower might want to utter for being in the right soil, a bird in the right sky. The concomitant responsibility (what a weird word for conscious flower or human) to wear the true colors of one's existence, to trace the right geometry in the heavens, the pure form following on the purity of existence. Knowing that to die in such circumstance is to lodge that in the earth which shall enrich the earth, that the risen Christ is the invigorating which allows these lives to occur, and the hand and smile behind them, in the lurid, meager light granted by the times and powers.

It is midnight. Fifty years ago my mother bore me. She could not have more exactly shot me to this place if she had loosed an arrow from a bow with the eye of an Iroquois. I thank her, and my father, who rests in Christ, and Philip, in whose heart I rest. I thank the living Christ. I adjust my bib and take prison for my choice birthday portion. And like Oliver Twist, ask for seconds.

I can almost sense the prayer and thoughts of others straining in my direction tonight. I turn prayer gently around, for the children, the wounded, the dying, the bombed. The silence comes down like a gift, a benediction. Happy half century, Daniel. Would that all priests were as fortunate tonight as you.

LOIHD, 11–14, 17–20, 22–28, 31, 40–41, 52–54, 56–59,
65–67, 71, 78, 128–30, 171–72, 192, 211–14

POVERTY

A prisoner is very poor —
1 face, 2 arms, 2 hands, 1 nose, 1 mouth
also 3 walls
1 ceiling
10 or 12 bars —
then if lucky
1 tree
making it, making it
in hell's dry season

I almost forgot —
no legs!
contraband! seized!
they stand stock still
in the warden's closet.
There like buried eyes
They await the world.   —ARB, 361

TULIPS IN THE PRISON YARD

Many poets, believe me, could do better by your
sovereign beauty, your altogether subtle
transfiguration of blank nature —
so winds, nights, sunlight
colorless wraiths, are drawn into
what can only be called a "new game."
Well. I will not glory
in infirmity. Yeats, Wordsworth would look once
breathe deeply, sharpen their quills,
with flourish pluck you from time.
But.
You are jail-yard blooms, you wear bravery with a difference.
You are born here will die here;
making you, by excess of suffering
and transfiguration of suffering, ours.

I see prisoners pass
in the dead spur of spring, before you show face
Are you their glancing years
the faces of wives and children, the yin yang of hearts
to fro like hanged necks
perpetual cruelty, absurdity?

The prisoners
pass and pass; shades of men, pre-men,
khaki ghosts, shame, futility.
between smiles, between reason for smiles, between
life as fool's pace and life as celebrant's flame —
aeons.
Yet, thank you. Against the ships
of ignorant furies, the slavish pieties of judas priests
you stand, a first flicker in the brain's soil, the precursor
of judgment.
Dawn might be, humanity may be
or
spelling it out in the hand's palm
of a blind mute

God is fire, is love.   — ARB, 149

STATEMENT UPON RELEASE
FROM DANBURY PRISON, FEBRUARY 24, 1972

My first word is naturally one of gratitude — to Congressman
Anderson, the lawyers, my friends and fellow prisoners who
petitioned, worked, fasted, and prayed to make my freedom
possible.

Freedom, however, is an unfinished business, whether it be my
freedom, the freedom of other prisoners, or the freedom of the
Vietnamese. I mean no exaggeration therefore when I say that
today I am only half free, that a large part of me is still captive in Danbury, still captive in the courtroom of Harrisburg, still
captive to the warmakers.

It is this unfinished business of victims and prisoners that I wish to dedicate myself anew. American prisons are bulging with human misery, attrition, and waste. In Harrisburg, the theater of cruelty is playing on and on, an indefinite run it seems, the imperial lions versus the inedible Christians. And in Southeast Asia, a war that was supposed to wind down, ticks on and on, its spring tightened by determined duplicity and violence and fear.

Unfinished business indeed. The president would like to declare the business of the war finished, but we have learned to measure the distance between his words and deeds, his diplomacy and his bombers, his promises and his jails. We refuse to cover the faces of the dead, to be distracted by his travelogues and his economic games. The war is still the first fact of life for the living — as it was when I went to prison, as it was when I went underground, as it was when I went to Hanoi and Catonsville, as it was when I went into exile. There is no issue comparable to the deaths of innocent children — neither the economy, nor good fellowship in China, nor cancer, nor pollution, nor taxes, nor political campaigns.

Mr. Nixon, hear us. You will hearken to the voice of the people, or, like your predecessor, you will go the way of political and moral oblivion.

Today we begin another journey together — a pilgrimage to Harrisburg. Let our walk declare the deep resolve of our hearts. We will never rest until sanity has been restored to the mighty and power to the powerless. This is our pledge of allegiance, to God and to humanity.

— Unpublished

5

They Shall Beat Their Swords into Plowshares

SWORDS INTO PLOWSHARES

On September 9, 1980, the Plowshares Eight, including Daniel Berrigan, entered a General Electric nuclear missile plant in King of Prussia, Pennsylvania, and hammered on two nose cones of the Mark 12A reentry missile, following the biblical mandate of Isaiah, chapter 2. Theirs was the first of over seventy-five Plowshares disarmament actions around the world. Daniel Berrigan faced ten years in prison for his act.

September 9, 1980. We rose at dawn after (to speak for myself) a mostly sleepless night. In and out of dream, in and out of nightmare. We had passed several days in prayer together, an old custom indeed, as old as our first arrests in the late sixties. We were mostly vets of those years, survivors too, survivors of the culture and its pseudo and counters, survivors of courts and jails, of the American flare of conscience and its long hibernation, survivors in our religious communities, in our families (they have survived us). By an act of God and nothing of our own, survivors of America — its mimes, grimaces, enticements, abhorrences, shifts and feints, masks, counter-masks. Survivors (barely) of the demons who challenged and shouted their name — legion!

We knew for a fact (the fact was there for anyone who bothered to investigate) that General Electric in King of Prussia manufactures the reentry cones of Mark 12A missiles. We learned that Mark 12A is a warhead that will carry an H-bomb of 335 kilotons to its target. That three of these weapons are being attached to each of three hundred Minuteman III missiles. That because of Mark 12A accuracy and explosive power, it will be used to implement U.S. counterforce or first-strike policy.

We knew these hideous cones ("shrouds" is the GE word) were concocted in a certain building of the General Electric complex. The building is huge: we had no idea exactly where the cones could be found.

Of one thing we were sure. If we were to reach the highly classified area of shipping and delivery and were to do there what we purposed, someone must intervene, give us a lead.

After our deed, a clamor arose among the FBI and state and county and GE (and God know what other) police who swarmed into the building. "Did they have inside information? Was there a leak?" Our answer: of course we had Inside Information; of course there had been a Leak. Our Informant is otherwise known in the New Testament as Advocate, Friend, Spirit. We had been at prayer for days.

And the deed was done. We eight looked at one another, exhausted, bedazzled with the ease of it all. We had been led in about two minutes, and with no interference to speak of, to the heart of the labyrinth.

They rounded us up, trundled us out in closed vans. We spent the day uncommonly cheerful in that place of penitence, in various cells of police headquarters. We underwent what I came to think of as a "forced fast," the opposite of forced feeding and undoubtedly less perilous to life and limb. The atmosphere in that spiffy new building (we were in GE country, the local economy is 40 percent GE, GE "brings good things to life") was one of barely concealed panic. How the hell did they get into the building so easily? How about the jobs of those of us who were purported guarding the nuclear brews and potions?

Lines of Justice Department, Pentagon, FBI were red hot. Why can't you get your act together up there? And what are we to do with these religious doomsayers? Let them go, let them off light, let them off never? Please advise!

About noon another ploy got underway. They loaded us in vans again, back to the scene of the crime. It devolved later they wanted the identification of the employees. But they wouldn't talk, so we wouldn't walk. They carried five of us out of the van into that big warehouse room with the bloody floor, the bloody torn blueprints stamped "Top Secret." And then the missile cones, broken, bloodied, useless. No more genocide in our name? And the wall of faces, police, employees, silent as the grave, furious, bewildered, a captive nation.

Under shrill orders from somewhere, the charade was halted. The procedure was illegal. A district attorney said it might endanger their whole case. Indeed.

So back to durance vile. They locked us up, they kept saying: "Sure, we'll feed you, presently we'll charge you." And nothing happened. By 5:00 p.m. the more inventive among us were ready to close their eyes, strip their shoelaces and pretend we were eating spaghetti Rossi in the West Village.

Then something happened. One by one we were led out. Take off your shoes. And (to the six males) take off your pants. It appeared that, these objects being stained with our blood, they were severely required as evidence. So, like the bad little boys in the fairy tale, supperless and shoeless, we were led off to our destiny by Stepmother State.

An intuition that we and others have been pondering for a long time grows on us, presses closer. To wit: in a time of truly massive irrationality, one had best stop playing the old academic-ecclesial game of scrabble, as though merely putting words together could make sense of moral incoherence, treachery, and meandering apathy, could break that spell.

Rationality? Reason? If these were ever in command, they had certainly fled the scene during the Vietnam War. I would be willing to venture that sanity and reason have never sat in the catbird seat again.

In the saddle of power and decision we have instead a kind of "Eichmania" analyzed by Merton, a tightly hierarchical, spiritually captivated, ideologically closed insanity. In it are caught the multicorporations and their squads of engineers and planners, on and up to the highest responsible chairs of command — the Pentagon and White House. All so to speak (so to doublespeak) to "bring good things to life."

And then outward into society, the malaise touches all with a leprous finger — meandering apathy, at least as complex an illness as rotten power. Apathy, the natural outcome of such authority so used.

We have evidence of such indifference to moral and physical disaster in other modern societies whose citizens, under whip and lash, or under a rain of bread and a politics of the circus, stood helpless to win the nod of blind, deaf fate, to speak up, to force a hearing.

Such apathy shows face today in our inability to summon resistance against nuclear annihilation. Screen out the horror, a shutter comes down. Best not to imagine what might be, best to act as though the worst could not be.

The phenomenon before the catastrophe is remarkably like the phenomenon after the catastrophe. Many of the survivors of Hiroshima, afflicted with radiation sickness, conceal their illness as long as possible, "act as though" they are not stricken. They go so far as to falsify family history, conceal the fact that they were in the orbit of death on the day of the bomb.

No wonder that today Americans find it more plausible, more conducive to sanity to ignore our nuclear plight, to fight survival in areas where the facts are less horrid, the cards less stacked. Economic woes, job layoffs, inflation — we have enough trouble drawing the next breath. And you with your little hammers and bottles of blood go out against Goliath? Thanks, good luck, but no thank you.

Blood and hammers. The symbolic aspect of our GE action appealed to some and appalled others. But almost no one who has heard of the action lacks an opinion about it, usually a passionately stated one. In pondering these passions, so long dormant, newly released, one learns a great deal — not about passions in a void, but about vital capacities for survival, sociability, spirituality. Some who hear grow furious; some of the furious are Catholics; Catholics also guard us, judge us, prosecute us. This is an old story that need not long detain us.

What is of peculiar and serious interest here is the use and misuse of symbols, their seizure by secular power; then the struggle to keep the symbols in focus, to enable them to be seen, heard, tasted, smelled, lived and died for, in all their integrity, first intent.

Their misuse. How they are leveled off, made consistent with the credo of the state. Thus, to speak of King of Prussia and our symbol there: blood. Its outpouring in the death of Christ announced a gift and, by implication, set a strict boundary, a taboo. No shedding of blood, by anyone, under any circumstances, since this, my blood, is given for you. Blood as gift.

Hence the command: no killing, no war. Which is to say, above all no nuclear weapons. And thence the imperative: resist those who research, deploy, or justify on whatever grounds such weaponry.

Thus the drama; the symbol outpoured implies a command. Do this; so live, so die. Clear lines are drawn for public as well as personal conduct. Church and state, the "twin powers," always in danger of becoming Siamese twins, are in fact kept from a mutually destructive symbiosis by imperative and taboo. More, they are revealed for what they in fact are — radically opposed spiritual powers, as in Revelation 13. Church can never be state; state is forbidden to ape or absorb church. And this mutual opposition, this nonalignment, this friction and fraying, erupts from time to time in tragic and bloody struggle. The church resists being recast as Caesarian icon. The state, robust, in firm possession, demands that the church knuckle under, bend knee, bless war, pay taxes, shut up. Church, thy name is trouble.

The choices are not large. Toil and trouble or — capitulation. In the latter case all is lost. The symbols are seized at the altar and borne away. Now the blood of Christ, the blood of humans, is cheap indeed; for what could be cheaper than blood the church itself has declared expendable? That blood is now a commodity, a waste. When Caesar speaks, blood may be shed at will, by Christians or others, it makes no difference. Which is also to say: there no longer exists any distinction in fact between armed combatants and citizens, between soldiers and little children. Killing has become the ordinary civil method of furthering civic ends. The sacred symbol of blood, whose gift urged the command "Thou shalt not kill" — that blood is admixed, diluted, poisoned. It is lost in a secular vortex, immensely vigorous and seductive, urging a different vision. Labor is commodity, the flag is a sacred vexillum, humans are productive integers, triage rules the outcome. Finally, a peremptory secular command: "Thou shalt kill when so ordered — or else."

It seems to me that since Hiroshima, to set an arbitrary moment, this debasing of the sacred symbols into secular use and misuse has proceeded apace.

To undo the blasphemy, what a labor.

We have been at this for years — dramatic events, deliberately orchestrated, arbitrary but intensely traditional, liturgical, illegal, in every case wrenching the actors out of routine and community life to face the music, face the public, face the jury.

Is it all worth it? In measure the eight who acted at King of Prussia have already answered the question. At least for themselves, and for one another. One of them said in the course of our discussion, "Even if the action went nowhere, if no one understood or followed through on it, I would still go ahead."

Worth it for ourselves. Each of us had, before the act, to plumb our motives, consult loved ones, care for the future of children, arrange professional and community responsibilities, measure in fact all good things against this "one necessary thing." And decide.

The eight so decided — yes. Such an act must be taken, even though it disrupts almost everything else, calls many things in question. The value of the act is thus measured by the sacrifice required to do it; an old and honored Christian idea, if I am not mistaken.

For us, going as we did in fear and trembling from the Eucharist to General Electric had the feel of the last hours of Jesus, his journey from the upper room to death. We held our liturgy the night before, broke the bread, passed the cup. Light of head, heavy of heart, we nonetheless celebrated by anticipation the chancy event of the following day; and the trial to come; and the penalty. Our logic? The body was "broken for you," the cup "poured out for all."

But what of the larger meaning of the action, its value for the church and the public? Here one must go slow. The value of the act for those who propose it, sweat it out, do it — this is more easily determined. Value is created, so to speak, in the breach, in a decision to gather, unite voices in an outcry, to precipitate a crisis that, at least for a time, will strip away the mask of evil.

But I know no sure way of predicting where things will go from there, whether others will hear and respond, or how quickly or slowly. Or whether the fact will fail to vitalize others, will come to a grinding halt then and there, its actors stigmatized or dismissed as fools. One swallows dry and takes a chance.

People gifted with our nefarious history must remind themselves that at King of Prussia, hammers and blood in hand, we set in motion a lengthy and complex drama. One should speak perhaps of three acts.

The first act belonged in the main to us, an early morning curtain raiser, the action underway. In a sense the adversaries have not yet appeared; only a few subalterns act on their behalf, in their name; the guards and police and employees. But GE has not yet turned on its voltage. No official appears in justifying garb to bespeak the ancient myths, to invoke sacro-secular outrage at the violation of a holy place, property off bounds, the shrine accessible only to initiates. (Antigone has buried her brother's body, but Creon has not yet flogged his way to condemn her.)

Then a second act opens. It marks the marshalling of forces of law and order, the involving of daemons of natural law, secular karma. Anger, retaliation are in the air, the gods of property buzz furiously overhead. The actors all but tear up the script of act one; and assault is mounted on the earlier reliance on "higher

law" or "conscience." Behold true conscience, behold the highest
law of all, the law by which all citizens must live, the law that is
our common safeguard against anarchy!

So in the manner of Shakespeare or Pirandello or Sophocles,
act two is a kind of play within the play. The audience is bewildered, thrown off guard. It had read a certain kind of admirable
moral truth in the face of the young woman Antigone (in the
faces of a nun, of a mother of six, of a lawyer, a professor, a
seminary graduate — faces like the credentials of moral worth).
Now it hears another kind of truth. This is not the truth of
"symbolic action," which from a legal point of view is always
murky, easily discredited, and reaching troublesomely as it does
into dark existence (the forbidden burial of a brother, the breaking and bloodying of icons) must be exorcised, discredited — by
measured, relentless argument.

The example of Antigone, the example of the eight, is deliberately magnified, made stark. Behold their act, performed under
clerical guise, under the guise of virtue. Behold their act, as
viewed by the state, the guardian and interpreter of public morality. You are in court, this audience, as extensions of the jury, who
are in effect extensions of the judge. You are not here to indulge
in murky existential probings, but to consider the letter of the
law and in your hearts to approach a verdict....

Finally, act three. Many scenes and changes; the great world,
a time between events (action/trial), the agora, a courtroom,
the many places where people discuss, argue, make up their
minds and unmake them again, slowly or with speed come to
a conclusion, the knotting of the action.

In court, the crime of the eight is segregated from the world,
the faces of the defendants, mirrors of conscience, are hooded.
The inert symbols, hammers, empty bloodied bottles, lie there,
tagged, soulless, mere items of evidence. They are relics of moral
defeat, emblems of legal punishment; as such, the prosecutor will
refer to them with disdain and handle them with distaste. They
will be compared, subtly or openly, to the tools of safecrackers,
to bloodied knives and guns. What if such implements became
the common tools of so-called conscience? What if all citizens,

under whatever itch of notoriety, took up such tools (like the soiled hands of Antigone, heaping foul dust on her brother's body) against the law of the state? How sordid a venture!

In the course of this act, the classic Greek formula is verified, the purging of pity and fear. These must be purged, for pity and terror get in the way of spiritual change. They are obstructive emotions, to be taken seriously, no doubt, but strictly as preliminary to the main event.

The event, in a larger sense, is destined to occur neither on stage nor in the court. It is rather the unending passionate pursuit of moral good, the righting of injustice, the ousting of death; the reordering of an ethical universe and of its social and political forms. But in order to be purged, pity and fear have first to be aroused.

How acute the Greeks were! In the first days following our action, friends invariably spoke of their forebodings, their dread of the harsh sentences that undoubtedly would befall us, their fear that our action would be ignored or misconstrued.

Pity and fear. The pity narrows emotional largesse, the fear spreads out inordinately, claims all minds. Fear of the future, fear for children bereft of parents, fear of the state and its legal savageries.

One emotion is too narrow, the other too diffused. Neither finally is useful; that is to say, neither serves to heighten the truth of the universal predicament (which is not defined by prison sentences, but by nuclear annihilation) — or to grant hints and leads as to a way out.

I must inject here a message from the jails of Pennsylvania. If the eight have insisted on anything, it is that their trial and imprisonment are not the issue at stake. Pity for them gains nothing. Neither does fear for them or for their children and spouses. The eight go their way, a way meticulously chosen and after much prayer. But the issues they raise will continue to shadow their lives and vex their hearts. It is the corporate crimes of General Electric, the race toward oblivion that this monstrous entity both fuels and illustrates.

Finally, what drove us to "such extremes"? To reach the truth, one must turn from Creon to Antigone; from the prosecutor, in our case, to the Gospel. In America, in 1980, it could hardly be called useful to the common weal or a mitigation of the common woe that a group of religious folk enter a mega death factory — in vain proof that they are in possession of some kind of magical counterforce. Why then?

Let us say merely because they hungered for the truth, for its embodiment, longed to offer a response to its claim on us. That even through us, an all but submerged voice might be heard, the voice of "the God, not of the dead, but of the living."

—POTIL, 148–58

WE COULD NOT NOT DO THIS

In March 1981, Daniel Berrigan and the Plowshares Eight stood trial in Norristown, Pennsylvania, and were convicted on eight of thirteen counts. These are excerpts from Daniel Berrigan's court testimony.

The question of why we did our action takes me back to those years when my conscience was being formed, back to a family that was poor, and to a father and mother who taught, quite simply, by living what they taught. And if I could put their message very shortly, it would go something like this: In a thousand ways they showed that you do what is right because it is right, that your conscience is a matter between you and God, that nobody owns you.

If I have a precious memory of my mother and father that lasts to this day, it is simply that they lived as though nobody owned them. They cheated no one. They worked hard for a living. They were poor, and perhaps most precious of all, they shared what they had. And that was enough, because in the life of a young child, the first steps of conscience are as important as the first steps of one's feet. They set the direction where life will go. And I feel that direction was set for my brothers and myself. There is a direct line between the way my parents turned our steps and this action. That is no crooked line.

That was the first influence. The second one has to do with my religious order. When I was eighteen I left home for the Jesuit order. I reflect that I am sixty years old, and I have never been anything but a Jesuit, a Jesuit priest, in my whole life. We have Jesuits throughout Latin America today, my own brothers, who are in prison, who have been under torture; many of them have been murdered. On the walls of our religious communities both here and in Latin America are photos of murdered priests who stood somewhere because they believed in something. Those faces haunt my days. And I ask myself how I can be wishy-washy in the face of such example, example of my own lifetime, my own age.

This is a powerful thing, to be in a common bond of vows with people who have given their lives because they did not believe in mass murder, because such crimes could not go on in their name.

Dear friends of the jury, you have been called the conscience of the community. Each of us eight comes from a community. I don't mean just a biological family, I mean that every one of us has brothers and sisters with whom we live, with whom we pray, with whom we offer the Eucharist, with whom we share income, and, in some cases, the care of children. Our conscience, in other words, comes from somewhere. We have not come from outer space or from chaos or from madhouses to King of Prussia.

We have come from years of prayer, years of life together, years of testing — testing of who we are in the church and in the world. We would like to speak to you, each of us in a different way, about our communities; because, you see, it is our conviction that nobody in the world can form his or her conscience alone.

What are we to do in bad times? I am trying to say that we come as a community of conscience before your community of conscience to ask you: Are our consciences to act differently than yours in regard to the lives and deaths of children? A very simple question, but one that cuts to the bone. We would like you to see that we come from where you come. We come from churches. We come from neighborhoods. We come from years of work. We come from America. And we come to this, a trial of conscience and motive. And the statement of conscience we would like to present to you is this.

We could not *not* do this. We could not not do this! We were pushed to this by all our lives. Do you see what I mean? All our lives.

When I say I could not do this, I mean, among other things that with every cowardly bone in my body I wished I hadn't had to enter the GE plant. I wish I hadn't had to do it. And that has been true every time I have been arrested, all those years. My stomach turns over. I feel sick. I feel afraid. I don't want to go through this again.

I hate jail. I don't do well there physically. But I cannot not go on, because I have learned that we must not kill if we are Christians. I have learned that children, above all, are threatened by these weapons. I have read that Christ our Lord underwent death rather than inflict it. And I am supposed to be a disciple. All kinds of things like that. The push, the push of conscience is a terrible thing.

So at some point your cowardly bones get moving, and you say, "Here it goes again," and you do it. And you have a certain peace because you did it, as I do this morning in speaking with you.

One remains honest because one has a sense, "Well, if I cheat, I'm really giving over my humanity, my conscience." Then we think of these horrible Mark 12A missiles, and something in us says, "We cannot live with such crimes." Or our consciences turn in another direction. And by a thousand pressures, a thousand silences, people begin to say to themselves, "We can live with that. We know it's there. We know what it is for. We know that many thousands will die if only one of these exploded."

And yet we act like those employees, guards, experts we heard speak here; they close their eyes, close their hearts, close their briefcases, take their paychecks — and go home. It's called living with death. And it puts us to death before the missile falls.

We believe, according to the law, the law of the state of Pennsylvania, that we were justified in saying, "We cannot live with that," justified in saying it publicly, saying it dramatically, saying it with blood and hammers, as you have heard; because that weapon, the hundreds and hundreds more being produced in our country, are the greatest evil conceivable on this earth. There is no evil to compare with that. Multiply murder. Multiply desolation. The mind boggles.

So we went into that death factory, and in a modest, self-contained, careful way, we put a few dents in two missiles, awaited arrest, and came willingly into court to talk to you. We believe with all our hearts that our action was justified.

We have never taken actions such as these, perilous, crucial, difficult as they are, without the most careful preparation of our hearts, our motivation, our common sense, our sense of one another. This is simply a rule of our lives; we don't go from the street to do something like the King of Prussia action. We go from prayer. We go from reflection. We go from worship, always. And since we realized that this action was perhaps the most difficult of all our lives, we spent more time in prayer this time than before. We passed three days together in a country place. We prayed, and read the Bible, and shared our fears, shared our second and third thoughts. And in time we drew closer. We were able to say, "Yes, we can do this. We can take the consequences. We can undergo whatever is required." All of that.

During those days we sweated out the question of families and children — the question of a long separation if we were convicted and jailed. I talked openly with Jesuit friends and superiors. They respected my conscience and said, "Do what you are called to." That was the immediate preparation. And what it issued in was a sense that, with great peacefulness, with calm of spirit, even though with a butterfly in our being, we could go ahead and we did.

This enters into my understanding of conscience and justification, a towering question, which has faced so many good people in history, in difficult times, now in the time of the bomb. What helps people? What helps people understand, in difficult times, now, in the time of the bomb? What helps people understand who they are in the world, who they are in their families, who they are with their children, with their work? What helps?

That was a haunting question for me. Will this action be help-ful? Legally, we could say that this was our effort to put the question of justification. Will our action help? Will people under-stand that this "lesser evil," done to this so-called "property," was helping turn things around in the church, in the nation? Will the action help us be more reflective about life and death and children and all life?

We have spent years and years of our adult lives keeping the law. We have tried everything, every access, every means to get to public authorities within the law. We come from within the law, from within.

We are deeply respectful of a law that is in favor of human life. And as we know, at least some of our laws are. We are very respectful of those laws. We want you to know that. Years and years we spent writing letters, trying to talk to authorities, vigiling in public places, holding candles at night, holding plac-ards by day, trying, trying, fasting, trying to clarify things to ourselves as we were trying to speak to others; all of that within the law, years of it.

And then I had to say, I could not not break the law and remain human. That was what was in jeopardy: what I call my conscience, my humanity, that which is recognizable to children, to friends, to good people, when we say, "There is someone I can trust and love, someone who will not betray."

We spent years within the law, trying to be that kind of per-son, a non-betrayer. Then we found we couldn't. And if we kept forever on this side of the line, we would die within ourselves. We couldn't look in the mirror, couldn't face those we love, had no Christian message in the world, nothing to say if we went on that way. I might just as well wander off and go the way of a low-grade American case of despair: getting used to the way things are. That is what I mean by dying. That is what we have to oppose. I speak for myself.

The Jesuit order accepted me as a member. The Catholic Church ordained me as a priest. I took all that with great serious-ness. I still do, with all my heart. And then Vietnam came along, and then the nukes came along. And I had to continue to ask myself at prayer, with my friends, with my family, with all kinds of people, with my own soul, "Do you have anything to say today?" I mean, beyond a lot of prattling religious talk.

Do you have anything to say about life today, about the lives of people today? Do you have a word, a word of hope to offer, a Christian word? That's a very important question for anyone who takes being a priest, being a Christian, being a human being seriously: "Do you have anything to offer human life today?"

It is a terribly difficult question for me. And I am not at all sure that I do have something to offer. But I did want to say this. I am quite certain that I had September 9, 1980, to say. And I will never deny, whether here or in jail, to my family, or friends, or to the Russians, or the Chinese, or anyone in the world, I will never deny what I did.

More than that. Our act is all I have to say. The only message I have to the world is: We are not allowed to kill innocent people. We are not allowed to be complicit in murder. We are not allowed to be silent while preparations for mass murder proceed in our name, with our money, secretly.

I have nothing else to say to the world. At other times one could talk about family life and divorce and birth control and abortion and many other questions. But this Mark 12A is here. And it renders all other questions null and void. Nothing, nothing can be settled until this is settled. Or this will settle us, once and for all.

It's terrible for me to live in a time where I have nothing to say to human beings except, "Stop killing." There are other beautiful things that I would love to be saying to people. There are other projects I could be very helpful at. And I can't do them. I cannot. Because everything is endangered. Everything is up for grabs. Ours is a kind of primitive situation, even though we would call ourselves sophisticated. Our plight is very primitive from a Christian point of view. We are back where we started. Thou shall not kill. We are not allowed to kill.   —CW, 221–27

WHEN HAMMERS COME DOWN

Everything enhances, everything
gives glory — everything!
between bark and bite
Judge Salus's undermined soul
betrays him, mutters
very alleluias.

The iron cells —
row upon row of rose trellised
mansions, bridal chambers!

Curses, vans, keys, guards — behold
the imperial lions of our vast acres!

And when hammers come down
and our years are tossed to four winds —
why, flowers blind the eye, the saints
pelt us with flowers!

See, the Lord's hands heap
eon upon eon,
like fruit bowls at a feast.   — ARB, 359

6

The Question of Peacemaking

THE SOUL OF PEACEMAKING

The trouble with would-be peacemakers, I reflected, was a grievous one. They had no true center. Many souls, a multitude of good souls, but no soul. Warmaking, on the other hand, required no center. Its reality was that of a machine, which we rightly called a war machine. And a machine had no center; it had parts, which were required only to mesh and move in gear.

And so with those who researched, constructed, tinkered with, the machine: they required no center. They needed only the machine, which proceeded from them and acted, from its inception and form, in place of soul or center.

The artificers evicted their soul, and the machine moved in on monstrous tracks, and took over. The phenomenon was called, in the biblical sense, possession; psychologically, obsession. And in the drug trade, a fast fix.

In any case, and again speaking biblically, those who made war must believe in war, as others believe in God.

The warmakers believed in god, the god of war. They marched to the common whip, in time with the military, and made a brave and colorful and glorious thing of sanctioned murder. The soul was in lockstep, for the machine and those in the image of the machine, had to ape one another; in efficiency and uniformity, within and without. For this was the soul of war, and no one could be exempt.

194

All this may have been realized by the peacemakers, the anatomy of war and the transformation of those who made war from the human to the machine. But the realization, if arrived at, failed to offer an alternative. And that was the real point, as peacemaking was the alternative to warmaking, and not merely its cozening, tolerant, or parasitic appendage.

The question for me, as peacemaking came to be a question, was one of soul, of center. Peacemaking did not require a charismatic leader or a resplendent public personality, though that might occur. The soul of peacemaking was simply the will to give one's life.

As war sanctioned the taking of life, peacemaking must sanction the giving of life. The gift might be a notorious, public act, as in the assassination of Dr. King. Or it might be a state execution of resisters, as in the White Rose group in Hitler's Germany. In the latter instance, the episode is hidden for a long time; at the time of the occurrence, it is received with contempt and indifference. The gift of one's life is simply unknown to all except one's immediate family, as the death of the Austrian resister Franz Jägerstätter illustrates.

One can go further and consider the mass anonymity of the extermination camps, where, beyond doubt, multitudes of unknown heroes gave their lives, whether to salvage honor or save others or resist debasing conduct. The century offers a mad and bloody variety of human valor, of those who go under in possession of soul and wits and the unimpeded power of choice. Souls, wits, choices; all of which the machine, in its rampageous blindness, seeks to claim for its own.

Many believed, many still believe, that peace will come through a certain nice adjustment of warmaking power, through diminished stockpiling, through a nuclear freeze. We still have not found our soul, or created a soul, or been granted a soul. We arrogate the metaphors and vocabulary of warmaking, and call it peacemaking. For the warmakers want peace too, and always have; which is to say, they seek a tolerable level of warmaking, one that will protect hegemonies and self-interest. And we too seek a certain level of

peace, one that will protect our self-interest, modest as it may be—
our ego, our good name in the world.

We are still unable to attend to the considerable and central
question: that of soul. Or more precisely, of the spiritual change
required for peacemaking.

The machine is incapable of this because it is a machine,
and the peacemakers are incapable because they are afraid. And
each of these, the fear of consequence and the fearless machine,
conspire in the end to the same thing, which is to say, war preparation and war. Or at best (in the case of the peacemakers), a
pallid mitigation of the full-blown fury.

It came to this, as far as one could judge in those tumultuous
times. Violence was the norm, war was the norm. The times, the
bloodletting, these were normal. Their (always regrettable) "inci-
dents" were the responsibility of no one in particular. What was
one to do, what was a president to do, or a bishop, or any citizen? Alas, war was a very old story, and this one must be seen
through, to the end.

Normal meant, morally acceptable. What was abnormal,
morally unacceptable, was—ourselves. Nonviolence.

One thing, Americans say, whether warmaking or peacemaking, leads to another. We were drawn into peacemaking as
the nation was drawn into warmaking. It was all but a law of
nature. The law was total in principle: if not immediately (it took
years for the war to "rev up," it took years for us to come to the
point of life)—then inexorably.

War, even so called conventional war, constantly blurred the
moral sense, the sense of limits: inevitably, war became total war.
More troops, more firepower, more bombings of civilians, more
everything.

And at home, equally and inevitably, more lies, more dis-
claimers of guilt, a constantly shifting language of justification,
shoddy politics, the corruption of once decent public conscience.
A growing unease, in a public used only to its ease. The unease
moved for a long time in a void. It was as though a sleepwalker
wandered about, wringing hands in a darkened house, seeking, in

inarticulate plaints, solace for the crimes of conscious life. What to do, O where to go? The implication, the guilt, were plain: there was a corpse in a house locked and empty and dark. But there was, as yet, nothing to do: so the sleeping one wept.

We found a few things to do. Something in us insisted: there were tasks, we must come on them. The process was largely improvisational. We tried something, it failed. No matter, try again.

Which is not to say that we had no guidelines. At our best (which we attained only now and then, by fits and starts) we saw this, and paid tribute to our stars or landmarks or titular gods. They had left us a good legacy, we knew right hand from left, we need not wander witless in a witless world.

Nonviolence first and foremost, with its fiery trail of implication: compassion for the adversary, care of one another, community discipline, prayer and sacrament and biblical literacy. Long-term carefulness and short, care of little matters and large, the short run and the long.

It was easy to set down a formula, and devilishly hard to live by it, even in minor matters.

We had to discover such things for ourselves — by reading the lives of the saints; pondering their secrets and spirit and tactic; what they had come on, what accomplished; the place of trial and error, the great winnower and humiliator. And by pondering the Gospel. And by listening to one another, and talking. But listening more than talking, a rare proportion, and difficult to honor.

— TDIP, 163–74

TAKING STOCK

Taking stock of
such as myself —

and enduring as I must
the dark quandary
named here, named now —

until a knell sound
and the sea give up its dead
and continents
heave like a pummeled dough
with exiles revenant —
and eternity's throat
like a bell take note
"all all is well" —

look, it were better
in bitter meantime
to smile
and lift a glass —

the starts and stops,
brisk, becalmed,
distempered, sweet,
the sojourn short or long —

the outcome
in better hands
than ours.   —ARB, 322

THE GREAT SIGN

*About this time, Herod proceeded to arrest Peter. He put
him in prison, delivering him to four squads of soldiers.
So Peter was kept in prison, but prayer for him was made
unremittingly by the church. And on the very night when
Herod was about to bring him out, Peter was sleeping
between two soldiers, bound with a double chain, and
guards were in front of the door. And behold, an angel of
the Lord suddenly appeared and a light shone in the cell.
The angel struck Peter's side, roused him saying, "Get up
quickly." And the chains fell off his hands.* (Acts 12)

Deliverance by the power of God, whether from illness, travail,
danger, accident, malice, and, above all, death — these are hard

to give ear to, let alone belief. The times are such that a far different voice than that of Peter's angel whispers in our ear. It is a voice of presidents, judges, juntas, shahs, executioners, torturers, deceivers, prosecutors, and others of like mind and mindlessness. Prison is the order of the day, not the opening of gates. Torture and starvation and disappearance, rather than freedom, dignity, the dance of life. And death above all, beyond all, at the end of all; death the universal threat, the universal solvent, the darling of dictators and abortionists and star warriors. The money is on death, death hedges no bets. It is life that is endangered and even despised, thrown away, pushed between the cracks of the great cities. Death in war, death equally in peace, or what passes for peace. But life worth living, life cherished, life given its chance, given place? How rarely!

Confronted with such a world, choices are made, leading in either of two directions. On the one hand, some choose not to see. Blunting of conscience occurs, consciences grow heedless and selfish. They achieve a kind of spurious normalcy, suffocating and single-minded. Since the world is a mess, the reasoning goes, one had best rein in high resolve and broad ideas — for the duration.

Others look on the chaos of the world, are struck with horror, and shortly become sources of chaos. They plunge off in all directions, charging at windmills. Needless to say, they achieve nothing, or next to it. And finally, moral exhaustion overtakes them.

There must be a better way. In the midst of dead ends, moral detours, there must be a way of living humanly, of obeying one's faith, of remaining sensitive and firm, thoughtful and courageous, of healing and being healed, of standing somewhere, in the honored phrase.

I remember one sign of peace, a sign of peacemaking, more accurately. And a sign of deliverance as well.

In the summer of 1984, seven friends went on trial in Syracuse, New York. On a November morning of the year previous, they entered the guarded acres of Griffiss Air Force Base nearby, and proceeded to damage an enormous B-52 bomber, taking to it with household hammers, marking the monster with their own blood, incapacitating its horrid threat of nuclear murder.

Practically everyone said in one way or another that it couldn't be done. Most said it shouldn't be done. Many in fact shy away from even discussing such acts; they dread the thought of entering on such toilsome and perilous ground. A very welter of objections is raised like warriors springing from dragon's teeth. There are religious objections, practical objections, legal objections, aesthetic objections. All unknowingly, some object from simple confusion, others from an over refined conscience. Some wince because the tactic lies so close to the gospel bone; others because the tactic is not laid out biblically, jot and tittle. Still others declare that the whole mess of arms, arms makers, armories, arms researchers — this is beyond all rational control, anyone's control.

Some haul out alternatives; the dusty pieties of secular recourse. Isn't it best to stay within the law? Have you tried writing your president? Some point to blood obligations or property obligations or responsibilities; as though indeed, blood and property were very images of God. Some had bought a farm, some traded in oxen, someone had taken a wife, another had to bury his father. And finally, there were those who confessed, ruefully and honorably, to dearth of courage.

Perhaps I can venture a moral profile of my seven friends. They lay no great claim to bravery; indeed, they confess to fear and trembling, to second, and even third thoughts; to a shaking hand as they grasp this fierce and harrowing sword, which they purpose somehow to transform into a plow.

Indeed, they tend to see themselves in those Gospel stories wherein nobility or high resolve or holiness are celebrated — but off to one side, less noble side. They waver between what can be done and what should be done. They breathe meantime, almost with ecstasy, the spice of life, loving their spouses and friends as they do, begetting and raising children, in some cases seeing their children's children born in the world. They dread jail as a necessary evil, no less evil for being necessary; indeed, if anything, more evil for that. Finally, they are by no means detached from their good repute, which they regard, with Shakespeare, as a peerless jewel.

To them also occur, in full force and logic and moral weight, the multiple objections stemming like very umbilical, from community obligations, from professions, from vows and priesthood — perhaps most of all, from longed for normalcy. Yet they have cut the cord and moved into the shadows.

Not, if I may speak for them, in any expectation of miracles. At least not in the spectacular sense, that judges will awaken to the dawn of truth, that icy prosecutors will melt under the sun of justice, that prison gates will spring. Such things may conceivably come to pass; in all likelihood they will not. And for sanity's sake, one had best proceed on the assumption that they will not.

What occurred during the trial went something like this. The seven were tried according to the rules of law; which is to say, a kind of straitjacket bound their free souls in the court room. They were convicted and sentenced in accord with laws designed to protect a public building against vandals, a home against armed robbery, flesh and bone against rapists and muggers. No miracles here, to be sure, but only "justice." In due course they were locked up, some for three years, some for two, under the assumption that rights of property and person are better served with such as they segregated from decent humans. Children now will be safer, intact, since the notorious Seven are behind bars.

My friends, in other words, despite all courage, altruism, outcry, are a long way from anything resembling miracles. They have not evoked a change of heart in officials or improved public understanding. The world goes on. Bombs and bombers and bomb makers prosper and multiply. Prosecutors continue to prosecute, judges to judge, juries to convict, marshals and guards to "do their job." And in the great world, at the far frontier of the empire, peasants disappear, torture grows more exquisite, the homeless beat at the walls in vain, presidents smile and beguile. My friends are a long way indeed from the springing of the prison gates. Our nuclear winter, a matter of degradation in nature and destruction of soul, proceeds.

And yet, and yet. In so reflecting, I am leaving something out. I remind my soul — I am recounting only "the facts." I am writing like a court reporter, in the cockpit of event, mechanically tapping out a kind of shorthand; words, words, words. This is the world's news, laid before the world's eyes; the world as the world sees itself. And the news, given the world, is bad.

But this is not the way Christians are to read, or to write, the news. Especially not, as the news, its power and ploys, its revengeful blows, falls on them. What then? Let us say for a start, we are to view "the world, the way it goes," through the eyes of Peter the prisoner, calmly sleeping the night away. When Herod was "about to bring him out to the people" (a euphemism, indicating a public execution), are we to conclude that Peter slept on, indifferent toward his fate: or that he was merely stupefied with terror? In either case, we had best attend, with the attention urged by desperate circumstance, to a single sentence of the episode. "All the time Peter was under guard, earnest prayer was made for him to God by the church."

Simply stated, we have here the absolute clash and conflict of oppositions, of powers and reliance, of practices common to church and state; all these, and an outcome. The prayer of the church prevails; against principalities and powers, against proximate capital punishment, against all odds.

At the same time: a caution. The story offers no inviolate pattern. The church is at prayer, but no miraculous or infallibly favorable outcome can be adduced. Indeed, we are to remember that angels notwithstanding, Peter, along with his friends, will suffer capital death in due time. Only once, and for a time, was this outcome interfered with. Peter has won a precarious stay of execution only.

We knew all along that in the Syracuse proceedings the odds against even minimal justice were overwhelming — and prevailed. Yet we were by no means hopeless, only perhaps chastened, and wary of magic. For we trusted that our friends would hold fast to their resolve; and we were not deceived. We believe that the God of life is with them, and that they will stand firm in that faith.

Their ordeal is only the first stage of a vast, seismic shift in public understanding; in it, all the living must have a part, eventually. Meantime, such first steps as our friends have dared cannot but be costly. God does not absolve them of the cost, but helps them pay up, in a good spirit, to the last farthing.

And beyond all doubt, the church is called, continues to be called, to unremitting prayer. To stand with the prisoners, to attend to their conscience. Standing as our imprisoned friends do, with the voiceless humans, so brutally disregarded, shrugged off, imprisoned, cast aside, perishing of starvation, tortured, capitally disposed of. Utterly powerless, in need (like ourselves) of a delivering angel.

In a sense that makes sense to me, my friends are already delivered. They are delivered from fear and trembling before the power of the state; also from inertia and moral amnesia. They are fit subjects for the miracle we call resurrection.

In the Gospel of John, we have constant reference to "signs." There are certain occurrences, interfering with the normal course of life. These are the very opposite of a dead end. They are meant to lead somewhere. In an obvious sense, the "signs" lead from illness to health, from sin to innocence restored, from death to life. But something even deeper underlies the matter. The signs offered by Jesus are symbols of healing of spirit. They offer a way out of despair, out of the hopeless numbing that halts the will in its tracks.

To put things mildly, few people any longer are inclined to look for miracles, for signs leading somewhere. Yet according to the Gospel, despair cannot claim the final word. We are offered something else — signs of a breakthrough.

It may be that the "sign" is not offered until we have reached the depths, lost all hope of things worldly, powerful, efficient. Perhaps we must let go, in a sense most un-American, of all signs and signals that tell us in so many ways — that we are in charge, that the world yields its mystery and grandeur and riches to our open sesame, that we can indulge in evil means and still bring good ends to pass. All the while of course, we deny spiritual realities and traditions and modes of conduct; deny the possibilities offered by nonviolence and compassion and the call to do justice; deny to ourselves the fruits of prayer, uncommon sense, ecstasy even. We open arms and hearts to the foul signs of the culture, welcome them, buy them, pay for them, place security and hope in them. Even in nuclear arms; which is to say, we scuttle the biblical security of faith in Jesus Christ, taking to heart and soul, the atrocious symbol of Omni Death, agreeing in effect, that the Bomb is our savior, along with its makers and hucksters and political slaves and satraps, and the madly bright who squander their talent at the forge of Mars. We declare with all these: we are the miracle makers, believe in us! The Bomb is our security, our Savior, our Sign!

I open the Gospel. Do I believe in miracles, in miracles of social and personal healing, in exorcisms of the self-damned, in the multiplying of bread, in the liberation of prisoners, including our prisoners of conscience? There is a greater miracle than any of these. We are told that the crowning "sign" of Jesus was his own rising from the dead.

Now I take it that this sign, like all others, leads somewhere. Must lead, by ways tortuous and long and uphill, through prayer and purified understanding, straight to our own time and place. Here, now, the "sign" of the dead man who walked away from death, when the worst had been done, when the tomb was sealed and the case closed — this sign has become a countersign.

It is for us, here and now, a countersign. It is a sign that goes directly, stupendously counter to the times (the clock of doom, the countdown first-strike ethos; time as inevitability of doom); counter also to the places where death stakes its claim (the Pentagon, the nuclear white train, the Trident fleet, the bunkers and bases and laboratories where the props and furnishings of hell are deployed).

Our time and place; people mesmerized walking toward death. And in the same time and place, something else occurring. Some people (not yet all, nor even a large majority) walk in another direction — away from the nuclear mortuary. In the blazing light of Jesus the Countersign, the people go counter. They refuse the doom assigned to them and their children. They renounce hell, that final impasse, and the signs that lead to hell.

The Great Sign, the sign par excellence, the sign that breaks up, like whiteness into all hues, into all lesser signs — is the rising of Jesus from the dead. And the great sign I hope for (and work on behalf of, and go to jail in view of) is that I and all the living might rise from nuclear death.

The Pentagon, that sign of a dead end, that non-sign of non-life, remains, polluting the atmosphere, a vast hecatomb consecrated to the end of the human adventure. The resurrected Christ, were he to appear there, for healing, or conversion (many of us believe he does appear there) would promptly be arrested. Conversion, we are told, comes hard in hell. Still, I reflect that the sign of resurrection was first raised, not in the heart of Pilate or Herod or the Sanhedrin. It was spelled out first, this sign of hope and rebirth, in the heart of Christ, his beat of love, restored, restoring.

But neither did resurrection stop there. The beat is taken up; it becomes the rhythm of the universe. Our Pilates and Herods and Sanhedrins are not immune from the holy contagion of love. Nor, all thanks to Christ, are we.   — WWA, 200–211

BLOCK ISLAND

Walking by the sea
I put on like glasses
on a squinting short-sighted soul
Your second sight
And I see washed ashore
The last hour of the world
The murdered clock of Hiroshima
          — ARB, 365

PILGRIMAGE TO
ROMERO'S EL SALVADOR

None of us were willing to leave Salvador without improvising a Romero pilgrimage. So, by way of a start, we trekked to the cathedral. I wanted to pray at his tomb, a simple matter, as I would want to pray at the tomb of Martin King, or Dorothy Day; the former because he, like the archbishop, survived for awhile to do extraordinary work in a witless and bizarre world. And Dorothy, because she, like the archbishop, knew that injustice and violence are wreaked first of all on the poor of the world — whose plight, contrary to common belief, is no creation of God, but of our "rotten filthy system," as she put things so pithily. I wanted to pray for friends at the tomb, possessed as I am of a nearly childish confidence in the saints — a confidence born perhaps of near despair that we mortals, unaided, will never undo the bloody mess of the world.

We knelt there like Chaucer's motley pilgrims, at our Canterbury shrine, this uninviting impregnable tomb, imbedded like a time capsule in our mad century. It was festooned with messages, banners, all manner of plaques and grisly cutouts of limbs restored. It was like skywriting on the air, like tattooing on the body of creation. Even in death, he gave voice to the voiceless. Their cry: all honor to the fallen one, veneration to Romero, the loser in the great chancy lottery of tyranny!

The cathedral is, as Joan Didion wrote, the clearest political statement in El Salvador. This being admitted, how is one to characterize the tomb? Pope John Paul II, no mean political figure, was by all accounts unimpressed by Romero. On the occasion of the papal visit to El Salvador, he visited the tomb only privately and in passing. The practice of *Romanità*, one concludes, does not require such personages as Romero. In life they were better played down; and in death their vindication by way of sainthood will be long in coming. But such reflections are perhaps beside the point; which is, after all, the perduring phenomenon: Romero and his people, in life and death. It would be redundant, even idle, to report that for millions of citizens, he is already a saint.

The news is out. He is revered as such, invoked as such; a living presence, requiring no foreign intervention or encouragement, even of the highest.

Dennis [Leder, a Jesuit traveling companion] was insistent; we must also visit the chapel on the hospital grounds where Romero was shot. Through the gates, up a hill verdant with spring foliage, to an altogether neat and attractive place. The chapel was undistinguished, conventional modern; that is to say, it strained after a style, and achieved only a monumental accumulation of brass, marble, and paint. Angles were sharp, paint vigorously applied in unlikely combinations. An unlikely scene altogether, for an event that shook the world.

The message of the killers was conveyed with the cleanness and finality of a bullet. If the bishop could be murdered at Mass, what scene indeed could be named a sanctuary, who was safe, and where? A universal message indeed, in mockery of the universal church: Beware, in modern war, everyone, regardless of station, age, merit, is fair meat.

The truth surrounding Romero's death is badly served, I believe, by recourse to theories of conspiracy or extragovernmental anarchy. The truth lies nearer home, anyone's home, a home truth so to speak. Which is to say, the warmaking state (a term which reality today renders redundant) *is* the conspiracy; such authority is anarchic. Such authority as then held Salvador in its grip could not for long survive if Romero did. It was as simple and brutal as that.

The Mass of the archbishop was underway, the chapel door lay open in the clement weather. The sharpshooter, a black clad hellion out of Cocteau's inferno, zoomed in. Romero stood at the altar, facing his sparse congregation of nuns and lay folk. One shot sufficed. He fell in his bloodied vestments. The gunman revved up, disappeared. It is stale news that several years later he has never been apprehended; nor is there evidence that he was ever seriously sought; nor, indeed, is it likely that if apprehended he would make clear whether the inspiration for the deed, or its motive, initiated in him.

The reasons for all this need not detain us. The murder of the archbishop, like any flagrant crime, does not occur at the whim, or at the serious initiation, of this or that gunman. Powers other than the murderer decreed the crime; decreed as its necessary adjunct that its trail be allowed to cool, until it is all but obliterated.

We stood silent at the chapel entrance; a nun approached us. Would we wish to visit the house of Romero? This was a rare privilege, the house being in custody of the sisters, and seldom opened to outsiders for any reason. I was reluctant, being less than enamored with visits to dwellings of the formerly living. The reluctance is no doubt instinctive, beyond reasonableness; some obscure feeling that I do not belong in the precincts, almost an awe in the presence of a very absence.

When a death has brought great personal loss, my reluctance becomes almost insuperable. And at that moment, the death of Romero, the brute incalculable fact, obliterated all lingering curiosity — to encounter his ghost, or even his ghostly walls and garden. I hastened my steps through the rooms, and exited again, as quickly as decently possible.

A tidal wave of memory, as I stood there amid the hospital traffic. I was back at Merton's monastery, some eight years after his death. The monks had invited a group of friends, scholars, poets to pass a day there, in a course of workshops and discussions on Merton's life and writings. It was the first time I could trust myself to return.

One feature of the visit was a walk through the Kentucky woods to Merton's hermitage. There we were invited to tour and tarry, to read the poetry of the renowned hermit. Or otherwise, as we might choose, to pass the autumn afternoon, bathed in haze and monastic quiet.

I chose the otherwise. Atavistic beyond doubt. But I could not bear to linger in those rooms, where friendship had flowered, spontaneous and hilarious at once, where an unbreakable thread was spun, a lifeline I still held in hand. Those unlikely monastic hours could not, for all of longing, be summoned back, could scarcely even be spoken of.

I wandered alone in the woods, ablaze with gold. In the cottage, Bob Lax, Merton's hermit friend returned from Greece for the occasion, read in his understated monotone selections from Merton's late poems. It was the plangent voice of autumn, hovering over the hazy fields of goldenrod, ragweed, honeysuckle. And the reality lay heavy on me. Merton was gone, and why should I trick and mistreat my soul, like a Halloween ghost; as though, at times, in certain moods (the summer, dying like a splendid phoenix), as though death and loss do not presume and preempt nearly all of life? Marveling, the guests moved through the cottage. Nothing was disturbed: fireplace, icons, the desk and its books. And in the inner room, the narrow cot and its woven coverlet.

And in Romero's house, two or three small rooms, a celibate neatness and order. A few changes were obvious. His portrait hung in the entrance; most of his books were removed by his family. And on the cot lay an inert, moving symbol, the wooden crozier of the fallen shepherd.   —Summer 1984, SS, 66–71

WITNESS OF THE MARTYRS

Let us conjure for a moment the image of a beleaguered Salvadoran peasant. His life and that of his family are precarious. Death, to be sure, is nothing new to them. Starvation has made stalking skeletons of his ancestors while they worked the earth, has brought them low before their time. Now the Guardia and its hired killers offer a like service, only more quickly, cheaply.

But this is not the whole story. Being quite helpless where he stands, he has sought help elsewhere. Better, he has been forced to seek his hope beyond the mischance of this world. Indeed, were his hope drawn only from the facts of life, it were as shallow as the soil he belabors.

Behold that deeper hope. He is literate. The first book he learned to read, perhaps the only at his disposal, is the Bible. More; he belongs to a *comunidad de base*. His friends and he, through diligent study, have come upon a precious insight. It takes in account the possibility, indeed the likelihood, of death by violence. Small matter, great matter, there you are, death being by no means the only word that reaches them, nor the last.

The promise, the Spirit. He lives by the promise of the Spirit. This, he will tell you, is enough to live by, or die for, if required.

Providence is a large word, perhaps he does not even know it. But he believes, and hopes on. God will have care for him and his people. He has only to take seriously the word of God, to love and cherish his family and friends. That will be sufficient, on the Day.

This is Christianity, one might say, stripped to bare bones. Helplessness, then a mysterious "power," the power of the promise, irrevocable, lived by.

For ourselves, another power looms. The Bomb, that nefarious symbol of the power of death, threatens more than our lives. It symbolizes what the Bible calls the "second death," the death of the spirit, of self-understanding, of very sanity. It threatens those precisely in virtue of its claim to all sufficiency, to protect our misbegotten spoils, to vindicate and justify, to require of us nothing of remorse or moral change. It leads us radically away from God.

It follows that the race toward nuclear oblivion is not to be understood as a merely human deviation, a going awry of political, social, military arrangements. This is the language of "flesh and blood," stone blind as to its own predicament.

Nor is the nuclear arms race to be thought of as a "problem" to be set right by experts, diplomats, the dissolution of the age of war, a cannier distribution of the world's goods and markets. The great powers are quite skilled in rearranging the world, even to admitting the existence of a less violent world, should the new shuffle accord with their interests. They might well arrive at an understanding that nuclear weapons are an anomaly, a waste. And so must be eliminated.

And nothing of reality would change. Neither on behalf of the beset poor, not in the plight of the enormously more beset rich.

The arms race is to be understood by Christians as a mystery of that evil we name death. It is the expression and symbol of the activity of "principalities ... of this dark age ... the superhuman forces of evil in the heavenly realms."

To assert this is by no means to acquit human forces of the evil they sponsor in our midst, in our time — they and their atrociously abused freedom. It is rather to indicate their enslavement (and ours as well) to the powers of death at large in a fallen world: powers alert to delay, to becloud, to deceive, to win over, to enlarge their claim and dominion.

Christianity was obsessed from the first with the bitter facts of death in the world. Here was the true, bare contest. Just as obsessed, or more so, with the sweet fact of life; there resounded in the bones of believers the call to take sides, to stand for the one against the other. *"Mors et vita duello conflixere mirando."* "Death and life in awesome conflict joined." Peter, like Jesus, must enter the house of death which is the world.

This was the heart of the matter. The resurrection of Jesus was their talisman, their credential, their warrant. They were like sheriffs sworn to break and enter the house where death had claimed the living. They entered and searched out death. And the dead walked again — because He was risen.

Life was thus, then and now, granted a slight edge over death; though the conflict would go on, bitterly, and without massive final outcome — the Outcome, which is also sworn. Thus we have signs to walk by.

Death by napalm, death by carpet bombing, death by starvation, death by sorties, death in prisons and precincts, death by disappearance, death by the inadvertence of power ... we know the horrid, necrophilic catalog of the century. And we know too a slight, all but invisible, all but voiceless alternative. By this we shall know it: it will not join the crush and rush, not climb aboard the death train, not sign up for the ideology, not join ranks, not fall into step. It has another word, a mere whisper to pass along and along: Life. Consequence. Fear not....

In San Salvador on November 16, 1989, as is known around the world, six Jesuit priests, together with a cook and her daughter, were dragged from their beds and murdered. The event was hardly unforeseen or even unchosen by the priests.

For at least a decade, the space of the horrendous civil war, they had dwelt under the livid threat that at length broke through their doors and exacted their blood. At one point several years ago, an ultimatum was issued against them: thirty days to leave the country, or be killed. They chose to remain and take their chances. The word of the Spirit, one concludes, was: Remain.

Instead of leaving the country, the Jesuits sent a modest appeal to their brothers around the world. Please be apprised of our predicament. Please come, if possible, to El Salvador. International attention is our only hope. A slight interference, the presence of outsiders, might, just might, delay discharge of guns already cocked and aimed.

Grief impels these lines. It was at that point, some five years before their deaths, that another New York Jesuit and I resolved to go. In the course of our visit we met the six who were subsequently murdered. It occurred to me at the time that it might be useful to survival to publish a small account of the journey, of the friendships we formed, of the dangers and complications of life in that tormented country. I did so. But nothing we did turned the guns aside, as we were to learn to our horror and grief.

After the murders, many of us were arrested in attempts to call those responsible to an accounting. And since little likelihood exists of a just outcome in their case, we concentrate on a single outcry: stop the murder of the innocent!

Jesuits who attended the funeral of the priests in San Salvador, brought to our country a portion of blood-soaked earth, and in procession, bore the emblem to the White House. There, they anointed the pillars. There could hardly be a clearer assigning of responsibility.

The martyrs test the church. The church knows itself, which is to say, knows its own voyage, has mapped the path by water or by land toward Jerusalem; has also calculated to a nicety the consequence of the journey. But this, it must be said, only insofar as it knows, embraces, honors, exonerates its own martyrs.

This attitude and activity in regard to our own can only be called crucial. It implies at the same time that the church rejects the ideology which the state invariably, for its own perverse delight and to cover its crimes, attaches to the believers whom it marks for destruction. This is an insulting tag attached to a noble corpse: "ideologue" or "troublesome priest" or "disturber of the public order."

Thus the sequence: the state executes the martyrs, then denigrates their death behind a meticulous (or foolish) scrim of duplicity and doubt.

It was thus in the case of Jesus. He must not only die, Roman law must be vindicated in his death (and he be dishonored, his memory smirched) by charges of subversion, threats of destruction of the Temple, endangerment of law and order.

In his death, we have something more shameful even. The state can be counted on for depraved conduct. But here we have a classic instance of religion abandoning the martyr, joining the vile, secular chorus of dishonor.

The church can react only with scorn. Martyrdom is included in the church's catechesis; the church knows why martyrs die, and says so. More, the church makes it clear that in certain circumstances, such violent death is the only honorable witness and outcome.

Then, their death accomplished, her task continues. She raises them to the altar for holy emulation. They are now inscribed in the calendar of saints. Her supreme act of worship proceeds under their invocation. For they are, after Christ and Mary, her chief glory. She knows it, and (at least sometimes) says it boldly, defending the martyrs against all comers.

The defense is risky. Honor of the martyrs places the large community at risk. Often guns again are lowered, the terror is renewed, others are placed in danger. The mere declaration of how and why the martyrs perished, heightens the immemorial struggle between the church and the worldly powers — a struggle in which the martyrs were forerunners. It is in this sense that the whole church is called to martyrdom to understand and vindicate the nobility of the noble dead.

In El Salvador and elsewhere, noble tongues are silenced. But the truth must continue to be spoken, the truth of their death, the cruelty and injustice of it, the precious connection between their death and the integrity of the Gospel. This is judgment; the heavy tolling, not of a passing bell, but a presentiment of the last day itself. The bell tolls for the defeat here and now of the violent victors, for the triumph of the victims.

The martyrs, all said, stand surrogate for Christ and the church. Their crime is their firm withstanding, on behalf of an irresistible word of love. In this they have spoken for the whole body of Christ. Then, their death accomplished, the community takes up the task; not to justify the innocent death, nor to seek justice (a case improbable of success at best, since the unjust and violent sit also in the courts).

The task is otherwise: to confront the powers with judgment, a call to repentance. Even murderers, and the powers which impel them, must be salvaged, those who are furthest from the saving truth, from the mercy and compassion they have gunned down.

The consonance between church and martyr: the martyr standing witness for the church, the church vindicating and honoring the martyr.

An ordination photo of the murdered Jesuit Ignacio Ellacuría shows him prostrate on the sanctuary floor while the litany of saints is chanted. A photo dated Thursday, November 16, 1989, shows him murdered outside the Jesuit house in San Salvador. His body is prostrate, face down. It is exactly the position of his ordination rite.

The church, from time to time, and wondrously in our own time, earns the name: church of martyrs. The title signifies the living consonance between the witness of those who die and those who survive. Both speak up, both pay dear; some in blood, some in the bearing of infamy and danger.

The death of the martyrs urges a scrutiny of conscience on the part of all. This includes a self-scrutiny of authority, of its ideology and behavior. Especially an ideology which inhibits the truth concerning the murder of our sons and daughters, the "honor and dishonor" of their deaths.

Let us for Christ's sake hear loud and clear, and let the assassins hear, and the faceless politicos and oligarchs hear, why our martyrs stood where they did ("the standpoint is the viewpoint"), why in consequence they, whether known or anonymous, were eliminated. Let us hear praise of the martyrs. Let us hear an unambiguous call to the faithful: "the holy dead must be emulated."

—WS, 29–30, 113–14, 124–25, 171, 224–26, 231–35

BLESSED FRANZ JÄGERSTÄTTER

In February 1943 Franz Jägerstätter, a young Austrian farmer, husband, and father refused to be inducted into Hitler's army and was promptly arrested. He wrote brilliant letters from prison and was beheaded on August 9, 1943. He was beatified in Linz, Austria, in October 2007.

He came alive under that murky, ambiguous sign: not a double cross, so to speak, but a bent cross, disabled, tampered with, horribly altered, crooked, nightmarish. A swastika. Dare we admit it: this is the cross which (despite all frantic denials) we too are born under? Or the one we create for ourselves? The one we bend around, to our own crooked uses and whims and frenzies. What do we make of the cross?

I would not venture that Franz saw this from the first (who does?), only that he saw it eventually. That cross hideously altered in form: a cross that favors deception, warmaking, unaccountability. He saw. And he told what he saw. And then he died resisting what he saw.

What happened to Franz that this came to pass? One thinks that a burning glass was granted him for soul, in place of the soul of a good citizen, or the soul of a hell raiser (he had been that, for sure). Something else.

He told in his letters what happened, that momentous turnabout. Franz's life went this way: (1) adolescent hellion in a backwater village, then (2) in spite of all, a conversion. Now the real act gets underway. A wife, Franziska, who loves him, clear-eyed, determined to bring to life all that submerged goodness in her beloved. So she beckons this wild-eyed colt to a maturity, a wholeness, a kiss with consequence. Three daughters are born. He becomes, by little and by little — himself. And in that measure, and for the first time, problematic to those he loved, to public authority. Realization dawns in him; one must live for the sake of the next generation.

He has a job: village sacristan. Now of all uneventful events, this is surely the winning yawn. A sacristan in a village even God couldn't name. Couldn't the story of Franz end here, for embarrassment's sake, for ecumenism's sake? Not yet.

Summer, toward midday, the church is empty. Franz sitting there, kneeling there, an open Bible in his hand, he is quite alone. He's trying to make sense of a certain text. On the one hand, he sees the words violated or ignored or trivialized all over Austria. This is astonishing, for the text seems simple and clear.

What can it mean, this business of "loving enemies, doing good to those who do ill, turning the other cheek, walking the extra mile?" His brow is furrowed; he's looking for light in a midnight tunnel. He gives the words time, a long time. Days, weeks. Eventually he realizes: all this thinking is going nowhere. Then he starts to let go. And his heart begins to breathe. Now his mind dwells on love. Love that opens doors, opens texts, means what it says, does not counsel lightly, matches words with deeds. And above all, is not fooled, but scrutinizes — the heart, the public situation. The heart that, so to speak, sees something, then makes up its mind. And follows through.

Indeed, Franz is under the gun. His world is going to very hell. In a blitzkrieg. One night, he sees it all in a dream of a great train. He could never forget it. That train! The "All aboard!" sounding, everybody scrambling to climb aboard, to go with what's going. Or as he wrote bluntly, as a voice in his dream said bluntly, "To go to hell."

To hell on earth. This is the appalling thing, the unbearable thing. Christians are climbing aboard. Priests and bishops. And then the faithful, assured that the ride is free and fast and safe. Hitler, Nazis, war, death: All aboard the train to hell.

What to do? The burden of asking one's soul, again and again, and with little help from others — what to do? And what of Franziska, and the children?

No slogans could win him over, no command to fall in line. The priests tried, friends tried. But neither church nor state could shunt his conscience around. The time came, the notice of military induction. And Franz uttered his great, though modest and generally despised, refusal.

What was the source of that refusal? One could speak of timing, of solitude, of steadfastness, of a purity and clarity of soul no contempt could besmirch.

Millions of Christians rode along on the monstrous train, while one among them trudged alongside the tracks — to his death. Many among them saw him through the train windows. He walked and they rode free; in time, they learned the consequence of both choices. Such knowledge leaves a bad taste in the mouth, a kind of heartburn in the guts. "We did no wrong," or "We didn't know,' or "Who was he to push heroism in our face?" or "Just look how he left his family unprovided!" And so on. It was as though the clarity that marked Franz had deserted the earth.

Was he right in refusing to board the train and others, who consented and climbed aboard, desperately wrong? Maybe. But this is cold comfort, this proving something, he the winner, they the losers. Let us say, rather, some of the passengers since his death have undergone a change of heart, stepped down from the train. They have come on an insight, not a comforting one, but salutary. The quality of his Christianity, and their own. The difference, but also, through him, the possibility. The possibility — of faith. Bedrock. Faith in the living God. And also, no more faith placed in the idolatrous state, the hideous "fatherland."

That ragged solitary figure trudging alongside the tracks! He beckons them. Get off the train!

To speak of today: it is no longer Hitler's death train we ride, the train of the living dead. Or is it? It is. The same train. Only, if possible (it is possible), the train is longer, faster, cheaper. On schedule, every hour on the hour, speedy and cheap and unimaginably lethal. An image of life in the world. A ghost train still bound, mad as March weather, for hell on earth.

The train beats its way across the world, crowded with contented passenger-citizen-Christians. And along the tracks, a few solitary figures, like animated scarecrows trudge along. On their own. The train hoots in derision and thunders by.

Everyone around is in possession of a ticket. Possession: nine points of the law. And if the possession is demonic, why then, ten points of the law. Drama, parades, flags, slogans, all becloud the soul. The law, homeland, purity, Heil Hitler! And if here and there, some malcontent like Franz, some besotted Hamlet in a nation of movers and winners, if such as he stands in the way, slows the rush to greatness, why, let him be cast beneath the great wheels and perish. And good riddance. The train speeds on, in no way impeded. And his memory in a few years, a few months even, is utterly lost.

We know something of the fate of the train. The train, the one Franz saw, and then refused to board — it did reach a destination of sorts. He had named the destination "hell on earth," and the proud cavalcade steamed into hell right on schedule. It delivered its passengers, millions of them, to the appointed place. They died. They died before they died. Indeed the destination lay in the decision, the end in the means. They died climbing aboard, died along the way. Died eating, died singing, died drinking, died talking (about everything except one thing), died beaming and smiling on the children (the children too died). Died of the worm that dies not, died of the serpent's promise (you shall not die). Died the second death, of which St. John speaks.

Alas, alas, had so many died ever before for so little? Died by common choice and no choice, by decision and no decision, by triviality and distraction, by routine and misreading of event? By...a shrug?

And then Franz, the obscure refuser. The pilgrim, the non-passenger on the train to oblivion. Was his No a private whim, inconsequential, a minor change of plans, as though at the last minute, he decided to travel by another route, a later train?

No. His No was a crime. A capital crime. In wartime, matters are made plain. Everyone must be aboard. Every train is a troop train. The barque of Peter is transformed into a troopship. This is a matter of the integrity of citizenship, the survival of the state, the national honor. A matter, as the priest told Franz, too weighty for uneducated simple folks (like him). All aboard! Or else!

Franz was summoned for an accounting. The church, that awesome shadow, stands behind. The Nazi officials sat, brows furrowed, portentous, confronting the delinquent. One voice, one command, church and state: Obey! All Aboard! These are awesome principalities, not to be underestimated. They bring a flush and paling of fear to the most upright frame.

We summon his image. Neither flushed nor pale, he stands in court. Not arrogant, not 100 percent sure, but sure enough to stand there, to withstand. A simple man, all said. Direct speech: Yes, no, when required. In his Bible, he reads how Christ did the same: "You shall love your enemies," and so on. That must mean something! Or why did he say it? That must mean something, here and now, in Austria, in wartime. Or if it means nothing, if it means we can climb aboard the express train to war, and Sieg Heil! with all the others, and reach the end of the line, killing, killed (a butchers' train, a slaughterhouse on wheels) — then why did he say "love your enemies"?

Hearing the great despairing wail of that engine, wild and featureless and ghastly as the beast of Apocalypse — that engine named War, battening on darkness, sweeping all into its maw (all but himself, all but a few), he said his "No."

The "No" was a modest low-toned refusal, aspiring to nothing great, nothing of renown. Reticent, wishing he could make sense of it all, wishing above all he could return to his family. He knows the limits of that "No": a word small as a grain of sand cast in the wheels of the mammoth engine. A "No" surrounded, hedged in, cornered; like a prisoner under the blade. Not loud, not world-shattering, unheard above the great seductive roar of Heil Hitler! (And yet heard.)

All aboard! On the instant! The train after all is quick and fast and safe and cheap. It leaves punctually and arrives on the minute. There are ample, even luxurious, first-class accommodations (remarkable, in view of a country at war). The second class is entirely satisfactory. Even, the third class is acceptable. And all arrive in the best of spirit! It is just like the start of a holiday — half the fun is getting there!

There is only one refuser, this villager. He shakes his dummkopf stubbornly, walks away from the train, this splendid symbol of the good life, the genius of the Fatherland! Where he goes, off there in the dark, the passengers do not inquire. Why bother, what business is it of ours. Our destination is secure, the tracks are direct as a well aimed arrow.

But as for that one, who dares oppose a great and complex system, an immortal generator of heroes, an empire such as the world has never beheld: *Anathema sit!* Let him be cursed.

Nevertheless, the warriors, the complicit, those who saw nothing, heard nothing, were mum as doornails, they all perished. A peculiar irony attaches to the outcome of the free ride. They perished, every one, whether in the course of the journey, or at the destination they, and their churchmen and their nation sped toward. That train! It was as though one by one, and then a few more, and then by the score, they were pitched overboard by an immense centrifugal force, and ground to a pulp under the wheels of Mars. Today, only the most infamous are heard from. And their names recalled here and there are invariably uttered with a curse.

Franz, locked up. For the most part, abiding in a kind of level calm. One who has little more to lose. Except of course, his life. He is no longer surrounded by a modest aura of achievement, a sort of village glow (family, work, stability, worship, sowing, harvesting, the plod of an unspectacular tradition). Most of this is gone.

Doing time, time to count his blessings. Former blessings, as he knows. Those welcomed entrances and regretted exits, those autumn days, those harvest fields, the welcoming cry of a child, running pell mell to his arms. All such memories, sweet, bitter as gall in the losing.

We think of his losses, the negotiable currency of faith. One by one, good things are plucked from him. Family, approval, the blessing of the church. He is treated like a neophyte of disaster. Then several more losses. Then an avalanche takes everything in its tide, everything of that fullness we inherit named life.

The haunting thing is — Franz will not go away. He will not go away from the church that sent him on his way, alone. His way, which should have been the way of the church. So he lingers, and is eventually welcomed, and heard.

Listen: "Love your enemies, do good to those who maltreat you. Walk another mile. Refuse the easy ride, damnation as destination." Is this to be accounted the resurrection of Franz, that the Gospel should at long last gain a hearing?

We have so much to thank him for. Thank you, Franz, non-hero, anti-hero, true Christian. All else having been rendered irrelevant, or poisoned, or compromised; all that loud talk, those national heroes, princes of the church, all in line, all in lock step, as Bonhoeffer wrote — "the leaders who have become misleaders," and then inevitably, "the led who have been misled."

If we choose to walk (and not to fall or give in or give up or climb aboard for that free ride), how few there are who walk along with us. Thank you, Franz.

— original version, *The Bride*, 99–107; revised for a lecture on the occasion of Franz's beatification, Philadelphia, October 26, 2007, unpublished

SOME

Some stood up once and sat down.
Some walked a mile and walked away.
Some stood up twice and sat down
I've had it, they said.

Some walked two miles and walked away
It's too much, they cried.

Some stood and stood and stood.
They were taken for dummies
they were taken for fools
they were taken for being taken in.

Some walked and walked and walked.
They walked the earth
they walked the waters
they walked the air.

Why do you stand?
they were asked, and
why do you walk?

Because of the children, they said, and
because of the heart, and
because of the bread

Because
the cause
is the heart's beat
and the children born
and risen bread.   — ARB, i

WALKING WITH THICH NHAT HANH

In the early 1990s, Thich Nhat Hanh and I led a retreat at the
Omega Institute in New York. I'd not sighted Nhat Hanh for
a number of years. I was affectionately greeted. The little Vietnamese Buddhist monk hugged and hung on as though I were the
last Christian on the teetering globe. He looks fabulous, and this
at the end of a punishing tour. It was a matter of careful diet, he
said. "Lots of brown rice, and chew and chew and chew. Then
the little stomach can manage." He smiled with a gesture in the
direction of that sometimes recalcitrant organ.

Some four hundred had gathered for the retreat. The considerable facilities of Omega were stretched. I was to learn that the unprecedented outpouring was quite typical, West Coast to East. "Ten thousand came out in Berkeley. Something like that everywhere," he said in noncommittal tones, a Buddhist air of numbers-come, numbers-go.

We walked together toward the big conference room, he and I, my arm around his shoulders, my free hand in his. Quite an entrance! I was touched to the quick. He walked along to the stage, was wired up, then seated himself on a pillow. The multitude filled the hall to overflowing, seated on cushions of one sort or another or on kneeling benches. Expectation hung lightly but palpably in the room.

Then, at least to me, came the first of many surprises. Children were shepherded in, some twenty of them, ages perhaps five to twelve. Pillows were produced, the youngsters grouped themselves around Nhat Hanh. Then a few quiet elders took up a song. The children joined. Shortly their treble dominated; then the retreatants took up the melody.

Another song. The themes urged breathing in, breathing out, the well being of earth, love for one another. The singing ended and the children quietly departed. And Nhat Hanh commenced his reflection on Buddhist psychology. Today's theme: the Buddhist worldview, rooted in compassion and political responsibility.

It all went along gently as Avon stream. As an old stager, I took in account the skill that governed the morning. The rhythms of the long (two hour) presentation varied masterfully. Every fifteen minutes or so a chime would be struck and Nhat Hanh would grow silent. Let the soul also have her food.

He sat, he stood, he strode to a blackboard and wrote, he walked stage front. These words occurred; dignity, simplicity, a disarming unmistakable air of take-it-or-leave-it. His instruction was of a tradition older than America, older even than Christianity. Something like a living root lodged in rock. Something tested; something that, like the little monk himself, trod the fire and ice of the world — and came through.

He was a survivor, an exile. His companions had been slaughtered. One could easily forget the anguish and loss; the level melodious voice went on and on, no notes in hand, everything literally by heart. Metaphor, metaphor. It was as though a river of blood, purified at last, had found its voice. Could one forget the Buddhist immolations in the Saigon streets, the altars confronting the tanks, the destruction of the shrines of Hue, the School of Social Service decimated, its young students slaughtered, by whose hand only God and the Buddha knew?

And why had they come, I asked myself, those four hundred American folk from far and near, to hear this monk, a Vietnamese, a citizen of the nation of the quondam enemy? Had something, religion, hope, prospects, failed the retreatants? Even for those who were camping out, the cost of the week was high.

War. This was the clue, of course. The lies, the affright and affront, the dislocation of spirit, the air assaults, the contemptuous hasty mustering of the forces for outright mass murder.

And here before us survivors of America stood the little monk. He too had survived — the harrowing, decades long, of his land. And a generation later, still living in exile. Refusing to give up. A world voyager, a presence among the desperate boat people, a reminder of what one can bear and survive and live to celebrate.

After the meditation, we were invited to accompany Nhat Hanh on a walk through the fields and woods. He beckoned me to his side as we moved out of the hall.

Outside, the children waited and joined us hand to hand. And so we walked and the chime sounded every ten minutes or so and we paused and moved along in a wave. Until we came to the lake and were motioned to sit in a circle and the singing started once more.

Fifteen minutes or so of that. We rose, and a gentle series of calisthenics followed. I watched Nhat Hanh. Years earlier he had been depleted, ill, sleepless with anguish. And here he was, stretching this way and that, for all the world like a practiced ballet artist. And there alas stood I, wobbly, scarcely able to balance on the spongy turf.

It seemed to me that something quietly momentous was at work. Given our unmiraculous world, something approaching the miraculous was bestowed on one among us. Let us say that his story and prospect invited a conclusion. The little monk, anonymous as say, an egg, was an equally unlikely agent of a momentous event. The egg was fertile.

And yet, and yet, a question teased. Why had a throng of four hundred Americans, many Christian, gathered to hear him? The quondam victim, the monk, this classic private spirit of hagiography, has taken on the postwar world.

Time has passed, sponging the memory clean. Among Americans, the Vietnam War is a more or less confused hodge-podge of purpose derailed, of presidents trapped in a tiger cage of barely functional despair.

Time is time, merciful and merciless at once. And the hands that keep the hands of the clock, delight in turning time around, in changing vastly the roles; ally, enemy. Nhat Hanh, ever so gently, unnoticed by most, cast off his role of victim. Now he is helping the "victors" cast off their role as well. Neither role could well serve the wearer; each was wrapped in a rotting shroud, signifying death.

Maybe nothing short of tragedy could bring such things to pass, and that too is an old story, instructive and painful. Astonishment at its coming is a kind of measure. It is laid against my plight and the common plight.

Every war in history, in the minds of practically all those who prepare for it or initiate it or respond to it or make money from it or propagandize it or research it or deploy it or go off to kill in it or are wounded in it or survive it — or write encyclicals about it or mount the pulpit to sanctify it — all of these find a way to set down the same thing.

Namely. The current war is a good war. It is a virtuous war, a just war, an oil war (self-justifying), a war to end all wars.

And the above justifications, from the point of view of biblical understanding, are pure scandal. At the flash point, when religion once more plays its immemorial role and falls in line, a stone is fastened about the neck of churchgoers and taxpayers and priests and popes. And they are cast into the sea.

It is better that way, says Christ. They are a scandal.

In such wise, according to primordial biblical images, religion joins the fishes and whales and dolphins and other beings, down, down to the rim of creation. Joins with those, among many others, endangered by the present course of events.

Cast into the sea like Jonahs, we must begin all over again, the task of evolving into our lost humanity — if indeed the above gentle creatures consent to our presence, thrashing about bewildered as we do.

Let's see where it all may go. For a start, let's spend a thousand years listening to the eerie voices of whales. Saying nothing. We're all talked out, all lied out, all freaked out. All done with killing and being killed. All done with — whatever it was we called Christianity.

Even at long last, centuries lost, learning something? An improvement over present savageries? Who knows. Maybe, with the help of friends. It's worth a try.   — TDIP, 352–55

7

The Word Made Fresh

GENESIS, THE DAWN OF ALL THINGS

For seven years I have pondered this — our sublime, notorious, at times noxious — Book of Beginnings. Pondered, read, dug, dunged, planted. The text became a kind of background music in my life, now a low hum, again a furious cacophony. I was enduring (and sometimes even managed to celebrate) membership (it could hardly be dignified by the noble word citizenship) in these United States. Enduring barely, as multitudes of innocents across the world were dying under American sanctions and bombs.

Seven years. A number of friends, together with members of my immediate family, were standing in draconian courts and prisons. I went on, a more or less presentable Jesuit. Tasks, some blessedly quotidian, some less so, occupied my days — teaching here and there, leading retreats, writing. I also was arrested constantly, as U.S. interventions blundered on with ungovernable force — Central America, Bosnia (with NATO), and at present writing, Afghanistan and Iraq.

And, to our story of beginnings, I was searching in scripture for a version of ancestry which would shed a measure of light on dark days. A version of cosmic, primordial beginnings. What were we humans like at the start, what went right (for awhile), what in short order went drastically wrong? And above all, what of this deity who purportedly (if one can credit a Jewish-Catholic pulse) had set things in motion, all manners of being —

intelligent, living, inert — a veritable cornucopia of variety and beauty?

The book of Genesis, I thought, was by no means an "objective" biography. As the story developed through Exodus and on to Kings, the image and behavior of the God, I concluded, were strongly colored by the ideology of the imperial sycophants, especially of the Davidic and Solomonic era. In the hands of court scribes and priests, the deity of the realm emerged as a project, useful to the designs of the empire. He chose this people over all comers. His ethic curiously resembles that of his powerful sponsors. He was pleased with punctilious worship, especially when it preceded military forays; the two were closely joined, a prosperous outcome guaranteed by intercessions.

Such themes lie of course in the future, outside the purview of Genesis. Still, a hint shadows the text — the malfeasance of patriarchs, the betrayal and murder of brother by brother, the bickering and envy and deceit, the sacrifice of principle in favor of pride of place. The lengthy story of Joseph is particularly instructive and disturbing: sweet innocence yields to experience of a certain kind. Power beckons, enchants, and corrupts.

These themes hit home, and hard, distressingly contemporary. Power corrupts. We are the woeful citizens of a world power in the images of Joseph's Egypt, of his Pharaoh and of a transformed Joseph — no longer the provider, now a tyrant on the move. War ravages. It destroys the civilized skills, so long and laborious in the making, of give and take, mutuality, respect, love of creation.

Someone has said it well: the barbarians are no longer at the gates — they are running Egypt.

"In the beginning, God created..." Momentous, majestic.

The Hebrew word for "create," *bara*, is used here as elsewhere, for a properly divine action. And in the first verse of all, "created" sums up the entire process. We are in the realm of poetry, in this sense at least — the author(s) "imagine reality." Images are offered, an answer (better, a hint of an answer) is proposed to the questioning mind, as the "first week" unrolls.

It is as though the author knew that one day a question would be raised — how can it be that all things are? Further, how can it be that prior to a "point of time" (including time itself), all things were not? And who, or what, made the momentous difference, who brought to pass the time of all things, time included?

Raising such questions implies, hints at an answer. Does not creation stand in a queasy balance, between an indubitable existence and the inability to contain or explain existence here and now?

Metaphysics was not the strong suit of our ancestors in the faith. Questions of creation and origins were of another realm; they were grist for the mill of the arts. Specifically, for the art of storytelling.

Let us tell a story, then, of a "first week." Let us sing it aloud, recount it to children, celebrate it in various sanctuaries. And let us do this long before "the story" and its consequence were made official, codified, centralized (and to that extent) set in stone in the Jerusalem temple-palace era.

These vaulting images of all things tumbling into being, flora and fauna and finally we humans, created in the image of great God — they were told and told again. They created song and dance and, eventually among Christians, fresco and mosaic and statuary and poetry and opera.

How did the images come to be? And more, how did they become so fruitful as to create endless forms and variations, images born of images? One theory of sources seems plausible. The first stories took form out of a sense of helplessness, of limits reached. Of limits that once reached, must then be breached. Every generation was beckoned to enter the awesome cave of the past and there "imagine the images."

But mere prose was helpless to encompass the stupendous *magnalia Dei,* the holy Wonders, beginning with the divine nod — all things, come forth! Poetry then, the ineffable imagined!

And a process was underway. Liturgy and its accompanying arts and cycles of feasts and fasts, mourning and celebrating, made of the year a cosmic wheel of light. The community mounted and rode the turning wheel, improvising, ever so gradually codifying what was seen and undergone and remembered. Summon the images of a palpable world. Know what to make of it, make ever more of it — see, hear, touch, feel! The wonders of the first week emerged — and the consequence thereof.

"In the beginning, God created."

Imagine then — the dawn of all things — including light and darkness, water and land, bird and beast. And ourselves! Placed last as we are (and apparently lords and mistresses of all) on the scale of the momentous first week — how greatly we humans are magnified!

God is serene and sovereign from the start. And even as the tasks of time multiply, God dwells in the great savannah we name eternity.

Creation. No great effort, no war in heaven or on earth. A mere majestic word: "Let there be..." and all things spring into being, in time and place.   — G, xvii–xx

KINGS AND THE PATHOLOGY OF POWER

Tradition has honored the books of Judges, Samuel, Kings, and Maccabees as "religious" or "biblical" or "divinely inspired" history. Puzzling indeed.

A question has lingered for centuries. What instruction from Yahweh may be conveyed in these accounts, steeped as they are in mayhem, slaughter, betrayal, intrigue, and bravado; rife as they are with fractious sons and foolish fathers, brothers betraying and killing brothers, women deprived of status and dignity, predatory enmities periodically erupting, and wars breeding wars that breed wars?

"Religious history," this brimstone brew?

Only a minuscule portion of the books could be deemed edifying. Few ideal humans emerge from among the kings and generals and counselors; few in the teeming "schools" of prophets.

A further question, the most grievous and puzzling of all: What to make of the Yahweh of these stories, a being who in no way disapproves of vile behavior, is inclined rather to bless it, to account more delinquent his "chosen," and with prodding from on high, to urge base instincts into action?

What then of "divinely inspired" history? Why are blood-ridden pages uniquely honored in church and synagogue, honored under the blessed cope of "Word of God" — so entitled, along with the stories and teachings of sublime prophets, martyrs, and truth tellers?

To speak of Christians, can our God incarnate in Jesus be one with this Yahweh, a deity of kings and their wars, enthroned in a cloud of moral ambiguity, implicated in wickedness trumpeted as virtue?

Let us stand back from the stories and venture a suggestion. The books of Judges, Samuel, Kings, and Maccabees imply that we humans must move in great darkness before we are blessed and enter the light. This, it would seem, is the law of the Fall. We must undergo the anti-human, the inhuman enthroned, wielding life-and-death authority. Behold the ancestry from which we spring, we children of primal catastrophe. Let us ponder such forebears, and weep.

We must suffer the anti-human as well in ourselves. Here and now. The warriors, tricksters, and betrayers are not only our ancestors; they are ourselves, our present awful authorities, our likely progeny and descendants. The wars of the Kings are our wars today — these awful days of the wars in Afghanistan, Iraq, Lebanon, Darfur.

Tears, then, for the victims, and for our unredeemed selves. Tears, before we are enabled to cry out in redemptive song, "O grant us a life that merit's the name human!"

All in due time. Within our timetable, whether marked by despair or the hope that hopes on.

But first, it would seem, we must undergo a harsh, even shaming pedagogy. Through these books, we must come to know the worst of our ancestry — as well as the worst that lurks in ourselves. We must come to know also the truth of structures and systems, throughout the ages and today. To know that even those approved by popular opinion and attested as winning divine approval — that such, given time, swamp grace and claim, like kings of a jungle, the spoils.

We are to know that rulers are not the more virtuous for being powerful. (As if we did not know it, as if it were not a fact of our horrendous years and the military rush toward oblivion.)

And what of ourselves, the governed? We too dwell in moral darkness, deep and often unapprehended; we who approve such rulers or are prudently silent in face of their crimes. We who offer, in our secret longings, small relief from theirs. Tendencies in leader and follower are often alike, and hold firm: self-interest, ego, lust, greed, duplicity, the common mire from which spring the wily and witless among us.

And all unlikely, saints and martyrs as well.

In such a spirit, we are urged to ponder these books of the Kings, are invited to dwell on hardly attractive matters — our common ancestry and plight. In those pages, willy-nilly we enter a scene of recognition. We see ourselves, Americans; we witness our own behavior in the world. Behavior that is for the most part shameful.

Do our leaders differ, in any large degree, from the rulers of old? They are hardly different at all. Today too they create an economic divide of riches and rags, systems of stigma and exclusion, of racism and sexism. And endless wars, incursions, bombings, sanctions.

Let it be said plain. The era of the kings is cursed of God — of true God, I mean.

The god of the kings, we are told, curses the enemies of the kings. But does not the god also curse his own, including the great kings? The curse is implied — and the inference left to us.

The curse takes these forms, among others: a moral void, the truth of human life denied — or derided. And (surely a related matter) the all but total absence of prophets.

The few who raise voice against royal misbehavior must be accounted feeble forerunners. Generally, these pre-prophets speak ambiguously, or remain silent, colluding with the crimes of their patrons.

Let us pause in wonderment as the kings contrive an image of their god. They make of the deity a kind of glorified ventriloquist's dummy, placing in his mouth words by turns cunning, ferocious, calamitous, and vengeful, words that proceed from the darkness of their own hearts.

Let us look long, and lament the implications that lie half-revealed in the ancient story. Unsavory, relentless is this tale of us humans, ever so slowly and painfully emerging into the light. What a difficult birth, millennia long!

And bearing what into the world, in this our millennium? A social monster, yet another voracious empire?

An honest totting up of the crimes of our nation, in our lifetime, raises such questions. A torment, as yet a strange relief. The relief of recognition and confession.

Let it be confessed. Despite the strong interventions of the prophets (and, as Christians believe, One Intervention surpassing all others), the books of the Kings stand like a record of our own benighted century, bloody as beef newly drawn and hung.

In essentials and main driving forces, the account here set down is being enacted before our eyes. Thus the meaning behind the text.

The meaning, the warning, escapes the attention of most — including most scholars. Nonetheless, let it be said plain, even unto ennui. The system that fuels our world coincides with, even surpasses, the crimes — social, military, economic (and yes, religious) — recorded of the Kings.

It is as though we opened a Book of Kells and found there — in caricature, to be sure — our own faces. Among the demons and gargoyles and maidens and kings and spooks and monks, the sad and solitary, the gaping, concupiscent mouths — and among the angels as well. Like it or not, confess it or not, we behold in these books of the high and mighty our ancestry. And ourselves.

The compassion of the Word of God is thus revealed. A strange compassion, seemingly devoid of mercy. The method is irony, truth concealed in paradox, all the more striking for being masked. Hidden often humiliated and put to scorn, the Divine awaits the mindful.

The Bible measures the mystery out; "a time, double time, half a time."

And let it also be said: the god of the Kings shockingly resembles the Baals. Like them, a deity of the realm of death, the realm of the Fall.

The Kings seek the divine, to a point. Who the search leads them to is another matter. They come on their god in a distorting mirror, reflecting back their own moral vagaries. Flash, flash back. A god in accord with whim, vaulting ego, profitless violence, peevish morbidity, at times a peevish resentment, a stroke of vengeance.

No prophets, as yet.

In these pages, how rare is the true and integral and tested, the man or woman of virtue, the saint. And when such a one shows face (often a woman, uncelebrated and unnamed), her fate is sure: she is ignored or crushed.

Let a prayer arise out of the void opened by these pages: "Grant us knowledge of our crimes. Help us take our true bearings in the world, to confess how rarely, in public life and private, in religion and statecraft, in temple and marketplace and home — how rarely authority is joined with virtue. Grant us knowledge of our plight, that we may cry out for relief, and be drawn forth."

In these historical accounts, I suggest that the Bible is in the process of "deconstructing" itself. Ironically, the Word of God acts like a fiery lens, placing the empire under scrutiny.

Thus the biblical method: let the kings wage wars; let them worship an approving deity lodged in a stupendous temple (the first "National Cathedral"?). Let them join religious sacrifice and battle, legitimating, even sacralizing plain slaughter. And in this imbroglio let them drown the eye in pieties. Allow them all this. The Word of God — audacious, subversive.

Believers are to act as judges, prophets. Deuteronomists, if you will. Jews who take Torah seriously; Christians who take Jesus seriously. Who summon the law (love of God and the neighbor) to judge violators of the law.

When this occurs, the Word emerges from the page as rebuke and judgment. The Spirit who breathes upon the Word breathes likewise upon the believer. We pause and grow thoughtful. A tale of wickedness, whether ancient or contemporary, is imputed for what it is — wicked.

In these pages, the "human," as defined and enacted by those in lofty places, often proves profoundly inhuman. In the warrior, diplomat, magician, court prophet, scribe, we see deception, betrayal, alienation, blind obedience, military and diplomatic chicanery, the will to multiply victims and lay waste the earth — these lauded and puffed, seldom renounced.

Open the Bible, then. Let the believing community see there the worst. More, see the worst presented as noble, virtuous, raised aloft in honor. And let conclusions be drawn — based on a later tradition, nobler icons, the prophets, Christ on the cross.

Out of darkness, light. But not yet.

In sum, we are offered in the books of Judges, Samuel, Kings and Maccabees a diagnosis of the pathology of power. Thus is implied a biblical anthropology, a biblical version of the human, conveyed in a stark *via negativa*.

The books of Kings, as they reach us, are a prime example of "theology from above." The final editor, an undoubted genius, sounds the imperial note like a trumpet blast. Triumphalism, invincibility, sway and glory, a sense of "Behold and rejoice — here, now, the ideal, sole, irrefutable, unique ruler and system."

Eventually, overt judgment will come to bear. Prophets will offer a saving midrash. They will denounce the ambiguities and crimes of high culture, raising a cry "over against." Isaiah, Jeremiah, Ezekiel, Daniel — withstanding the worst, they raise a fierce protest against the otherwise unaccountable Kings.

And another gift of these noble spirits. Through them the moral physiognomy of the Holy stands clear. God is advocate of the "widows and orphans and the strangers in your midst."

Still, "My ways are not your ways." The prophetic word confronts an absurd claim: that the behavior of a Solomon dovetails with the divine will. No. God is the utterly Other. Let no mortal presume to stand outside judgment.

Today. The Word of God is spoken for the sake of today, for us. If not, it lies dead on the page. Lift the Word from the page, then; take it to heart. Make of it the very beat of the heart. Then the Word comes alive; it speaks to commonality and praxis. Do it. Do the Word.

Thus too, judgment comes home. It is lodged against our own culture, against our contempt for the poor, our wars and injustice and greed.

As we read, Jesus stands at our side. He speaks for the victims, the forgotten ones, those who live and die in the margins of the text, in the footnotes, the silence, the space between letters. Be attentive. In the scroll hear the voice of the dead, the unborn, the expendable.   — KTG, 1–9

JOB'S SUMMONS TO LIVE HUMANLY

"I know that my redeemer liveth...." Not much to hang one's hopes on, we are told. The words are a limping translation of a corrupt Hebrew text.

And yet, and yet, how the words resonate, amid conflict and opposition, luminous, teasing with hope!

The story is ancient — and new. A chieftain, a giant among his people, grows prosperous. He is favored of God, honored among his own. Then, a sea change. In multiple guises, from above and around, from Deity to demon to companions, from bodily illness to ecological ruin, death moves on him. Job is stricken ill, family and goods are snatched away. His scene of torment, an ash heap, or a town dump.

And in the midst of such travail, those words, "I know that my Redeemer liveth..." are left hanging there; a future vindication, integrity restored, a sane universe, restoration of all.

On the cusp of old age, I took a serious, extended look at the book of Job (rather ruefully, and with an eye over the shoulder, knowing I'd already exceeded the biblical allotment by years).

It was perhaps inevitable, that tardiness; at least I so console myself. I had first to make my way through the *silva oscura* of Dante's purgatorio — a tortuous passage through American alarms and wars, bombs and incursions. Meantime, for years, I studied Job. By common consent of the ages, it offered a singular version. Better, a vision.

Job, an exemplary human being, persuasive, bracing — and hard to take.

A character unlike any other in the Bible. Of no prophet is so excruciating a story told, in such relentless detail. Job stands under a veritable firestorm. It assails his physical integrity, his virtue, his faith. God, Satan, and a coven of humans bear down on him. Each is intent on a curious, not altogether admirable project — the "testing" of the just.

An awful book, in the biblical sense. A book that made me pause in the reading, ponder, often tempted to lay it aside. Simply too much.

Too much, this laissez-faire God. Who was he anyway, by what right did he bargain his friend away? This sinuous world-weary Satan, too clever by half. And that trio, pouring a salt of contempt into a friend's wounds.

And too much — Job himself. A mighty protagonist, a prince among men. And more; one who, as is strongly implied, speaks for us all, speaks in our name, bespeaks the human predicament.

Speaks for my condition, and yours? The notion is appalling. He confronts the illusions we live by, the empty fealties we offer a culture of death, our dismal, rote pieties. The book is a judgment. We meet our match. We, the masters of the world's game, as the game is rewarded — and punished.

The quintessential American game. For every winner, many losers. Winners inside the borders, losers beyond. The military thrives on such assumptions, in principle. So does the world economy, runaway, set in fast-forward gear.

We know there are losers in the world. In an honest moment we might even admit that Americans create them, multitudes of losers. But the fact is after all, somewhat inert. Hardly impinging or breaking the skin. Or leading to ethical change, as goes without saying.

Thus comes this book of Job, the drama of a born loser. And, perish the thought — what if we ourselves were, in someone's eyes, losers? What if Job were an image, straight from the hand of the Maker of Images — an image of the American plight, the first world plight, of our uneasy place in creation, our larcenous wealth? What if Job bespoke the effect on the flesh of humanity, of our spiritual "underdevelopment," our intractable violence?

Job, image of the human — precisely as loser. Job afflicted — and as such commended to ourselves. Figure him out.

I studied Job, and I learned a few things. A summons to live humanly in a bad time. A faith that verges on despair, that looks that dark eminence in the face and is not turned to stone. A faith desolate before the injustice of the world. A faith that survives a barrage of nostrums, accusations, insults. A faith that would not be put to silence. A faith kindred to the one discovered by Jacques Sommet, a French Jesuit who died at Dachau: "A new faith, the faith of the charnel house."

Job's faith. A faith that in conventional eyes — those friends again — very much resembles blasphemy.

Job the loser, and Job the teacher. I was put off by contradictory, litigious squabbling, by endless entrances and exits, doors that open only to slam shut, refusal of comfort or assurance, argument and counter-argument, characters insulting and demeaning one another, even as they invoke competing gods.... What a welter!

I longed to have done with this imbroglio, a drama that dares question my status in the universe, in history, before God — before the victims of American bombs-at-the-ready, a carnivorous world-throttling economics, an internal combustion machine of violence.

And questions. Not new ones by any means. I sense that somewhere in the dark spaces of the American psyche (in my own psyche) a question was lodged. What if a heavenly being, an eye resting on America, grew frosty? What if a thumb were to turn down on us? And we declared the unchosen?

The book brings such suspicion to the fore, mercilessly. It implies a radical reversal of roles, one after another. And this, even as everyone is apparently mortised securely in place. God in heaven, only slightly concerned with the plight of his friend, more concerned to prevail in his shady bargaining. And Satan prowling the earth, a hand of death laid on Job.

And the plight of Job, for forty-two interminable chapters, is driven home. Followed by a brief scarcely believable summary of relief and restoration.

Unsettling, shifting, no firm ground underfoot. Every character, no matter how high and mighty, every lofty repute, held up for fierce reappraisal. No one, not even God himself, justified, approved, allowed to come off as morally admirable, untinged by selfishness or ego.

God enters into a vile bargain whose prey is the life and well-being of — a friend. Satan is thoroughly — Satan, which is to say, twisting goodness to bizarre ends. And Job, complex, truculent, near blasphemous, his moods veering between despair and ecstasy.

And of those friends, less said the better — surely among the least attractive companions ever assembled around a figure of woe. Cocksure, petrified in orthodoxy, discrediting the suffering one, peddling their version of God as judge. And they sum Job up, dissect him like a corpse on a gurney. He is self-deluded and secretly given to wicked ways.

One can only advise: beware, sensitive souls, this cast of characters! But the author asks in effect: will you understand? He presents a human passing through the knothole of actual, awful life. Not Job, the prospering chief secure in possessions (only slight attention is lent that circumstance, a prelude to the main act).

The main act is terrible. Utter downfall, wounds, pettiness, and grandeur, bursts of anguish and fear and dread. A story that shocks, a kind of Greek recognition scene, a devastating cultural critique. And an offering too, of a possible healing, even a kind of rebirth, a new sense of ourselves in the biblical "scheme of things."

Connections. When I turn from the book to the world, I see Job as a social image. He is multiplied, from one era and culture to another and another — and on to our own.

Today Job is an image of those who dwell in a world we Americans have both named and created: the "third" world.

But more than "out there," he dwells in our own assaulted humanity. As well as in the slain, the bombed, the refugees, the unwanted, and undocumented. The expendables.

We will never have done with him, this semblance, this haunt. He stands at the end time, the time of no recourse, of no mercy.

We are never done with him, with the summons to stand at his side. In solace, in binding up wounds. In resistance against a vile bargain ("let him prove himself, let God and Satan judge him, and his friends to boot"). A bargain sealed in heaven — or in hell.

Ironically (and this is only a beginning of ironies) we are told that Job was an enemy of the chosen, an Edomite.

A "Thank you" is due, then, to an unlikely benefactor. And a muted "Alleluia" as well.   — JADND, xiii–xviii

WHO ARE WE,
THAT YOU TAKE NOTE OF US? /
PSALM 8

Through all the universe
your glorious name resounds

I raise eyes
to the lofty tent of the heavens
sun stars moon
        Foil of your right hand

I see rejoicing
beast and dolphin
eagle, cormorant, condor
triumphant plowing the seas
in the plangent air godlike

I bend to the faces of children
they lisp your name

And I ponder;
mere mortals, who are we
that you
take note of us
have care of us?

fragile, fallible
vermicular, puny —
crowned now, sceptred now
conscious now, exultant now!

Through all the universe
how glorious is your name!

THEY CALL YOU BLIND MAN:
CALL THEIR BLUFF / PSALM 10

Lord, why   stand on the sidelines
silent as the mouth of the dead, the maw of the grave —
    O living One, why?

Evil walks roughshod, the envious set snares
high and mighty the violent ride
Applause for maleficence, rewards for crime
    Yourself set to naught

Eyes like a poniard impale the innocent
Death cheap, life cheaper
The mad beast is loosened, his crooked heart mutters
    Fear only me!

Lord, they call you blind man. Call their bluff

    extinguish their envy

See; the poor are cornered
marked for destruction, grist
    for a mill of dust

        At the bar of injustice
        they tremble, wind-driven birds
        under the beaks and stares
        of the shrouded Big Ones —
        No recourse but you; no recourse
        but your faithful love!

SHOW ME YOUR FACE, O GOD /
PSALM 61

At land's end,
    Where the sea turns in sleep
       ponderous, menacing
         and my spirit fails and runs
       landward, seaward, askelter

I pray you
    make new
this hireling heart
    O
turn your face to me
—winged, majestic, angelic—

    tireless,
      a tide
    my prayer goes up—
show me your face, O God!

I LOVE YOUR PROMISE / PSALM 119

A double heart be far from me, Lord
I love your commands
my hope is your promise

A lying tongue be far from me
I love your promise
my hope is your law

Far from me a violent will
your will is my hope
I love your commands

To witness your law
to love your commands
be my first love.

MAY I TO MY LORD HASTEN /
PSALM 131

Lord cut my cloth
   to a human measure —
big schemes, big follies
   the dark ground of connivance
   be far from me

   Come my soul
     like a bird to the hand
     like a child to breast
I will nurture you, mother you

   As my soul hastens
     to breast, to hand
     may I to my Lord
     hasten. Abide.

HAND IN HAND, HEART IN HEART /
PSALM 133

Sisters and brothers dwell in peace
What joy, what an omen!
Hand in hand, heart in heart
a double strength

A waterfall pausing, various, ever moving,
roses, surprising strawberries
A closed circle, an enclosed garden, a universe —

There
war's hoarse throat is silenced
and praise goes up night and day
and the stanchions of slaves in the hills
gather dust, spring ivy.

                 — ARB, 179, 184, 188–89

JEREMIAH AND THE PROMISE

My thesis is simple and, I trust, audacious: each of the prophets, in the present instance Jeremiah, is an "other" of Yahweh.

As God's compassionate and clairvoyant and inclusive image, each prophet strives for a divine (which is to say, truly human) breakthrough in the human tribe. Lacerating, intemperate, relentless, the prophets raise the question again and again, in images furious and glorious, poetic and demanding: What is a human being?

We are unready for God; we are hardly more ready for one another.

And yet, and yet...Through the prophets, Yahweh strives mightily for a breakthrough on the human landscape of history, to bring light to our unenlightened human tribe, to speak the truth, unwelcome as it is, of who we are, who we are called to become: friends, sisters, brothers of one another.

This is a tough proposition that goes against the odds of our history, our wars, injustice and greed, our idolatries. Again and again, these venturesome spirits, the prophets, are warned of the odds: strive as they may, no one — from top to bottom of the social structure, "kings, prophets, priests, people" — will hear; they will turn in despisal from the message of Yahweh.

Worse and worse the warning goes: scorn and obloquy will be the lot of the truth-teller. Frequently the authorities of temple and state will unite against the prophet, invoking the "law of the land." And when the iniquitous law allows it (or even when it does not), the authorities will seek a capital sentence.

Jesus stands in this line of these hapless heroes. Willy-nilly, the afflictions of the prophets are his own. He will echo, some five or six centuries later, the awful word of Yahweh addressed to Jeremiah.

The word of Yahweh to Jeremiah is altogether ominous: you will speak, and no one will hearken. Inhibited from birth they are, stalled in a false tradition, morally deaf, dumb, and blind. Insist as you will on a summons from Yahweh to works of justice and compassion; persevere, intercede, and risk all — the response will be indifference, even hatred.

Jeremiah, Isaiah, Ezekiel, and the other great ones press on through a trackless thicket of adverse will. Nothing, or very little, changes. And, despite all, they are never won over to the world's ways, never — short of death — put to silence.

For all their moral greatness, we shall not make of the prophets a species of moral superhumans. True, awful events daunt, discourage, and dishearten. Terrible misfortune and loss befall Jeremiah, Hosea, Daniel, and Isaiah. Suffering is the price exacted of them in their quest for a fuller and deeper humanity — for others, but for themselves first of all. This realization lurks there, between the lines. The great ones admit to it. And someone, against all the odds of Yahweh's prediction to the contrary, nonetheless hearkens to the word and records it. We are left with that record and with its implication for ourselves: What price the human?

They give us one price: to perish, and to have the record of your life and death set down by another. This at best. At worst, to have no record at all. To perish in memory also. That you ever lived. This is the threat.

"The Lord spoke to Jeremiah . . . and spoke again . . . and spoke to him many times." What a claim! Such assurance: that "take it or leave it," the word of Yahweh — undeviating, polemical — will thunder away for more than forty years!

Who, we ask, was this daring one? He was the worthy, even surpassing, soul brother of the likes of Zephaniah, Habakkuk, Nahum, and Ezekiel. All bear a similar burden of awful events, the downfall of a proud people, exile, and humiliation. Jeremiah sees that catastrophe is imminent, is bound to be. Again and again, with the persistence of a clairvoyant or a madman, he shouts the threatening word — repentance or ruin. And inevitably the shout is lost in contrary winds. It falls on our ears as well, brief, laconic, the bad news that at length came true.

For years, no one took heed. Indeed, who at any period is inclined to take heed of such news as he uttered, who to take it seriously? They turned away, fed up and angered.

All sorts of expediencies are at hand for those who choose not to hear. This naysayer must actually want the worst to occur! He must be guilty of concocting his own brand of bad news, guilty by presumption of ill will, malice, envy, whatever. Like discord at the king's banquet, he cannot bear that people should prosper. Darkness is his element. And the last extreme: let the law be invoked against this malefactoring manufacturer of our darkness. Thus we may with impunity persecute the messenger.

Nonetheless, the awful event Jeremiah warned of is finally at hand: the prophet of doom survives to witness it: "And in the fifth month of that year (the eleventh of the reign of Zedekiah), the people of Jerusalem were taken into exile." It was the third roundup of Jeremiah's lifetime. Ten thousand Jerusalemites, we are told, including the royal family, artisans, and nobles, were driven down a road of tears into Babylon. And a puppet is set over those who linger on in the holy city, destroyed and sacked. The national humiliation is complete.

What a harsh announcement! It falls, a bolt from the blue: "Before I formed you, before you were born, I appointed you." Does the choice preordain the chosen to joy or sorrow, or both?

Such a word from the Most High, one is tempted to say, were better left unspoken until the point of death, a kind of consolation prize in one's last moments — or perhaps an emollient word offered to survivors. Then it could be borne! But to hear it uttered in one's youth — a word determinant of the entire future? The hundredweight of that!

Jeremiah can only protest: "I don't know how to speak. I am too young." Does he protest too much, as some have claimed? No matter his age, the sense goes deeper. Who, at any stage of life, issued such summons, would not feel callow, inept, a stutterer?

Suddenly everyone in the world seems more qualified, more gifted, superior, wiser, more apt to win the divine pleasure. Only look about you, young Jeremiah. There are in Jerusalem divines and nobles, savants and saints, priests, elders, prophets — each and all planted in a fruitful soil. There is wisdom aplenty, access to the powerful, instructions handed down with assurance, law, order, honorable service in temple and court. And in face of this ample wit and wisdom, you are the chosen? Yahweh speaking to you? All these others passed over, redundant, of lesser moment?

"I will be with you." From beginning to end of scripture, the echo never dies. The first promise and the last. With daring we lift the promise from the page and claim it for ourselves.

God with us — we know so little of what the promise might mean in practice, what gift it implies, even what form it takes. God, we are told, stands with the poor, the victims, those buried deep at the base of the human pyramid — and with the friends and champions of these. Still, for all that, history is somber; victims go on being victimized; the best so often go under.

While time lasts, the promise must be taken as ambiguous, dark, all but impenetrable to the logical mind. In this wise: if the power of the Most High is "with us," how comes it that such power so often takes the form of — powerlessness? We look to the martyrs, we hear their outcry.

Perhaps a measure of light dawns when we open the book of Jeremiah. If the promise bears a crucial weight in one thus assured, if the word of Yahweh is accepted as a promise on which a great spirit proceeds to build a life, to risk all — what weight might the same words exert on us?

My sense at the outset of the book is that the promise is one matter, the shape of a given life, another. Will the promise shape the life? It all depends. As to Jeremiah, the promise seems meaningless. Would he fare differently, for the better, for worse, had it not been uttered? As posed, the question itself is meaningless. Rightly understood, the promise touches on imponderables.

I venture that the meaning and measure of the promise are clarified in pondering the book itself — taking careful note of Jeremiah's reaction to the atrocious suffering that befalls him. Then the gift shines, the promise holds firm — moral coherence, consistency of word and behavior, undeviating patience, faith and trust though the skies fall.

No one of us has seen the promise vindicated in the lives that beckon us on, over a long, often bitter, haul. Friends keep at unpromising labors; or harder by far, at peaceable confrontations with death-dealing law, ventures that earn only contempt and punishment. We take note of their noble detachment — from successful outcome, self-justification, honor, wealth, the credit of a great name. This in virtue of the promise.

The hearts of such are fixed elsewhere than in the cultural wasteland. Thus they see good work through to the end, quite simply for its own sake: for its goodness, its human substance, its serviceability and good sense — its being "for others." All in virtue of the promise.

Jeremiah, yes. And as to ourselves, we shall see.

—JTWTWG, xi–xii, 1–5

EZEKIEL AND THE LANDSCAPE
OF DRY BONES

With Ezekiel the great era of the prophets is in full tide. And what a relief, after the predatory era of Judges and Kings!

The heavens opened before him, a vision appeared, sublime and grandiloquent. The vision, ironically granted in exile, is the first in a series of opaque, even hallucinatory, images. Ezekiel embraces his vocation, pays dearly for it, passes it on.

His own tradition long has distrusted him, sought to exclude him from the canon. Even today his code all but resists breaking; one reverts time and again to the offensive, shocking vision that strikes like lightning in the opening verses.

The mimes he must perform — humiliating, absurd. It is as though Yahweh would pull him down, a sort of public clown, wan and dispirited, possibly mildly insane. What he must undergo to lay open the wounds of soul and society!

He is bidden to "lie on your left side, . . . lie on your right side," to "clap your hands, stamp your feet, and cry 'alas!'" In fine, he must show in his humiliated body, for the sake of the body politic, what is to come — exile. Yahweh instructs: "Dig a hole in the wall and pass through it. While they look on, shoulder the burden and set out in the darkness."

Ezekiel was destined to hear a decree of Yahweh, iconoclastic words such as were uttered to no other prophet. They signaled what looked like God's ultimate repudiation of the people and the temple. (And he a priest, cherishing both temple and liturgy.)

The anger of Yahweh came to an unexampled, dreadful climax. Like a gravely offended regent, Yahweh abandoned the holy place. It seemed like the end of the world, and to all appearances it was. An era was crashing about the prophet's head.

The land was overrun by a merciless enemy, bent on extermination. And the people, whose proud boast was of a special status before God were rendered — literally — godless. By God himself.

At the point of disaster, Ezekiel is commanded to accompany his repudiated people into exile. And it is in Babylon that he receives his vision and its charge. A cruel setting for his vocation; he alone among the prophets is anointed outside Jerusalem.

He must taste the fate of his people. It is as though nothing of relief or repentance could befall until the worst had come to pass. Or from another point of view, it is from "the remnant," those who have lost all, the despised and enslaved, that a human future will take form.

As to those images of his: after initial shock, they seem apt and helpful. What a relief, one thinks — a new way of seeing, of understanding! As when, immediately after the initial vision, "a hand stretches out to me, in which was a written scroll.... Written on it was lamentation and wailing and woe."

He is instructed to "eat the scroll," which he finds (and so strangely, given its purport) "sweet as honey in the mouth." Could it be that the image is a deliberate oxymoron? To this effect: the truth (exile is inevitable) is a bitter dose indeed. Still, truth is a gift, especially so in face of prevarication and cover-up. So there is sweetness too.

The truth: quite a menu. The strong image of scripture as literal food, filling mouth and gut with its suave vitality!

His image of a whitewashed wall — a wall that like Israel itself barely stands erect, is cracked and unsteady. And must be repaired, if not totally rebuilt. The image is drawn out, dramatic, wonderfully apt and biting.

A coven of false prophets arrives at the wall. They are sedulous, skilled — in covering the truth over. They carry big brushes and pails. A touch here, a stroke there — they set to work. Soon the wall gleams like new!

But Ezekiel has news for them. The rains will roar down; the wall will collapse in a rubble. Then what of the whitewashers and their silly talk of "all's well," of "peace, peace, when there is no peace"?

A true prophet endures the divine thunderbolts. Ezekiel knew it, to the bone. He must suffer with his people. If he did not, how could he venture to speak for them? Endurance, survival, bare and unsung, became his lot. Babylon, exile, the worst years. Nothing of shame or defeat was spared him. Yet he was guiltless, faithful to the end.

Still, failure was not the whole story. There was also the great prevailing event at the start. Where others were rejected and cast aside, Ezekiel was singled out. From then on, he walked the sere landscape, stood firm, spoke an unrelenting word. He became a figure of redemption.

The irony is overwhelming. God's historical choice of this people, once so firmly in place, seemingly irrecusably, was negated, canceled. Ezekiel alone was the chosen one. That choice, election, vision, assurance: To what end was it granted?

"A figure of redemption." The meaning of the phrase is necessarily obscure, even as it is certain. Perhaps this: his task was, against overwhelming odds, to keep hope alive. Whether in Jerusalem or in Babylon, he uttered a word of hope. Of necessity it was a dark word, ominous, at times threatening. A terrible event hung over the horizon. The decision of Yahweh was irreversible; they must lose all. In due time, yes, return, restoration would come to pass. But only in due time.

And his people, who in their heyday had been deaf and blind to the word, at length achieved a wisdom of sorts, and responded. Realization dawned, a new day after the bleakest of nights. Eventually it became clear that the repudiation by Yahweh was not final. A chastened people came to a new understanding. The exile was a disciplinary act, one phase of the long pilgrimage of sin and repentance.

But at what price to the prophet! He was spared nothing. In an unlikely, barren terrain of contempt and enslavement, he announced a further chapter of the saga. Relief was dawning; exile and despoilment were not to be granted the last word.

Such a mad hope! It took the form of a supreme vision, of the "dry bones" scattered in the wasteland. From exile, shame, defeat, a dead end — came the revelation. We must understand that for Ezekiel's people, all evidence, rumor, the false promises of yea-sayers, everything that shored up a kind of cultural optimism had been swept away, dissolved. Despair rode the saddle of the world; life had become its own "worst case." Ah, then it was that the heart of Ezekiel saw and his tongue was loosened. Hope stood free, sang its song of prevailing.

In a place of pure desolation, an entire ecology speaks of the prevailing of death. A sere landscape, dry bones. No sign of life.

And then — a sign. One after another, the bones stand upright, connect one to another, grow animate. Skulls speak aloud. And death lodged in cadavers like a parasite, in institutions like a colony of termites — death shall have no dominion!

Ezekiel (or Yahweh) had cannily chosen the occasion and locale: in a place and time when death seemingly had won every round, death, in the end, loses. Then and now, an image to confront (and confound!) a culture of death!

What if, what if! What if, one thinks, we could take the image to heart, name it for our own, walk with the dead who walk again, keep on keeping on, confront those not so hidden persuaders, the principalities — the entire cultural apparatus of death!

In my mind, gradually, as such thoughts occurred, the strange, even bizarre, quality of the book of Ezekiel gradually dissolved. His riches emerged, Lazarine and large.

Yes. He became for me an absolutely crucial voice, to help me endure, to interpret, to lend a helping hand. To survive the times, times that seem unredeemable, mad, collapsing like a wall. Ezekiel: a figure of redemption, a companion and witness, someone to stand with us.

I was grateful for this, perhaps a small favor: he allows room for a touch of madness, surrounded as we are by evidence of insanity in high places — addictions to death-dealing, domination, greed, ego, the forms of death that govern authority high and low today.

Ezekiel, truth-teller, points to another way. He resists every attempt to be "normalized, by wicked authority," "assimilated" by the world. He will not grow spiritually sodden; no business as usual, no war as usual, no waste and want as usual, no religious rote and rot as usual.

God, he declares, has another, far different, hope for creation, for ourselves. For the "widow and orphan," the abused and condemned and forgotten, those who count for little or nothing, "lives of no value." And we, the beneficiaries of such sanity, so talismanic an ancestor, can only give thanks.

—EVID, xvii–xxi

DANIEL AND THE CREDENTIAL OF NONVIOLENT STEADFASTNESS

How to take seriously the spectacular story recounted here of the youth in the fiery furnace (Dan. 3–4)? Let us regard it as of more import than, say, a tale told for the instruction of Sunday school children. (Perhaps we resolve the unsettling implications of the story by relegating it to youngsters, thus distancing, even trivializing it?)

The episode lies too close for comfort. Close indeed, and torrid. Scorching, a near memory of furnaces of our lifetime, stoked against the innocent. So we incline to put the image of the furnace at a distance, as we do other horrors of the age: cluster bombs, land mines, smart missiles, napalm, rubber bullets; successive incursions, whether in Vietnam, Iraq, Grenada, or Central America.

The plain fact is that our nation, along with its nuclear cronies, is quite prepared to thrust enormous numbers of humans into furnaces fiercely stoked. Of the preparation and commission of such crimes, of their technique and strategic advantage, we have learned a great deal. But of repentance we have learned precisely nothing.

As a nation, nothing. As a church, perhaps something. It seems impossible to keep one's own story from dovetailing with the story of Daniel and his friends. Always some peaceable action brusquely summons those I love into the hot belly of the legal juggernaut!

As I set down these notes, I girded myself for a journey to Syracuse, New York, to attend yet one more court appearance of my brother Jerry. His crime: he dared, in his stubborn way, to enter the Griffiss Air Force Base in Rome, New York, and to plead there for the children of the world. The action, it goes without saying, was not favorably received. The law concurs; his action was criminal.

The nuclear plague is of course legally protected. It is also self-engendered, deliberate, huckstered worldwide with a scientific sangfroid. Through the collusion of governments and scientists, the stoking of nuclear furnaces proceeds apace, at Griffiss as elsewhere. At that notorious base, surrounded by innocent fields and domestic animals, are stored tactical nuclear weapons in great numbers, destined (at the time) for export to Europe. From the same base at a later time "nuclear capable" bombers were launched against Baghdad.

In the Syracuse courtroom (or in any other courtroom in the nation) no mention of international law will be tolerated. Nor will the so-called argument from necessity, in virtue of which violation of a law is permitted in order to prevent a greater evil. Nothing of these. The fact that provocative weapons of Omnidestruction are lodged at Griffiss will not be in contention. Not even, so to speak, in mention.

Other topics will be explored. Arousing the prosecution to indignant rhetoric will be a minor infraction committed by a few fractious souls. Their crime is this — insisting, in whatever way is open to them (not many gates or hearts are open), that the existence of such places as Griffiss is morally appalling and tactically insane.

Meantime across our nation and world, research and deployment of such weapons continues. The fiery nuclear furnace is stoked to "seven times its heat." Despite momentous changes everywhere fomenting in the world, including many hopeful auguries of peace, the American race to oblivion proceeds.

That race has its own inner urge: ever more and more! It is as though a juggernaut has been launched downhill; it requires no other engine than its own massive momentum. It gathers speed apart from personality, political party, the second thoughts of the (few) thoughtful officeholders. It matters not a whit who inhabits the White House, who is appointed Chief of Staff, who sits in Congress or the Supreme Court; it matters not at all that former enemies have been quelled or overcome. The Bomb rules. Together with its "conventional" relatives and progeny, it rules the economy, decrees who is to be enriched and who is impoverished, and across the world, who is to live and who perish. The Bomb has even stolen a capital letter from the deity.

As to the golden image decreed by the king (Dan. 3:1ff), it is the absurdity upon caprice. The statue, we are informed straight-faced, is of enormous size. It is also badly, even hallucinatorially proportioned: "ninety feet by nine." Is there a conscious irony here? Does the royal pomposity not see how this form appears as the bizarre, larger-than-life sign of a demented self-regard, a morally grotesque ego?

It may fairly be taken, though left unmentioned, that the image operates on many levels. It is an image of a god otherwise unknown, not even named. It is also, as suggested above, an image of the king himself. (So also avers the first Christian commentator, Hippolytus.)

If the latter version holds, one may venture that the statue is erected to forestall the bad news implicit in the king's dream. The dream was unsettling in the extreme. So the disproportionate deific image attempts to offset the king's demise and the downfall of his kingdom as prophetically announced by Daniel. Also, one thinks, the colossus is concocted to forestall the advent of the final Realm, the rock that crushes and cancels in its wake every human intervention and polity.

Yet another aspect of the story: it is recounted to fortify and hearten a persecuted people. Let us be of good cheer, mock the oppressor, his pretensions to divine rank! In the eye of the beholder, the statue is rendered altogether ironic and banal. It is as though the image were despite all one of a surreal clown or a court fool.

The image in place, a command is issued. Let all and sundry fall before the statue to worship it! Time is collapsed; decree and obeisance are one. Daniel, tongue in cheek, catalogues "all peoples, nations, language" obeying on the instant. No interval, no second thoughts, no recalcitrants (except for a few!). We are in a nightmarish world of automatons. Citizenship as an idol? Daniel's is a theology from below, with a vengeance.

The account is mimicry, incantation, caricature, deconstruction all. As though to say in code, "Note, please, the superabundant foolishness of this would be superhuman and his minions!" To this has come the empire, emperor and citizenry both, bound in a single bundle of banality. It is as though a colony of termites were at work, bringing down a shack, long gone in wrack and ruin. The royal pretensions are denied and derided in the very fact of reporting them.

The king's glory reaches to high heaven. He has achieved an astonishing world conquest (Dan. 3:4). What more attractive to the imperial djinn than a celebration of his empery — that his victories be fused into permanence through an overpowering and dizzying image?

In the eyes of Daniel something more than a rampageous royal ego is at work here. Through its image, the empire is rendered demonic. Which is to say, a powerful political, military, economic (religious?) entity is raised to proclaim absolute dominion over life and death.

We have here an event, the Bible suggests, that is a constant of imperial history. In a parallel passage in Revelation, an otherwise unnamed tyrant issues a summons similar to that of Nebuchad-nezzar: worship the Beast, or perish (Rev. 5:9; 9:9; 13:7; 14:6; 17:15). A running thread binds one testament to another, and the behavior of an early empire with a later one. Are not all such entities genetically related? In attempting to seize the prerogatives of God, the empires are remarkably, lethally consistent. Or so the imagery and teaching would have us ponder.

Against these great odds the "faith of the saints" is called to steadfastness. Beware! Certain forms of fealty commanded by rulers are usurpations of the adoration due God alone. The godlings must be resisted, even at the price of capital execution.

In stark contrast to Daniel's community, all levels of dignity in the realm are promptly inducted into worship of the massive image. Rank and protocol are fastidiously observed, a charade of pomp, power, and prestige is mounted. The scene, reminiscent of later spectacles, is designed to bedazzle and stupefy and subdue, to bring to heel even mettlesome spirits. All are summoned.

The procession advances; it is as though the scribe were holding his breath in awe (or perhaps stifling with difficulty his derisive laughter): "princes, governors, lieutenant governors, commissioners, treasurers, judges, magistrates, and all other offi-cials of the provinces."

The implied message is clear as a trumpet blast. A vast impe-rial bureaucracy has closed ranks; it is one in fealty. Of what avail, then, the resistance of a few diehards, were such to occur? And even more to the point, what god could bear comparison with this colossus (Dan. 3:4–5)? Thus the scene unfolds, metic-ulously described, a catalog of folly, a travesty of the honor due true merit.

A great huffing and puffing is underway. Need it be added that the votaries are unprepared for the hard tumble to follow?

"You will prostrate yourselves and adore" (Dan. 3:6–12). (The appalling phrase is repeated word for word in Rev. 13:15). The high and mighty, along with the lowly and powerless, duly fall to ground. For Daniel and his community, the moment of truth approaches.

They are, by all indication, deliberately absent from the scene. The transgression is noted, and the resisters shortly denounced. The motive of the adversaries, one can judge, is envy (Dan. 3:8). Feet have been stepped on, aspirants thrust to one side. And outsiders, exiles, of no account, have been granted high powers and prerogatives. And now, O king, behold the ultimate arrogance. The same beneficiaries have dared spurn your royal will! Thus God is placed in contention versus the gods. So also Daniel's understanding of faith is verified: a faithful community will inevitably be subject to crisis, and to the impending threat of the mighty.

We would much prefer to freeze in its remote time and place such idolatry as is described here, as though to think (and thus we often are prone to think), "Good riddance, we've done with all that." Yet the exact opposite is true. We moderns continue fervently to construct our own pantheon, gods violent, voracious, greedy. Ancient appetites, grievances, hostilities, jealousies arise, a fury of greed, envy, ego, hypothesized in a technological setting. Numerous shrines are consecrated to the gods of the nation, to the gods of manifest destiny, nuclear security, and so on.

Is the shrine of national idolatry the Pentagon, the Congress, the Supreme Court, the White House? Or perhaps all these in concert, with their vast paraphernalia of weaponry, their network of acolytes, diplomats, scientists, engineers, economists, sociologists, apologists? And yes, their enemies — hypothetical, virtual, nonexistent, the dark saturnalia of the imperial psyche?

And the silent churches, what of them? Where can worship of true God be found intact? As for ourselves — indifferent, silent, and politically enlisted — what judgment shall be leveled?

Judgment is already leveled. Imperial misbehavior reaches down and down, into a rapacious economy, political corruption, cruelties exacting more and more tribute. The crime awaits the "day of Yahweh." In Daniel and the prophets, that day is anticipated, dramatized for our sober instruction.

It goes without saying that from the works and pomps of this political-military idol, God, the God of Daniel and Isaiah and Jeremiah and Jesus, is summarily excluded. Or if granted place, our deity is shunted to an out-of-the-way alcove reserved for a minor potentate. And the worship goes on. Placation, imprecation, intercession, adoration. Moreover, the tribute is offered strictly on a quid pro quo basis. The god is required to produce, whether the benefit be a successful war or a booming economy.

Too, the shrine of the god is neatly situated; it lies just adjacent to the market place, each provenance greatly benefiting from the prospering of the other. Is not commerce in need of a blessing, and is not the temple graced by the shower of gold released in its direction by this Croesus [the Lydian king of legendary wealth]?

It is helpful to clarify the question raised by Daniel and his companions as they confront the gods of the kings. The question is not precisely "one god or many?" Rather, "true God or false?" That the true God is one, and the false gods many, is only a partial statement of the terms of conflict. Conceivably, the king could regard himself as a monotheist, but his (one) god, his monstrous image, could hardly be thought of as true God. The image is in fact closer in spirit to the beast of the apocalypse.

Inevitably, belief in God raises questions of conduct, as Daniel and his friends well know. The king's behavior, his preposterous edicts tumbling out and out, unmask the base quality of his faith. He remains ethically unhinged, cruel, overweening, bellicose. So degraded a spirit raises the towering image of a supreme god. And not at all strange, this god resembles the king.

Shall we raise here the vexed question of forced conversion (even to the "true faith")? It is striking, the contrast between the conduct of the king and that of the three youths, vis-à-vis their respective faiths. For his part, the king would tighten the screws: believe or die! The youths, on the other hand, have little to say, even as, under the slings and arrows of adversaries, they have much to endure. They utter nothing of threat or reproof, whether against their tormentor or his complaisant minions. What kind of witness is this? Is the God they worship true God? Are others invited to believe as they do?

They are a silent trio. They neither raise questions nor offer answers. They force no one's hand. Simply, the truth of their lives speaks for them: they are prepared to die for their belief. Enveloped in a mysterious silence, they offer their inquisitor a true defense. In this exemplary moment they are thus commended to the generations, our own misadventurous one included. Their credential is a pure light in a dark time: nonviolent steadfastness.

—DUSG, 53–61

JONAH AND THE WHALE'S TALE

We note in the book of Jonah how the heart of God turns and turns about.

Ironically, spontaneously, mercy is offered the great ones of Nineveh, lost in idolatry and yet much beloved — this to the scandal of conventional religion and its practitioners, including Jonah. The prophet has grown callous, cynical, yes conventional, arbitrary. God and the prophet have become a scandal one to the other.

The spiritual ancestors of Jonah, as well as those who follow him, leave a consistent trail of heroism, obedience, sublime poetry and rhetoric, fulminations and comforts drawn from the heart of Jawe. And from this one? Something else, something of: grumbling, low spirits, absence of prayer, self-will, stonewalling.

Something of ourselves? The point of it all? Let us see.

Jonah is an anti-hero. In this he matches our mood — both rather dark of mind, melancholic, on the down side. And we're strangely grateful for this.

God is forever shocking the gods. In such ways as this: A people despised as furthest removed from grace, beyond the pale — these may come to surpass those commonly regarding themselves as snugly within the orbit of grace.

Nineveh, according to the true believers, is Sin City. The appellation may or may not be correctly conferred. Up to a point, Jawe seems to agree that such, alas, is the case.

But then, we are told, something happens. The Ninevites, one and all, are wondrously, instantly converted. Caution as to intemperate judgment is therefore advised. God delights in judging the judges.

Nineveh thus stands surrogate for all who are declared by insiders to be outside. Nevertheless, the citizens of Nineveh are to be shown compassion, to be sent a message: "You too count for much, to you I offer the dignity of accountability...."

It is an apt moment to recall again how the imagination of Jesus was suffused with the tale of Jonah. Jonah, persnickety and tardive — and Jesus, hastening toward Jerusalem — a likeness between the two? Indeed one would not have thought so. And yet the likeness is insisted on, both with respect to the death-resurrection theme, and the theme of judgment.

Jesus draws upon the broadly implied irony of the Jonah story. Something strange happened on the way to Nineveh. Or in a later and more tragic and actual event, on the road to Jerusalem. The believers, the chosen, the covenantal people — all those words and names and evidences of a special sense of being in the world, of credentials and privileges — these are shaken out, emptied (Matt. 12:41; Luke 11:32). "At the judgment, the people of Nineveh will rise against this generation and condemn it, because they repented at the preaching of Jonah...."

It staggers the mind. Nineveh proves more believing, trusting, loving, penitential, apt for conversion than all those true believers, the chosen ones of temple and Torah.

The analogy becomes a bitter pill indeed. The erstwhile pagans become witnesses for the prosecution, against the chosen. The neat scheme of salvation is unraveled, the sigil is reversed, truth is stranger than illusion.

The chosen have overdrawn their account; they are bankrupt on the day of Jawe. The beneficiaries, heirs, are the formerly despised, the goys.

As to Jesus' reference to "the sign of Jonah," there is an apparent difficulty (Matt. 12:40): "Just as Jonah was in the belly of the whale three days and three nights, so will the Human One be in the heart of the earth three days and three nights."

The imagination of Jesus! He summons the ancient stories, draws them boldly to his use. But if the story of Jonah is fictive and the story of Jesus factual, how can the latter call up the fiction as analogy? Deep waters here.

To His way of seeing, there are truths truer than fact. His imagination embraces the improbable, and lo, all is changed.

How else approach the resurrection, except by imagining it? There is no reasoning can touch that outcome, no earthly logic. But there is rhyme to it, His morning-beyond-death.

Therefore we imagine. In a stupendous ruction, Jesus and Jonah are cast forth from the maw of death. Then they meet, unlikely brothers, face to face, the one a mirror image summoned by the Other. There they stand, delivered, on the firm ground of a new existence.

We approach Nineveh at the side of Jonah. We see the great city through the eyes of popular legend. It is as though a tale of New York were bruited abroad, its grandeurs intact, indeed inflated, its shame and violence and greed vacated. And the tale, let us imagine, reached the ears of a remote Amazonian tribe.

Something like this: the word would filter down and down. "A divinely great city, three days' journey in breadth!"

We consider also Jonah's plight. He is a foreigner newly arrived, and from a people long at enmity with the inhabiting people. Worse, his message is hardly apt to render such an audience benign. It is an unlikely, even preposterous threat Jawe has entrusted to him. "Yet forty days, and Nineveh shall be destroyed!"

Undoubtedly destruction is not the entire message of Jonah. Nonetheless, his words sounded like a drum of doom. And on the instant — what? An effect out of all conceivable proportion to the cause! The words of this stranger are launched on the urban air. We imagine a small fire, no larger than a match flare, starting up. The flames pass, as though the very air had grown combustible. Jonah is heard, by one or two, by a few, by a multitude. It is astonishing, beyond all logic or experience. Beyond — hope?

Shall we venture something? The episode is an image of the wild, improbable hope of God?

Questions vex, trouble the heart, grant us no peace. The troubles of our time! The wars, the insuperable hold on imagination and energy; of violence, fear, greed, idolatry of death. Will there ever come relief, an end to our plight?

And then this image: the instantaneous conversion of Nineveh. It is improbable, impossible. It never happened, it never could.

Image, promise, vision. There it stands. In the (eventual) obedience of Jonah and its miraculous outcome, we see as though in a sublime elixir, a concentrate held to the light — a hint of meaning. Jonah, no longer playing a surrogate god, takes his measure at last. He grows modest.

And our implacable gross history comes alight, grows transparent. Nineveh is an image of all peoples and all time and of the end of time. Direction, outcome, non-absurdity, time and ourselves (God the chance taker!) — behold us, as such a God would have time and ourselves one day, one impossible day, to become, to be.

If we humans were capable of hearing, the miracle of Nineveh would "come true" in the classical sense of the words. Only imagine! Beyond brute facts, beyond the yawning boredom of Athenians and the distempered leaders of Jesus' time and the colossal blindness of most of us, stands the longing heart of God. Scheming, providing, preempting even.

How shall Jawe open on our behalf a less tragic course than we blunder along, a less awful ending to the human adventure than we madly pursue?

Behold Nineveh, the change of heart, of structures, of the fabric, the very soul of people and things. A vast tidal wave seeps filth and debris into a sea of mercy!

The heart of Nineveh beating to the rhythm of the heart of God. Ourselves, as shall be.

Even through such unlikelies as Jonah, even through such as ourselves. This the Nineveh story provides: a glimpse, more — a promise.

What might be. More, what shall be.

—MPMT, 175–76, 182, 186–87, 192–93, 197–98

THE IMAGINATION OF JESUS

There is more than one way of identifying ourselves. When speech is used, the most powerful (and highest) clue to "who I am" is imagery, metaphor, a poem. This is one way of understanding certain passages of John's Gospel. In a series of declarations, many of them metaphors, Jesus describes himself: "I am the bread of life," "I am the light of the world," "I am the door," "I am the good shepherd," "I am the resurrection," "I am the way, the truth, and the life," "I am the vine."

The images imply a profound communion between spirit and visible creation. In one image the communion is celebrated between aspects of earth's creation and spirit ("I am the way, I am the vine"). In another, between an artifact of one's hands and spirit ("I am the door"), or between a human occupation and spirit ("I am the good shepherd"). We all but conclude — spirit can only be imagined — and we are right! Or we might conclude: every humble or human thing is apt to lead beyond itself, or within itself — to spirit.

Note the incendiary implication of Jesus borrowing a phrase like "I am," unadorned, naked. Thus he takes to himself four times in the Gospel of John (8:24, 28, 58; 13:19) the divine Name announced to Moses (Exod. 3:14). He claims for himself the faith of the people of covenant. The daring words have struck fire; and not by any means a friendly one.

We have what seem to be two steps in Jesus' self-revelation. First, the naked phrase of the Jewish testament is taken to himself, quoted as true of himself. Second, the unimaginable Yahweh becomes subject of an imaginative addition: God is not simply "I am who Am." We are offered a series of images, a series of imaginative approaches to the mystery.

And this is sublimely fitting, if one pays heed to the claim "I am" as pressing upon us. For according to the claim, Yahweh, the God who is One, is now incarnate in this world. In Christ, God knows God, a knowledge infinitely beyond the human — and yet now announced by a human. In other words, in Christ, God imagines God.

We are right also in venturing that poetry is not necessary; prose is necessary. Which is to say, prose is an instrument of efficiency. It belongs to the "things which are seen." Prose is useful, moves things, gives orders, is logical, serves for argument, settles conflicts or makes war, is privy to special interests, makes money, passes information, and the rest.

Poetry, on the other hand, is unnecessary in the sense that God is unnecessary. Poetry is useless in the sense that God is useless. Which is to say, God and poetry are not part of the kingdom of necessity, of a world of law and order (of lawlessness and disorder) and sin and war and greed we name "the Fall."

Merely naming that world is not enough. It leaves us in the same world, the same plight, fallen amid the ruins. For we cannot name a prelapsarian world and still be true to our world. Events have caught up with our history. The first parents dwelt in a garden, but we are in another world.

The poetry of John does something more than naming that world. It imagines a fallen world, and thus is liberated from its malice. Thus the "Word," the "logos," "came among us" who are the fallen. He entered, not an Eden, but a world of sin and death. Of which matters he was destined to learn much, most of it awful, wrought in his own flesh. It was a sorry drama that ensued, a tragedy of whose end we know. "His own did not receive Him."

To say, "I am the way" is to say, "I am the way out. Come, imagine a way out. Then put foot on it."

To say, "I am the truth" is to say, "I am not the untruth. Come speak the truth."

To say, "I am the life" is to say, "I have risen from death. Come, don't get used to death, don't inflict death, get up, resist death, rise from death."

To say, "I am the light of the world" is a way of saying, "People lose it, lose their bearings, their direction, lose their humanity. I have struck a light. Come, light your mind and heart from mine."

In a sense, the primal command to "name all things" was badly understood, partially taken. Naming things, in the sense of a mere catalogue, devoid of affection or connection, ends in this: we consume instead of eating. That was the first sin, we are told. The first parents did not imagine creation; they only named it. They could not imagine boundaries as well as freedom, taboos as well as trees.

In the statements beginning "I am...," Jesus does not so much name himself as imagine himself. In doing so, he gathers us in, takes us along; sometimes implicitly, sometimes by name. He takes us far, farther perhaps than we would be willing to go on our own, far into nature, into the unknown.

Let us call it a Zen voyage, perilous, exhilarating, ironic. What would it be like, he implies, to live in a shepherd's skin, (or more properly) in the skin of "the Good Shepherd"? What would be the actions of such a good pastor? What would be the outcome of tenderness and solicitude when our charges are not sheep but children, the innocent, the victimized, the non-combatants, women, the aged, the refugees — from El Salvador and Bosnia to Nicaragua and Guatemala to Afghanistan and Iraq — all the endangered? What would it be like to be "the branches of a vine" — when the weathers of the world are as they are, sharp, unpromising, assaulting? What would it be like to be a light, when darkness covers the earth?

Christ speaks so confidently "I am...," rather than, "I look like...," or " 'I resemble." Can he speak this way because in fact, he has plunged to this depth of imagery, so that the images proceed from a life lived, rather than from a Godly superiority, over our benighted selves? Because perhaps he has taken to himself the torment and wounds of this world, and in so doing, imagined a better world, and in so imagining, has created a better world?

And more. In not one of his statements or images does Jesus name himself as one member of a species. There is a crucial, though subtle matter here. Which is to say, "I am not just any vine in a vineyard, 'a' vine, one among many. No, I am *the* vine." Which is to say, "I am all vines, I am the vine of all times and places, the Alpha and Omega vine. Is this impossible? Only to prose, to logic, to necessity, to the Fall, the non-imagination. To these, it may be impossible, but it is not beyond imagining, at least my imagining. For I am the — mythic vine."

"The mythic vine." There is a vine about which stories are told. The soil of this vine is the imagination of people. There gathers about the image all sorts of implications, as generations come and go, telling once more to children, the story of "a" vine which in the telling and retelling, has became "the" vine. In time, the vine became the people themselves. According to Isaiah and Jeremiah, they were one vine, they were an entire vineyard, kept by Yahweh. They produced well at one time, at another they fell to ruin and decay. But no matter weal and woe, (and these were all part of the story), the image was like a deep root. It went to the heart of the world, it could not be uprooted.

There were other implications too. At harvest time, the fruit of the vine became the symbol of the rejoicing of the last days. It was the cup of blessing, the fruit that rejoiced the spirit. By the time of Jesus, to say "I am the vine" is a stark claim indeed. It amounts to this: that the speaker is the protagonist of a myth. He has placed himself at center stage in the tribal story.

Jesus does not "imagine" himself in the world as one who is out to win adherents or to get people in line. His imagination doesn't function like a policeman's superego. Nor be it added, does ours, when ours is exorcised of illusions and fantasies of domination. The image, "I am the door," implies this non-necessity, this welcome and inclusion. The implication is: "I am the open door, not the closed door." Or, "I open a door long closed, locked. You are not trapped in the kingdom of necessity, the Fall. The door is now open."

We would say today, Jesus knows something about first things first. Let us start here with the improbable, if not the impossible. If he started by being "useful" to a project, founding something, proving something, squaring off against other orthodoxies, we would know rather shortly that something else of crucial import was being neglected, ignored, even despised. Something so simple as the truth. But he says simply, "I am the truth." That image, it might be thought, of "the" truth has its own native power; it sounds all the more powerfully on the polluted air of the kingdom of untruth, the Fall.

No need to enlarge on this; a nation rather continually at war will suffer a huge loss of capacity. The Greeks knew it; in war, the first casualty is the truth. Implied here is "I speak the truth." And more, for he claims more: "I embody the truth." And then, "I live the truth, I follow through on the truth." And from this good beginning all sorts of good things might follow, including a community dedicated to "the truth."

"I am the way." We are not to miss, as they say, the context. He is imagining himself in a fallen world. Chaos is implied, distemper and confusion. In such a world he offers a "way," that actually goes somewhere. Among the many ways, one deserves special attention. His way. Therefore he is justified in saying — "the way." And this in a world of great confusion as to ways false and true, conflicting signs, false road maps, of dead ends and land's ends, of detours and pitfalls, chasms and cunning twists.

On those ways, that tangle and web of purpose, appetite, misery, stretching across time and this world (the time after the Fall, the fallen world) travel the wanderers and the lost ones, thieves and robbers, priests and Samaritans, the wounded, the afflicted, the homeless, the mentally bereft, the shoppers and campers and so on. In this world, he makes his way, and makes way for us.

Make straight the way! was the cry of Isaiah. Even for the wayward? Yes. His cry might have been an ancestral command issued to John Baptist and Christ. So the image was passed on and arrives on other lips.

That is the first point of the image; to draw attention, to make us mindful. There is a way to go in the stalemated, bewildering world. It is "the" way, in proportion as it makes sense, offers companionship, leads us home. The way is the way of the heart; the world and time (even a fallen world and the time of the Fall) is the terrain of the heart of Christ.

To announce "the way" in a fallen world is hardly to propose a "way back" to some garden of innocence. The announcement is not nostalgic, in other words. To the contrary, it deals with memory, and remembering. (Nostalgia is a way of forgetting, of amnesia; but memory "brings to mind," "recalls," "calls us back" — mainly to our true selves.) Context is everything. The word on the page, even the image on the page, can be received as abstract, weightless. But the context of "I am the Way" is a real world; as real as our own; which is to say, risking the otiose, the realm of the Fall.

This "Way" leads somewhere; the arrival is one with the way. The image grew from the action. To comprehend the image, it is necessary to take in account the action. Which is to say, Christ walks the way before he commends it to us. The Gospel tells us so, he set his face steadfastly toward Jerusalem. Which is to say, toward death.

Now if that were all, Jerusalem and death, we were then allowed to grow nostalgic. But since that is not all, we are instructed to "remember Me," something entirely of another order. The way passed through a fallen world, toward a fallen city. In point of fact, that meant "the Way," whatever adherents or enthusiasm it had gathered in the countryside, was to come to an abrupt halt in that city.

Jerusalem, for the likes of Jesus, was land's end, time's end, life's end. It was the city of death; which is to say, of capital punishment, of foreign intervention, of religious collusion and temple religion. Such people as ran affairs there, we are told, bickered a great deal among themselves. But they were quite in agreement on one matter; any "way" that challenged their affairs — or worse, derided them and their authority — should reach a literal dead end. The Way was to halt there. But it did not. Something quite different transpired. The Way resumed from there, "to the ends of the earth," we are told.

Once the Way is proclaimed, we too may take our sounds. Our way, as we walk it today, is manifestly one way among many. There is the Buddhist way, the Hindu way, the Muslim way, the Jewish way. From a cultural point of view, there is the American way, much commended in song and story, by media and mammon. A way which leads straight in our time to the disasters named Vietnam, El Salvador, Guatemala, Bosnia, Afghanistan, and Iraq. And then among us Christians, there is the way of Mr. Bush and of Dorothy Day, of Jägerstätter and of, God help us, Hitler. Divisions, conflicts, warmakers, peacemakers, the many ways, including the abhorrent, the perilous, the heroic, the modest, the demented.

But for ourselves, here and now, a question or two may help clarify matters. Is our way also THE WAY? Does it make sense, offer companionship, lead us home? If so, is it parallel to, does it converge on THE WAY?

"I am the Vine." "You are the branches." In the other "I Am" images, our part was only implied. One might say, it was left to us to imagine where we fitted in, or responded or took part. He left it, in all courtesy, to our own imagining. Here, something else. We are part of the image, the tendrils and branches, also the harvest, the grapes. But this inclusion is a matter of emphasis rather than of "here we are, there he is, all nicely distinguished"; no matter of "we are something, he is something else." As though it could be said, the vine stops here, the branch starts there. Nature does not work that way. There is an equation, a continuity, a "we" that includes Him. There is root and vine and branch and fruit, one living being. There is a kind of ecology of the spirit here. He and we, deep in the earth, dependent on the earth, one with the earth; and deep in one another, dependent on one another, one with one another.

Context is everything. It is hardly by happenstance that "I am the vine, you the branches," is the last of the "I am" statements of Jesus. This one is placed by John at the supper of Holy Thursday. Which is to say, the image is to be verified, tried, and convicted (and to that point proven truthful) in a fallen world. In such a setting, the image is manifestly political as well as pastoral, tragic as well as comforting. It is as though the vine and branches were bare survivors in a vineyard torn to pieces, a battlefield littered with uprooted vines, the dismembered dead. Creation would have the vineyard brought to harvest; but in the world of the Fall, wine turns to blood.

The fruit of the vine is indeed the cup. But it is also, in a surreal and tragic transformation, something else. "This is the cup of my blood, poured out for you." Somehow, the fruit of the vine has been harvested, trodden, aged. It has reached this cup, this evening meal. And there, it has been transformed — "The cup of My blood." As if that were not enough, pressed down and flowing over.

It is not enough. As the Vine included us, the branches, so the cup of "My blood" includes us, by fervent implication. The cup contains blood, the blood is "given for you." The giving of one's blood supersedes the letting of blood. Violence yields to nonviolence. The illustration is clear, and passes into instruction. Say it again and again, in a world dissolved in a welter of bloodletting: "The cup of my blood, given for you." In the words spoken, the cup passed, the covenant is made new.

—TWMF, 45–52

LOVE YOUR ENEMIES, THE JUST COMMAND

Love your enemies? The Word of God in our midst? But we were at war! The moment the war was launched, we all became realists. The Word of God might apply elsewhere (or elsewhen) or to simpler times or to one-to-one conflict or to pacifists and religious (whoever these latter might be; for the most part they were mum as the others).

Love your enemies — a strange command, when you think of it. It is like the text of a drama, written with a mysterious ink. When the play is staged, the text disappears. It is in a sense self-canceling. You say it aloud, act it out and are struck by the tremendous, curt implication. The enemy disappears!

"Love," and then "enemies." The two cannot coexist, they are like fire and ice in the hand. The fire melts the ice, or the ice extinguishes the fire. The fire wins out (at least in the Gospel text)! The verb "love" transforms the noun "enemies." The enemy is reborn by the power of love. Astonishing. Now the enemy is a former enemy, and a present friend, brother, sister, lover even. Talk about rebirth!

Love, you, the enemy, and lo, the enemy vanishes where he stood.

Also, it is not only the opponent who undergoes a dazzling transformation, but myself as well, who against all expectation has learned love in place of hatred, who had once been stuck in the same plight as my enemy. Together we made a frozen mirror image, awful, redundant, implacable. I was the enemy of my enemy. A sound definition of hell.

Break the mirror! Christ commends, and confers, a mutual rebirth. Now for the hard part. If, according to Christ, there can be no just war because enemies have been transformed by love, something else follows.

No humans, not even those armed and at war against my country, can be regarded as legitimate targets. Christians may not kill, period. Christians may not be complicit in killing, period. May not hurl napalm at children. May not bury alive in the desert the nameless soldiers. May not launch the smart bomb against women and children in the shelter.

Are women and children the enemy? No sane person would declare so. (But we are not all sane.) Are the soldiers the enemy? The just war theory says so. But Christ denies it. He has granted the soldiers, too, a kind of deferment, an exemption from killing and being killed.

We heard stories of former wars, stories that underscore the absurdity and pathos of bloodletting. On Christmas day during World War I a cease fire was declared. The exhausted soldiers, allied and German, issued from the trenches, exchanged cigarettes, chatted, traded photos of their families. A day later they squared off once more, one imagines with half a heart — back to bloody business as usual.

Another episode. During the same war, we were told of a platoon of young French draftees en route to the front. They marched through a town. Local citizens came out in force to honor them. But then something bizarre: a wave — was it of grief or rage? — gathered in the ranks of the soldiers. Marching along, they began a strange bleating: "Bah! bah! Bah!" Sheep being led to the slaughter! The horrid truth, alas, too late.

And what of ourselves, Americans, Christians? We soldiers, civilians, church members, women, children, are called to be conscientious objectors against war. Against any war. Christian presidents are called too, and Christian generals — strange, bizarre, unlikely as it may seem.

Christians are called to be objectors against all and any war, against "just" war, invasive war, preemptive war, defensive war, conventional war (whose horrendous effects we have seen again and again).

The above declaration, admirably simple and to the point, would of course, put many exalted authorities out of work. So be it; better unemployed than so employed.

Let us remind them, and ourselves, that we are called to other tasks than killing.

The ethic of Jesus is set down in some detail and embarrassing clarity, in the fifth chapter of Matthew's Gospel. "Blessed are you makers of peace." And immediately, since we are to know that such a title is not cheaply conferred or claimed: "Blessed are those persecuted for the sake of righteousness."

The "good works" that follow the ethic are indicated in the twenty-fifth chapter. Summoned to love the (former, transformed) enemy — and thereby transformed, reborn, ourselves — we are to undertake the works of justice and peace.

There is another implication of what I call the "just command" to love our enemies — that terms such as "combatants" and "noncombatants" no longer wash. The terms imply that some, because they took up arms, stood outside the love invoked by Christ. As though others, for being disarmed or unarmed, were thereby, and solely thereby, judged more valuable.

So reasoning, we remain stuck in the pernicious language of the just war, implying that the unjust soldiers, enemies, tyrants, drug lords lie beyond the pale; that such lives can be wasted with impunity. The language is outmoded, passé, morally regressive. It will not jibe with the Gospel and its vision of the human; just, peaceable, compassionate.

More, such language condemns us to a cycle of violence and guilt, in which we are whirled about, off kilter, shamed, celebrating crimes we should weep for. The guilt of the generals haunts us, the pale implacable face of the wartime president, the mass graves filled with the living and the newly dead. The guilt of those who launched the bestial slaughter, the guilt of those who know of it, who parade and rejoice. The guilt of those who have no objections to register.

The time is short. Reject the errant history, the pseudotradition. There can be no just war. There never was one.

—TWMF, 59–61

THE TIME TO OBEY IS NOW

I was in Europe some time ago, speaking on the nuclear question. I came in the wake of an internationally known moral theologian. He said, "The Berrigans are off base. They are talking about the Sermon on the Mount as though it were realizable now. What we really need is an ethic of the interim." An ethic of the interim, as I understand it, would allow us to fill the gap between today and tomorrow with the bodies of all who must die, before we accept the word of Christ. On the contrary, I think the Sermon on the Mount concerns us here and now, or concerns us never. In whatever modest and clumsy a way, we are called to honor the preference of Christ for suffering rather than inflicting suffering, for dying rather than killing. In that sense, all "interim ethics" have been cast aside. The time to obey is now.   —TMM, 226

GOOD FRIDAY

You come toward me
prestigious in your wounds
those frail and speechless bones

Your credentials:
dying somberly for others.
What a burden —
gratitude, fake and true vows,
crucifixes grislier than the event —

and the glory gap —
larger than life
begetting less than life,
pieties that strike healthy eyes
blind; believe! believe! Christians
tapping down the street
in harness to their seeing-eye god.

Only in solitude
in passing tic of insight
gone as soon as granted —
I see you come toward me
free, free at last.

Can one befriend his god?
The question is inadmissible I know.
Nonetheless a fiery recognition
lights us:
broken by light
making our comeback
—ARB, 342

THE FIRST NONVIOLENT REVOLUTION

Once there was a dead man, a criminal, a subject of capital
punishment. And lo! He refused to stay dead. He stood up. As
the authorities shortly came to sense, this was an earthquake in
nature — in the nature of law and order, in the nature of death,
the nature of war. For in the nature of things, as defined by the
nation state (a great one for deciding what the nature of things
is) — dead men stay dead. The word from Big Brother, the word

that gives him clout, inspires fear, is: A criminal, once disposed of, stays disposed!

Not at all. Along come these crazies shouting in public, "Our man's not dead! He's risen!" Now I submit you can't have such a word going around and still run the state properly. The first nonviolent revolution was, of course, the Resurrection. The event had to include death as its first act. And also the command to Peter, "Put up your sword." So that it might be clear, once and for all, that Christians suffer death rather than inflict it.

All worldly systems and arrangements are simply by-passed by the Resurrection, declared passé. If death has no hold over people, in the sense that they've exorcised their fear of death, then what's left worth fearing, or worth hoping, from any worldly structure? They deserve, one and all, the feisty appellation conferred on them by a great modern Christian, Dorothy Day, "The filthy rotten system." I take it she was referring to their main function, multiplying the metaphors and means of death. The end of such a world, as she realized, and regarded it, was not only near. The end has occurred.   —BWB, 58

AN ETHIC OF RESURRECTION

One thing seems reasonably certain. Our ethic is a gift of the God who rolled the stone back, who beat death at its own game. If that be true, something would seem to follow. The death game is not our game. We are called to undergo death, rather than inflict death. And in so acting, to cherish life. And the vocation is no less urgent or valid in our stalled and death-ridden culture. A calling to works of solace and rescue.

The ethic of Jesus, as I understand it, issues from the ever so slight edge he grants to life, in the "life vs. death" conflict of the Easter hymn. He grants the edge (better, he wins the edge), from the edge. From his chosen place in the world.

The drama, in its raw original form, opened during the week we call holy. It has had a long run, and tragic. To these years of war and turmoil and sanctions and the death of children.

We are not to ignore the fierce "reversal of fortune" in the drama of Jesus, as history misses his point, and yet stages his story again and again. The script has been seized on, bowdlerized, deformed. We have a new script, different stage directions, and up to the bloody present, a far different outcome. Which is to say, the prevailing and victory of the Hero of life has been everywhere and at all times denied, proven absurd, shunted aside. His nonviolence, patience, reconciling love — these are deemed unworkable, impractical, unrealistic. In power politics, on death rows, in abortion mills, in a defunct and discredited "just war theory," in the churches as well. The word is — Out with all that!

Thus briefly, Friday to Sunday, the Lord of life is thrust offstage. We have a new and darker hero, icon, model. Death is our great protagonist. The power of death is the *motor mundi*, the driving force and fuel of event. This is what the world and its amortized religion have made of the drama. It is the legend stitched on the flag of every nation and principality, the Tao of death, the ethic of death, the ideology of death, the victory and prevailing of death. An infection at the heart of things.

Is it just at this point that the church is called to break and enter? To say No to death in virtue of, in hope of a larger Yes to life?

By and large, one must conclude in shame and confusion of spirit, we Christians intervene in the death game (if at all), with sparse understanding, grudgingly, with a foggy "maybe" on our lips, with a "just war theory." The clear words of our Gospel, "Blessed are the peacemakers," "Love your enemies, do good to those who do ill to you," "Peter, put up your sword," "This is the cup of my blood, given for you" — such words are among the first casualties of war. War is declared. We are suddenly inducted along with everyone else. We cannot utter a forthright, unmistakable No.

I propose that we reflect on the implications of that No in virtue of a larger Yes, that we undertake an ethic of resurrection, and live according to the slight edge of life over death:

- Ideologies of "the nations," political or economic arrangements however enlightened or democratic, can never be equated with the Realm of God. Indeed the Word of God addressed to the nations, as well as to revolutions whether of right or left, is always and everywhere the same: "Not yet. Not yet the Realm of God."

- And especially and always and irrevocably, the community of faith grants no compatibility, none, between the Gospel and the sanctioned slaughter known as war.

- The "just war theory" is in fact a cruel oxymoron. War, no matter its provocation or justification, is of its essence and nature, supremely unjust. The injustice of war implies a blasphemous inflation of human authority, that humans are allowed to decree who shall live and who shall die, to dispose of human differences by disposing of humans. We are done with that theory forever.

- Imperial ideologies always reduce themselves to this — the vindication, indeed the honoring of death as a social method.

- The ethic of Jesus is distrustful of any theory or praxis of social change that does not exact risk and sacrifice of Christians.

- Our faith confesses no debt to the law of the land, when that law is protective of the realm of death and its artifacts, its courts, jails, taxes, armed forces. When Christians enter such precincts, they are to reflect the scepticism of scripture. Can worldly powers attain, dispense, or honor justice? They cannot.

- As to law courts, Christians enter them under rigor of the law, as defendants and resisters. They enter in jeopardy, at the mercy of death's servants and sycophants, like the One they follow. But never in debt to the law, not a farthing.

- The best time for Christians, the most enlightened time, the time when ethical hairsplitting is halted and the Gospel rings clear, is the time of the martyrs. On the other hand, complicity with secular power, commonly and absurdly known as "normal times," implies only Christian decadence. We are to learn from, and follow, our martyred sisters and brothers.

- The Christian response to imperial death-dealing is in effect a non-response. We refuse the terms of the argument. To weigh the value of lives would imply that military or paramilitary solutions had been grotesquely validated by Christians. There is no cause, however noble, which justifies the taking of a single human life, much less millions of them.

- Our "no," uttered in face of imperial violence, takes the form of a non-answer. Our appeal, more often than not wordless, like the silent Christ before Pilate, is precisely to Christ Crucified. Which is to say, to God in trouble for being Godly. God under capital sentence. God sentenced to death, executed for being God, for being human. The crime: such acts, miracles, healings, stories, refusals, as serve to vindicate, honor, and celebrate human life.

- The "No" to the state, uttered by the unarmed Christ, is vindicated in the resurrection. Of this, the world can never be a witness. (The military be it noted, were in attendance at the event. The soldiers were struck to earth, and subsequently entered in collusion with the authorities, to lie about the occurrence; see Matt. 28:11ff.)

- In contrast, "Witness of the Resurrection" was a title of honor, self-conferred by the twelve (Acts 1:21–22). The meaning of the phrase is simple. The apostles were called to take their stand on behalf of life, to the point of undergoing death, as well as death's analogies — scorn and rejection, floggings and jail.

- This is our glory. From Peter and Paul to Martin King and Romero, Christians have known something which the "nations" as such can never know or teach — how to live and how to die. We are witnesses of the resurrection. We practice resurrection. We risk resurrection.

- We Christians have our own language and symbols. These properly understood are charged with life. They are life-giving, vessels of life. A few examples may be in order. When we pour blood at the Pentagon, we in effect renounce ideological bickering, concerning, truth told, who shall live and who die. We declare in fear and trembling our willingness to die rather than to take life. In granting and dramatizing the thin edge and advantage of life, we rest our case. The drama contains the entirety of our ethic.

When we spread ashes at the Pentagon, we mime the death ridden pollution of the place. The drama contains the ethic.

When we dig graves on the White House lawn, we pay tribute to the empty grave of Easter, even as we show forth the universal grave to whose brink humanity is being pushed. The drama is the ethic.

Such acts as these are ventured in favor of life, even as they say more loudly than words, our "No" to the inflation of death.

My teachers, among others, have been Martin Luther King, Dorothy Day, Gandhi, Thomas Merton, and my brother Philip, a continuity of nonviolence and non-ideology, stemming from the early church and the prophets, from Jesus himself.

My teachers are non-ideologues. They are attached to no self- or special interest, including the self-interest commonly considered most legitimate of all, their own lives. Simply put, they know how to live and how to die. They draw on the great earth-time symbols that offer both "mimesis" and "praxis" — "the image" and "the movement." Gandhi walked to the sea and took up the forbidden salt of the poor. King declared, "The church is the place you go from." He started in the church and went from there, breaking down segregation, economic injustice, and denouncing the Vietnam war.

Incomparably the greatest of these is Jesus, who for his part, took bread, broke it, and said, "This is my body, given for you." Then he took a cup and said, "This is my blood, given for you." The ethic of the body given, of the blood outpoured! The act led straight to the scaffold and to that "beyond" we name for want of a better word, resurrection.

We have not, in this century or any other, improved on this. More, being equally fearful of living and dying, we have yet to experience resurrection, which I translate, "the hope that hopes on."

A blasphemy against this hope is named deterrence, or Trident submarine, or Star Wars, or preemptive strike, or simply, any nuclear weapon. These are in direct violation of the commandment of Jesus: "Your ancestors said, 'An eye for an eye,' but I say to you, offer no violent resistance to evil. Love your enemies."

That is why we speak again and again of 1980 and all the Plowshares actions since, how some of us continue to labor to break the demonic clutch on our souls, of the ethic of Mars, of wars and rumor of wars, inevitable wars, just wars, necessary wars, victorious wars, and say our No in acts of hope. For us, all these repeated arrests, the interminable jailings, the life of our small communities, the discipline of nonviolence — these have embodied an ethic of resurrection.

Simply put, we long to taste that event, its thunders and quakes, its great Yes. We want to test the resurrection in our bones. To see if we might live in hope, instead of in the *silva oscura*, the thicket of cultural despair, nuclear despair, a world of perpetual war. We want to taste the resurrection.

May I say we have not been disappointed.

— TWMF, 220–25

8

Love, Love at the End

CONSOLATION

Listen
if now and then
you hear the dead
muttering like ashes
creaking like empty
rockers on porches

filling you in   filling you in

like winds in empty
branches like stars
in wintry trees
so far
so good

you've mastered finally
one foreign tongue

VISION

then showed me he
in right hand held
everything that is

the hand was a woman's
creation   all lusty
a meek bird's egg

nesting there   waiting
her work   and I heard it

new born   I make you
nestling   I love you
homing   I keep you

ZEN POEM

How I long for supernatural powers!
said the novice mournfully to the holy one.
I see a dead child
and I long to say, *Arise!*
I see a sick man
I long to say, *Be healed!*
I see a bent old woman
I long to say, *Walk straight!*
Alas, I feel like a dead stick in paradise.
Master, can you confer on me
supernatural powers?

The old man shook his head fretfully.
How long have I been with you
and you know nothing?
How long have you known me
and learned nothing?

Listen; I have walked the earth for 80 years
I have never raised a dead child
I have never healed a sick man
I have never straightened an old woman's spine

Children die
men grow sick

the aged fall
under a stigma of frost

And what is that to you or me
but a turn of the wheel
but the way of the world
but the gateway to paradise?

Supernatural powers!
Then you would play God
would spin the thread of life
and measure the thread
5 years, 50 years, 80 years
And cut the thread?

Supernatural powers!
I have wandered the earth for 80 years
I confess to you,
sprout without root
root without flower
I know nothing of supernatural powers
I have yet to perfect my natural powers!

to see and not be seduced
to hear and not be deafened
to taste and not be eaten
to touch and not be bought

But you —
would you walk on water
would you master the air
would you swallow fire?

Go talk with the dolphins
they will teach you glibly
how to grow gills

Go listen to eagles
they will hatch you, nest you
eaglet and airman

Go join the circus
those tricksters will train you
in deception for dimes —

Bird man, bag man, poor fish
spouting fire, moon crawling
at sea forever —
supernatural powers!

Do you seek miracles?
listen — go
draw water, hew wood
break stones —
how miraculous!

Listen; blessed is the one
who walks the earth 5 years, 50 years, 80 years,
and deceives no one
and curses no one
and kills no one

On such a one
the angels whisper in wonder;
behold the irresistible power
of natural powers —
of height, of joy, of soul, of non-belittling!

You dry stick —
in the crude soil of this world
spring, root, leaf, flower!

Trace
around and around
and around —
an inch, a mile, the world's green extent —
a liberated zone
of paradise!   — ARB, 205, 220, 217

MODERN SPIRITUAL MASTERS
Robert Ellsberg, Series Editor

Already published:

Dietrich Bonhoeffer (edited by Robert Coles)
Simone Weil (edited by Eric O. Springsted)
Henri Nouwen (edited by Robert A. Jonas)
Pierre Teilhard de Chardin (edited by Ursula King)
Anthony de Mello (edited by William Dych, S.J.)
Charles de Foucauld (edited by Robert Ellsberg)
Oscar Romero (by Marie Dennis, Rennie Golden,
    and Scott Wright)
Eberhard Arnold (edited by Johann Christoph Arnold)
Thomas Merton (edited by Christine M. Bochen)
Thich Nhat Hanh (edited by Robert Ellsberg)
Rufus Jones (edited by Kerry Walters)
Mother Teresa (edited by Jean Maalouf)
Edith Stein (edited by John Sullivan, O.C.D.)
John Main (edited by Laurence Freeman)
Mohandas Gandhi (edited by John Dear)
Mother Maria Skobtsova (introduction by Jim Forest)
Evelyn Underhill (edited by Emilie Griffin)
St. Thérèse of Lisieux (edited by Mary Frohlich)
Flannery O'Connor (edited by Robert Ellsberg)
Clarence Jordan (edited by Joyce Hollyday)
G. K. Chesterton (edited by William Griffin)
Alfred Delp, S.J. (introduction by Thomas Merton)
Bede Griffiths (edited by Thomas Matus)
Karl Rahner (edited by Philip Endean)
Sadhu Sundar Singh (edited by Charles E. Moore)
Pedro Arrupe (edited by Kevin F. Burke, S.J.)
Romano Guardini (edited by Robert A. Krieg)
Albert Schweitzer (edited by James Brabazon)
Caryll Houselander (edited by Wendy M. Wright)
Brother Roger of Taizé (edited by Marcello Fidanzio)

Dorothee Soelle (edited by Dianne L. Oliver)
Leo Tolstoy (edited by Charles E. Moore)
Howard Thurman (edited by Luther E. Smith, Jr.)
Swami Abhishiktananda (edited by Shirley du Boulay)
Carlo Carretto (edited by Robert Ellsberg)
John XXIII (edited by Jean Maalouf)
Jean Vanier (edited by Carolyn Whitney-Brown)
The Dalai Lama (edited by Thomas A. Forsthoefel)
Catherine de Hueck Doherty (edited by David Meconi, S.J.)
Dom Helder Camara (edited by Francis McDonagh)